D0745996

THE WAY OF THE SPIRIT

A Bible Reading Guide and Commentary

THE WAY OF THE SPIRIT

A Bible Reading Guide and Commentary

Vol. 2

TIMES OF REFRESHING

The Historics
(Joshua – 2 Kings)

Matthew's Gospel

Acts

Paul's Mission Letters

JOHN McKAY

Marshall Pickering

Marshall Morgan and Scott
Marshall Pickering
34–42 Cleveland Street, London W1P 5FB

Copyright © 1989 John McKay
First published in 1989 by Marshall Morgan and Scott
Publications Ltd
Part of the Marshall Pickering Holdings Group

All rights reserved. No part of this publication may be
reproduced, stored in a retrieval system, or transmitted, in
any form or by any means, electronic, mechanical,
photocopying, recording or otherwise, without the prior
permission in writing, of the publisher

McKay, John
    The way of the spirit
    Vol 2: Times of refreshing
    1. Bible
    I. Title
    220
    ISBN 0–551–01761–9

Text Set in Times Roman by Vine & Gorfin Ltd,
Exmouth, Devon EX8 1RU
Printed in Great Britain by
Camelot Press Ltd, Southampton

With gratitude to God for all who have
taught me about God's kingdom,
encouraged me in revival,
and sustained me in vision.

If my people, who are called by my name,
  will humble themselves
  and pray
  and seek my face
  and turn from their wicked ways,
then I
  will hear from heaven
  and will forgive their sin
  and will heal their land.
                    (2 Chron.7.14)

Contents

List of Maps, Charts and Diagrams

Acknowledgments

Correspondence courses? Never! That was my initial reaction to the Christian media consultant who suggested Volume One was ideally suited to become the teaching manual for a home study course. I dismissed the matter from my thinking instantly, unwilling to consider it because of the amount of work it would involve. Two days later I was awake very early in the morning knowing the Lord was asking me to do it. The course for Volume One, which can be taken with or without tutorial assistance by correspondence, was launched about two months later. This Volume comes with the course to go with it already prepared (see p. 248).

Once more I thank the members of our fellowship and the staff and students of Roffey Place for their patience and encouragement. I have particularly welcomed the constructive comments offered by some of the students who have taken the lecture-course on which this book is based. Some of their suggestions have been incorporated, both in the book and in the home-study course.

My thanks again to Pete Goddard who this time not only designed the cover with its illustration symbolising the refreshing water of God's Spirit flowing over and out from the pages of his Word, but also was responsible for the rest of the graphics in the book.

And finally I bless the Lord for the steadfast support I have had from my wife and sons. Marguerite has again read the manuscript and proofs, and has both encouraged and restrained my sometimes flagging, sometimes over-excited pen. A good wife is indeed her husband's crown! (Prov. 12.4)

John McKay
15th November, 1988.

Preface

If you were to ask me, 'What is the way of the Spirit?' I would have to answer that it is the way of God with men and of men with God according to the patterns found in the Bible.

Strange as it now seems, I used to study Israel's history almost as if God had no part in it, that is other than being someone the ancient Israelites worshipped at their temple. In fact, I was somehow able to gloss over the parts of Scripture that spoke about God being directly or miraculously involved in the affairs of men, almost as if they only reflected ancient man's primitive understanding of how things happened and therefore had to be totally disregarded, or at most reinterpreted according to our modern, more sophisticated thought-forms in which God has little or no place. For example, the miracles of the crossing of the Jordan and the collapse of the walls of Jericho in Josh. 3 and 6, I believed, must surely have had some natural cause, such as an earthquake, and it was simply their naivety that made the Israelites speak about God having a hand in it at all. And, of course, I applied the same measure to the miracles of Jesus, the utterances of prophets, the stories of conversions and successful church-planting, and so forth.

As you can imagine, baptism in the Spirit threw me into some confusion, for miracles began to happen around me in much the same way as in the Bible, and according to my standards of interpretation they should not have been happening at all. My first reaction was to think they must be coincidences, but when they continued to happen, I was forced to come to terms with the fact of God's wonder-working power.

Since these early days I have learned just how fully God does work according to the biblical patterns, particularly among men of the Spirit intent on seeing revival and growth in his kingdom. And that is what this book is all about: the way of the Spirit in kingdom-building, revival and church-growth. The story began in Bible times, but it continues today according to the same patterns and principles. I therefore pray that you will be able to discern these for yourself as you read and that you will then learn to enter into the thrill of sharing in the kingdom-revival work to which God has called us today.

The Overall Plan of Study

This volume is the second in a series of four covering the whole Bible. Each deals with a successive period of Old Testament history, concentrates on the books of the Old Testament associated with that period and examines particular aspects of faith related to it. Each volume then traces the sequel to the story told in the Old Testament section through books of the New Testament that seem to provide an appropriate follow up, and in doing so separately examines one of the four well-known portraits of Jesus as Priest, King, Prophet and Lord.

	VOL. 1 THE CALL AND THE CROSS	VOL. 2 TIMES OF REFRESHING	VOL. 3 HEIRS OF THE PROPHETS	VOL. 4 MY LORD AND MY GOD
OLD TESTAMENT	2000–1230 BC	1230–500 BC	1050–400 BC	600–0 BC
	The Pentateuch	The Histories	The Prophets	The Writings
	Faith, obedience and sacrifice	The Kingdom, revival and Messianic hope	Prophecy, revival and charismatic faith	The Lordship of God in history, worship and belief
NEW TESTAMENT	Mark	Matthew	Luke	John
	Romans and Hebrews	Acts and Paul's mission letters	Selections from Acts & various epistles, Revelation	1–3 John, Paul's captivity & pastoral letters, James Peter & Jude
	Jesus as Priest	Jesus as King	Jesus as Prophet	Jesus as Lord

The Purpose of the Series

The purpose is to provide a commentary-guide to *the Way of the Spirit* through the Bible. Christians who have been influenced over the past 20–30 years by the Charismatic

Movement have often spoken to me of a need for some such guide, one that would help them to understand their Bibles better in the light of their experience of the Spirit, and one that would help them to relate their Bible-reading to such matters as the Spirit's ways, the power of faith, the dynamic of the word, revival, healing, and so forth – in fact everything that relates to personal experience of God in the life of the believer. We shall therefore be endeavouring, as we trace the Bible stories, to lay bare the heart that pulsates within giving them life, to tap their dynamic source – which is, of course, the Spirit of God himself.

As we study the history of Israel, we shall see how, unlike secular history, it is very much a story about God's dealings with men. When we trace the accounts of individual lives, we shall find they too are stories about the working of God's Spirit in transforming men. And throughout we shall also discover just how much the Bible does delight in the very things many Christians love to hear about in the Church today: the miraculous, the prophetic, the visionary, the love and fellowship of Spirit-filled believers, and so forth.

Our aim is therefore to examine the foundations of Christian faith, vision and experience in Scripture. Hence, alongside the chronological and topical arrangement of each volume outlined above, there is another more embracing pattern relating to our overall purpose:
– Vol. 1 outlines the basic principles on which all Christian life and experience needs to be founded: faith in God's promises, obedience to his call and acknowledgment of the saving power of Christ's sacrifice.
– Vol. 2 traces the main movements of revival in biblical history, thus highlighting the principles by which God's kingdom operates and outlining the challenges and vision that inspire all men of the Spirit.
– Vol. 3 examines the experiences and teachings of prophets and other men of the Spirit in both Testaments more directly, demonstrating how their faith and vision are of the very essence of biblical hope.
– Vol. 4 looks at the common approaches of Spirit-filled Christians and the Bible to worship, service, pastoral matters, the challenges of daily living, and the like.

How to approach the Way of the Spirit in the Bible

These books are written as Bible-reading guides, hence for use in conjunction with the Bible. (A simple reading scheme is provided on pp. 242–7.) As you read the Scriptures, besides looking to the notes for guidance, expect the Holy Spirit himself to interpret what you read – and more than that, to lead you to the very source of his truth in the life of God himself. Remember the words of our Lord Jesus: 'You diligently study the Scriptures because you think that by them you possess eternal life. These are the Scriptures that testify about me, yet you refuse to come to me to have life' (John 5.39f).

The Bible can be read both for its information about the things of God and also for the enjoyment of its life. The first is theology, but on its own that can become the letter that kills, and so it needs to be coupled with the second, for 'the word of God is living and active . . . it penetrates even to dividing soul and spirit . . . it judges the thoughts and attitudes of the heart' (Heb. 4.12). Our theology has to be living, and it is only the Spirit that gives life.

Paul speaks about the difference between reading Scripture with and without the illumination of the Holy Spirit in 2 Cor. 3.14–18, where he says that those who read without the Spirit do so with a veil over their eyes. 'But,' he continues, 'whenever anyone turns to the Lord, the veil is taken away.' Then he adds, 'Now the Lord is the Spirit . . . and this comes from the Lord, who is the Spirit'. This removal of a veil is something Christians commonly experience after baptism with the Holy Spirit, and so my prayer is that you, the reader, will also know it being lifted as the Spirit enlightens God's Word for you.

Don't allow yourself to become too preoccupied with small details, the precise interpretation of individual passages, words or phrases, complex historical or theological issues, and the like, but rather see yourself walking on the stage of the ancient world, first with the men of Old Testament times, and then with Jesus and his disciples. Go with Jesus around Galilee, listen to him speaking, participate in the astonishment and excitement of the crowd, share in the puzzlement and the illumination of his disciples, get the feel of what you read. The information given in these pages is mainly intended to help you lay hold of that 'feel' for yourself, particularly as it relates to the vision, the power and the life of God these men of old knew.

Read your Bible in something like the way you would read a novel or watch a play. Take yourself into the life of its drama and let the feel of that life flow through your life as you walk and talk with the ancient men of God and with Jesus. Lay hold of their vision and let it become yours as well. Let their longings be your longings and their joys your joys, for therein lies the life God wants you to know in Christ.

All biblical quotations are taken from the New International Version of the Bible. To avoid confusion, the conventions of the NIV translators have also been adhered to beyond the quotations, e.g., 'he' rather than 'He' for God, 'the Most Holy Place' rather than 'the Holy of Holies', 'Spirit' (of God) rather than 'spirit' in the Old Testament (contrast RSV).

PART ONE

INTRODUCTION

1

The Story of God's Kingdom on Earth

Though the overall story of God's kingdom is one of progressive expansion, there are plenty of ups and downs on the way. Naturally the moments we enjoy reading about best are those of revival and growth, when 'times of refreshing' were granted by the Lord. However, despite the fact that many are excited about revival in the Church today, and despite the title of this volume, what God's people are called to first and foremost is not revival, but spreading his kingdom. Revival is something he grants along the way, when things begin to go wrong and we have to call out for his help. Because we are as we are, these occasions are not infrequent, and so revival becomes an integral and necessary part of our kingdom-calling.

Building the kingdom has, of course, always been God's own work, but it is a work he has never performed without man's aid. Perhaps we should say it is something he invites us to do in co-operation with and in dependency on him. But, however we express it, the fact is, it is not a work we can do on our own. As we follow the story we shall see that truth highlighted over and over, particularly in times of blessing or suffering, and as we read let us take its lessons to heart, for they are still valid today. God has not changed the rules by which his kingdom operates.

We shall trace Israel's history from the time it entered Canaan and became a nation with its own political identity down to the end of the kingdom in the sixth century BC. Our intention is not just to recount the facts of history, but to examine the relationship between God and his people that led to their establishment as a kingdom and to discern the principles in it that led to growth and revival.

We shall follow the New Testament story of kingdom-

3

growth through Matthew's Gospel and Acts. Whereas
Volume One drew out the portrait of Jesus as Priest and
Volume Three will show him as a Prophet, the main picture
here is naturally of Jesus as King, or Messiah, the promised
son of David who came to usher in God's kingdom and now
reigns at his right hand for ever.

1. IN THE BEGINNING, NOW, AND AT THE END

Repent, then, and turn to God, so that your sins may be
wiped out, that times of refreshing may come from the Lord.
(Acts 3.19)

Time is a peculiar phenomenon. Some believe it goes in
cycles, having no start and no finish, but repeatedly bringing
man back over the same ground again and again. Others
believe it to be endless, but not cyclic, holding that it is
aimless, unpredictable and without hope. The biblical con-
cept stands in complete contradiction to both of these,
proclaiming that it has both beginning and end, and that the
end is not simply the finish, but the goal, and so is completely
purposeful. But more than that, the picture of the end is
comparable with the picture of the beginning, for God's
purpose remains constant. The Bible story tells how God
wrote his purpose into the beginning and how, after sin had
spoiled it, he has been working towards its restoration at the
end. The story is basically of God seeking man's co-operation
for the restoration of his kingdom, sometimes finding it, but
often not, and yet always faithfully progressing towards his
final goal.

Gen. 1. 1: In the beginning God . . .

Gen. 1–2: . . . God created the heavens and the earth . . . and
repeatedly he looked on what he had created and saw that it
was good (1.4,10,12,18,21,25,31). He set man over it all to
rule like a king, which at first he did in a beautiful setting of

peace, and of harmony between himself and God, his wife and the animals. The Garden of Eden is a perfect portrait of what God intended his world to be like.

Gen. 3–11: With Adam's fall God's beautiful canvas is soiled beyond recognition: 'Cursed are you . . . Cursed is the ground . . . The Lord was grieved that he had made man . . . God saw how corrupt the earth had become.' (3.14,17; 6.6,12). The garden has gone, man murders his brother, sin multiplies on earth, God sends the Flood, and the proud tower of Babel is toppled leaving confusion on earth. Man is now alienated from man as well as from God. Sin's destructive work seems total and complete.

Gen. 12–50: But God now takes a first step toward restoration by calling Abraham and through him building a people to whom he can teach his ways. First they have to learn faith in the covenant he makes with Abraham, promising land, children and ultimately blessing for mankind. The story is of mixed success and failure – Abraham's descendants end up as strangers in Egypt. (2000–1270 BC)

Exod.–I Sam.: God calls another man, Moses, and through him brings his people out to freedom, teaches them his laws and their need for obedience, takes them (despite their constant grumbling!) through Sinai, and under Joshua leads them into Canaan, where, after initial success, they drift away from God and are repeatedly invaded until finally they end up under Philistine domination. (1270–1050 BC)

I Sam.–II Kings: When Israel decides to have kings, God calls yet another man, David, and makes a third covenant, promising the throne to him and his descendants for ever. At first, thanks to David's faithfulness, all goes well and the kingdom is firmly established for his son, Solomon. But the remainder of the history of the kings tells of repeated disobedience, first leading to the split of the kingdom into

Israel (in the north) and Judah (in the south) and then to the final collapse of Israel at the hands of the Assyrians in 722 BC and to the exile of Judah to Babylon after 597 BC.

During this period, particularly at times of crisis, God spoke to both nations through prophets, calling them back to his ways. The prophets also spoke of a new covenant that God would make when he would pour out his Spirit for all men, and of a coming King (Messiah) who would fulfil God's pattern of kingship entirely, and so usher in the kingdom of God on earth. (1050–597 BC)

Ezra–The New Testament: The exile resulted in Jews becoming scattered everywhere throughout the ancient world. Soon after the Persians overthrew the Babylonians in 539 some returned to rebuild Jerusalem, and their enthusiasm was encouraged by prophets such as Haggai and Zechariah, but gradually their faith became mainly one of quietly waiting for their Messiah and hoping for better days. Judah passed from the Persians to the Greeks in the fourth century, gained some independence for a while in the second, and finally came under Roman domination in the first. (597–5 BC)

The Old Testament story is one of successes and failures. Breakthrough often seems just round the corner, but then is lost. There are indeed high times of blessing, but repeatedly the nation goes into decline, ending in bondage. The promises of God are never removed, but also never fulfilled. It is an unfinished story – but that is because it is a story of preparation. God's primeval kingdom was snatched away by sin and here we have the account of how, using sin-bound men, he lays a foundation for rebuilding his kingdom on earth. By New Testament times we have a people strategically scattered throughout the world, believing in one God, taught in the ways of righteousness, knowing the need for faith and obedience, understanding something about the relationship between sacrifice and sin and so prepared for the sacrifice of the cross, and waiting for the coming of Messiah and the outpouring of the Holy Spirit. Moreover, the peace and religious toleration the world enjoyed in the early years of the Roman Empire made conditions almost perfect for the spreading of the Gospel. The materials God had to work with were perhaps far from perfect, but it must be admitted that he performed a marvellous work of preparation with them.

The Gospels: Jesus, born of the Spirit and baptised in the Spirit, came proclaiming: 'Repent, for the kingdom of heaven is near.' (Matt. 4.17). He taught with the authority and anointing of a king, he exercised the power of a king in his dealings with demons, sickness and nature. He spoke much of his kingdom in the parables. He gathered disciples and prepared them to go and call men into his kingdom, and he promised them they would operate with all the authority and power of the kingdom that he himself had. After his victory over death he commissioned them for the work and gave them final preparation for their empowering to do it.

(5 BC–30 AD)

Acts: The disciples, now empowered by the Spirit, continue the work of Jesus, proclaiming the kingdom amid signs and wonders. The Church spreads rapidly from Jerusalem, through Judea and Samaria, out into Asia and Greece, and right to Rome itself.   (30–64 AD)

The Christian Church has grown considerably since New Testament times, albeit with plenty of ups and downs, and so the kingdom continues to spread its influence and recapture territory lost through Adam's sin.   (64 AD–Today)

Revelation: About 95 AD St. John was granted a vision of things to come and of the end: after a time of final Christian witness and persecution, God will usher in a new age with a new heaven and a new earth where sin, suffering and death will be no more, where all the blessings of Eden will be restored, and where man in Christ will reign at the last as he was intended to do at the first.

(The End)

Rev. 22.4–5: In the end . . . God.

God's will is seen in the beginning and the end. History, the middle part in which we live, is about God restoring his will. Because of sin, man's part is mostly negative, but when he heeds God's call and turns from his sins, God sends times of refreshing for the progress of his kingdom work. That in a nutshell is our theme.

2. KINGDOM BUILDING, CHURCH GROWTH AND REVIVAL

In the story we have just reviewed there are two significant periods of growth and expansion. The first occurred between the time Joshua led Israel into the land and the kingdom was established under David and Solomon, the second between the time that Jesus led his disciples into what became the Christian Church and the end of the New Testament era (still continuing today). These are the periods we shall be examining in detail, and as we do so we shall be particularly seeking to lay bare the principles that make successful growth possible.

The Old Testament story is covered by the historical books: Joshua, Judges, Samuel and Kings. We shall not finish our study at Solomon's reign, but continue it down to the end of the kingdom, to the time of the exile, because it is just as important to learn the principles of maintaining what is built as those of kingdom-building. From the very start the Israelites found that demanding work, so much so that they repeatedly opted for what seemed the easier course of accepting the ways of the peoples around them rather than continuing to build their own kingdom in Canaan. The results were always disastrous and each time they had to relearn the need for turning back to God. Our story is certainly not a naive account of steady success, but also tells about decline and failure, and hence about recurring need for revival.

It is the clear witness of the Old Testament that both growth and revival are generated by God's power, not man's. The moment man tries to go it alone, decline follows

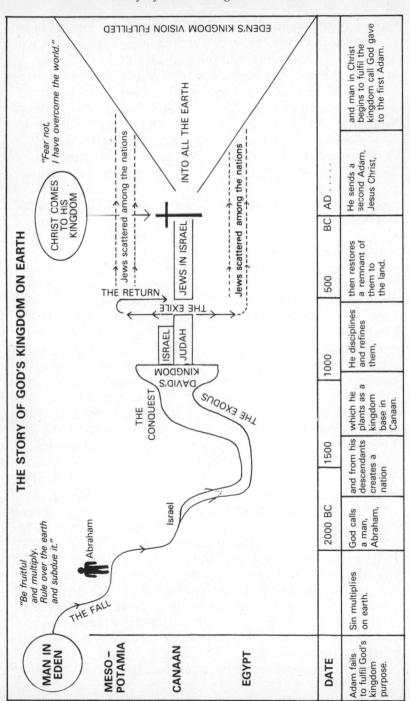

THE STORY OF GOD'S KINGDOM ON EARTH

EDEN'S KINGDOM VISION FULFILLED

"Be fruitful and multiply. Rule over the earth and subdue it."

"Fear not, I have overcome the world."

CHRIST COMES TO HIS KINGDOM

INTO ALL THE EARTH

Jews scattered among the nations

JEWS IN ISRAEL

Jews scattered among the nations

THE RETURN

THE EXILE

ISRAEL

JUDAH

DAVID'S KINGDOM

THE CONQUEST

THE EXODUS

Israel

Abraham

THE FALL

MAN IN EDEN

MESO- POTAMIA

CANAAN

EGYPT

DATE	2000 BC	1500	1000	500	BC AD......
Adam fails to fulfil God's kingdom purpose.	God calls a man, Abraham,	and from his descendants creates a nation	which he plants as a kingdom base in Canaan.	He disciplines and refines them,	then restores a remnant of them to the land.	He sends a second Adam, Jesus Christ,	and man in Christ begins to fulfil the kingdom call God gave to the first Adam.

Sin multiplies on earth.

automatically; though equally revival begins the moment he
turns back to God in heart-felt repentance. Similarly growth
and revival are maintained only so long as he continues to
walk with God in obedience and faith. From earliest times, in
the primitive years of the nation's birth and infancy, before
Joshua led them into Canaan, God had already shown
Abraham and Moses the standards of faith and obedience by
which he expected his people to live and had warned them of
the consequences of failing to do so. As we read through their
history we shall see the outworking of these principles in the
nation's joys and sorrows. But over and above all that we shall
also see clear evidence of God's own unfailing love and
faithfulness as he reaches out his hand time and again to
rescue his people from the terrible consequences of their
waywardness.

And the same general principles are also of paramount
importance in the story of the kingdom's growth in the New
Testament: faith in the power of God, obedience to the will of
God, and repentance securing refreshment and revival from
God.

When we begin to read the stories of judges and kings, of
war and peace, of the vagaries of human living and the
complexities of political institutions, it is important to remember that what the Bible tells us is first and foremost a
story about a people and their God, not just about a people
among other nations. This is not secular history, but the
history of God working among men to create and restore his
kingdom in their fallen world.

In Old Testament times the kingdom was, of course,
embodied in the geographically definable political state of
Israel. But unlike other kingdoms, Israel believed it was
begotten of God for a purpose, to be the expression of his
eternal kingdom on earth. At creation God had given man the
kingly authority to rule over the world, but as a result of the
fall, this world became dominated by sin and Satan. God's
purpose was therefore to replant his kingdom's rule, first in
Canaan, but then out from there into the rest of the world.
Thus, whilst Israel was certainly a national state, it was also
more than that, for behind its political facade lay the vision of
the kingdom of God.

In the New Testament it is this eternal kingdom of God that

surfaces in the work of Christ. The vision and purpose is the same, but the structural form changes, for in Christian times the kingdom finds its expression in the Church that begins to spread beyond Palestine into the rest of the world. That was always God's plan anyhow, that his kingdom should one day embrace all mankind, not simply one small national group.

3. STUDYING HISTORY

The historical writings in the Bible
Since the Jews do not recognise our New Testament as sacred Scripture, they do not refer to the Hebrew Bible as 'The Old Testament'. Their name for it is 'The Law, The Prophets and The Writings' (*Torah, Nebi'im uKethubim*).
   'The Law' refers to the Pentateuch.
   'The Prophets' refers to
      (i) the history books Joshua, Judges, Samuel and Kings ('the former prophets');
      (ii) the prophetic books of Isaiah, Jeremiah, Ezekiel and the twelve Minor Prophets from Hosea to Malachi ('the latter prophets').
   'The Writings' refers to everything else.

The books in the Hebrew Bible are arranged in that order, which is different from the English order.
   Our main historical source will be 'the former prophets', so called because they contain the stories of the early prophets. We shall also cross-refer to Chronicles, though it does not give us the same coverage of our period. It is essentially a history of the Davidic dynasty and the southern kingdom of Judah, and so gives no account of the conquest, the settlement or Saul's reign, disregards the history of northern Israel entirely and omits all the prophet-stories found in Samuel and Kings. However, it does provide us with additional information, particularly about the temple and its priesthood. Thus its accounts of David's and Solomon's reigns concentrate particularly on the building of the temple and the organisation of its worship, and the same interest in the affairs of the Levites continues through its account of the divided monarchy.

The books of Ezra and Nehemiah cover much of the history of the post-exilic era, but that will be reviewed properly in Volume Four.

We shall be covering the story of the establishment of the kingdom in the New Testament mainly by studying Matthew's Gospel, Acts and Paul's mission letters: Matthew because, although the same theme does run through all four gospels, it is particularly highlighted there; Acts because it is our only history of the early Church; Paul's mission letters because they provide some intriguing insights into the challenges of kingdom-planting and Church-growth.

Studying history as a Christian

Christians and Jews differ from non-Christians in their approach to history because they believe that God has been active in it. That should mean, for example, that they have little desire to seek alternative explanations for miracle stories, and yet, strangely as it may seem, many Christians do. In fact we find there are several different attitudes to history among Christians today, though generally they fall into two broad camps, each with a variety of shades of opinion.

1. *Evangelicals* on the whole are strong 'Bible-believers', but how much they believe and how much they are prepared to question varies a great deal.

Some describe themselves as *fundamentalists* and believe as a matter of dogma that everything must have happened exactly as the Bible describes because every letter of it is inspired by God – though they do not necessarily conclude that he still acts in exactly the same ways today.

Others would say they are *conservative*, but not fundamentalist, since, although they are of a fundamentalist bent, they are prepared to discuss some of the details of Scripture with an open mind about their interpretation and historical exactitude; for example, whether creation literally happened in six successive twenty-four hour stages.

There are even some who would describe themselves as *liberal evangelicals* and are prepared to question much more than their conservative friends, though they would still want to define certain limits to such open questioning.

2. *Liberals* are less attracted by 'Bible-believing' than

Evangelicals and in fact generally criticise them for believing too much or too naively. But again there is variety of opinion.

Radical liberals stand at the other end of the scale from fundamentalists, holding that the Bible is a very human book, containing, not supernatural revelation, but theological reflections of religious men who were trying to show how they believed God acted, i.e. that it is an interpretation of history – and so we are free to re-interpret it today according to modern ways of thinking that do not normally see God active in the affairs of men. Thus, for example, the miracles of Jesus, they would say, should often be explained in terms of our present-day understanding of medicine and psychology without involving God or miracle too much in the discussion.

There are, however, plenty of *liberals* who are of a more believing and less radical inclination, and they are often prepared to concede that God may have acted in some way in history, even if they may not always agree it was precisely as simple as the Bible tells it. For example, most liberals, however believing, would normally want to find natural explanations for such events as the plagues of Egypt or the crossing of the Red Sea. They would seldom be prepared to accept the accounts of Jesus' incarnation or his resurrection at face value without a great deal of discussion about the author's intentions in writing, about their theological presuppositions, about the value of their sources, and so forth.

Then finally there is a point somewhere in the middle where many Christians drift happily with one foot in the evangelical camp and the other in the liberal, neither

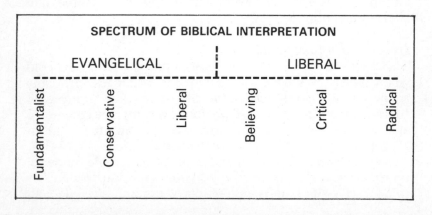

SPECTRUM OF BIBLICAL INTERPRETATION

EVANGELICAL   LIBERAL

Fundamentalist   Conservative   Liberal   Believing   Critical   Radical believing too much nor questioning too much, but intent on doing a little of both.

Charismatics often have problems with these different approaches to Scripture and seldom fit into any of their categories exactly. They do generally accept the validity of the biblical narratives and so give the impression of being fundamentalist in inclination, but unlike the fundamentalists their reason for believing is not normally because of some dogma about inspiration. Rather it is because they have found after baptism in the Holy Spirit that the same kind of things as the Bible relates – visions, prophecies, miracles, healings and the like – have begun to happen in their own experience and so they have found belief becoming unproblematic. That certainly tends to make them fairly conservative on the whole, but not always closed to discussion.

Perhaps the main difference between the charismatic and all the others is that he firmly believes that God still works today in the same kind of way as he did in biblical times. For example, charismatics, whether they be of a conservative bent or not, believe that the gifts of the Spirit are as available to Christians today as they were in the first century; non-charismatics, be they radical or fundamentalist, generally say they are not.

Our approach here will be to see how God has acted in history as the Bible tells it, firmly believing that in his eternal unchangingness he still acts in essentially the same ways today, and therefore seeking to draw from the biblical narrative lessons for our guidance in understanding his will and purposes for our own lives at this time in the late twentieth century.

Israel among the nations

The civilisations of Egypt and Mesopotamia were already old when Abraham's father left Ur of the Chaldees, probably round about 1950 BC, when the city was sacked by invading Elamites from the east. Ur was both a centre of commerce and of moon-worship, as also was Haran in Northern Mesopotamia where he eventually settled (Gen. 11.27–32).

Mesopotamia, after a period of considerable imperial power at the end of the third millennium, became divided into smaller city-state units in the early second. Assyria and

Babylonia first emerged as important political entities at this time, though it was mainly Assyria that showed expansionist tendencies. From 1500 to 1100 it was one of the leading states in the ancient world, but then it entered a period of weakness and only began to revive again about 900 BC. Up to that point, from the time Abraham left Haran to come to Canaan, the Mesopotamian civilisations played no significant part in the history of God's people.

Egypt was the main external influence on Israel in the second millennium BC. Although we cannot be certain about the dates, it seems likely that Joseph and his brothers went down to Egypt some time after 1720, when foreign kings, known as the Hyksos came to power. They were Semites, like the Hebrews, but they were driven out in 1570 by the Egyptians under Amosis, who turned Egypt into an empire that exercised control over Canaan for most of the following 350 years. During those long years the political climate began to change, and by the end of the fourteenth century the Israelites found themselves an oppressed people. They left Egypt in the following century, sometime during the reign of Rameses II, perhaps about 1270, and are first mentioned outside the Bible in a list of peoples his successor, Merniptah, fought against during a campaign in Palestine about 1220.

In those times peoples, who were spoken of as 'Sea Peoples', began to be dislodged from the islands and coast-lands of the Aegean by northern invaders and they came flooding across the Mediterranean into Palestine and North Africa, gradually eroding Egypt's strength and causing the collapse of her empire. *Canaan* was thus left free for the taking. Edomites, Moabites and Ammonites established independent kingdoms in the southern and eastern regions by the Dead Sea and across the Jordan; Philistines, who were newcomers from among the Sea Peoples, settled on the southern coastland; Israel took most of central Palestine; and, of course, the Canaanites continued to occupy a number of their ancient strongholds throughout the land.

Israel was finally established in strength under David, who built up his own empire incorporating the other little nations around his borders, though that was relatively short lived, for on the death of Solomon the kingdom split in two and the satellite states regained their independence.

About 900, *Assyria* began to expand its frontiers. In 853 the Assyrians engaged a coalition of Palestinian forces at Qarqar on the River Orontes; in 841 Jehu of Israel was obliged to pay them tribute. In 732 they took Damascus and finally they took Samaria in 722, thus bringing the history of Northern Israel to an end. Although they never took Jerusalem, the Davidic kings were their vassals until they were overthrown by the *Babylonians* in 612. Over the next fifteen years Judah was for a while subject to Egypt, and then to Babylon. Finally Jerusalem rebelled and was taken by the Babylonians in 597 BC.

Israel was a little country, not much larger than Wales, situated at the crossroads of the ancient world and for most of its history its fortunes were inseparable from the comings and goings of the super-powers on either side of it. It is impossible to read the Old Testament story intelligently without knowing just a little about them, but it is important to re-emphasise here that the story we are about to follow is first and foremost about Israel and her God.

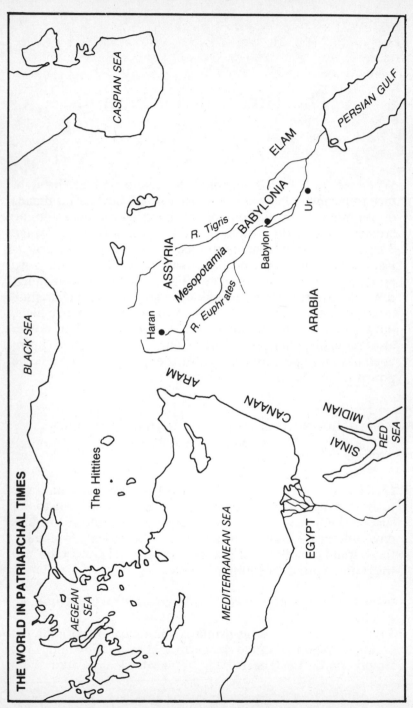

THE WORLD IN PATRIARCHAL TIMES

2

The Birth of the Nation

When we study God's purposes and activity, we are brought face to face with his Word and his Spirit. They are his means of communication and control, and have been so ever since he created the world by them in the beginning (Gen. 1.2f; Ps. 33.6). By them he has continued to direct and control its history through men who have been open to hear his word and receive his Spirit. The Church today is constantly reminded, particularly through its evangelical and charismatic members, of the power of Word and Spirit to change lives, but we shall see as we follow the Bible story that their power also radically changes history. The activity of the Spirit becomes more pronounced the further we go; at first it is the power of the Word that is more manifest.

1. GOD'S WORD TO ADAM, ABRAHAM AND MOSES (GENESIS – NUMBERS)

God has spoken to his people on many occasions, sometimes to impart new vision, sometimes to call them back to, or sustain them in vision he has already given. Before Joshua's day, among his many communications to Israel's forebears, three stand out above all the rest as of pivotal importance for the whole course of human history.

God's plan for his world – his covenant with Adam. (Gen. 1–11)
The first of these was his primal communication with man at creation. When he made the earth and everything in it, God simply said, 'Let there be . . . ' and each created thing

18

appeared. But when we read about the creation of man, it is different, for we are given some insight into the reasons why he was created: we are told something about God's thoughts beforehand and about his communication with man afterwards. And the heart of the matter is that man was made by God to rule over the earth as his viceroy. For that purpose he was made in God's own image and was given kingly authority over all animal and plant life (cp. Ps. 8.5–8). God created a good earth, a beautiful garden-kingdom, and in his goodness entrusted it to man to care for, enjoy and rule over as its king.

Such was God's purpose, but it was spoiled by the fall, after which man lost the fullness of his kingly authority. Life became a battle with his environment, as he tilled the soil with the sweat of his brow, cultivated it in competition with thorns and thistles, bore children in pain (Gen. 3.16–19), and eventually had to live in a relationship with the animal world governed by fear (9.2) and with the rest of mankind governed by suspicion, hostility and confusion (ch. 4; 11.1–9).

God's plan for redeeming the world – his covenant with Abraham. (Gen. 12–50)

For God to make earth his kingdom again, he had to start somewhere with somebody. We are not told the reason for his timing or his choice of Abraham, but one day, probably sometime soon after 2000 BC, God spoke to him, sketching in broad outline his plan for redeeming the world, and inviting him to co-operate in bringing it to birth.

The plan was very simple (Gen. 12.1–3):
1. God would lead Abraham to a land of his choosing;
2. there his family would so increase that one day they would become a great nation;
3. God would look after him and bless him in his co-operation;
4. and the outcome would be that blessing would eventually be restored to all peoples on earth.

God made no great demands of Abraham, other than that he trust him and set out for his new home. He did not say Abraham would have to work or try hard at anything; redemption would be God's doing, not Abraham's. All he had to do was make himself available to father a family in Canaan so that it might in turn become the nucleus of a nation through which God could re-create his kingdom on earth. God was only asking for his co-operation and trust – his faith.

The stories of Genesis show us some of the problems Abraham had in sustaining that co-operation. Shortly after his arrival in Canaan famine struck and he went down to Egypt, not where God wanted him to be at all, and the result was that he got himself into a mess from which God had to rescue him (chs. 14f). Later in his life he almost repeated the same mistake with similar consequences (ch. 20), but in the end he bought a plot of land and established his home in Canaan (ch. 21).

In the meantime he also had faith problems about becoming a father in his old age. Though God reassured him and he did respond in faith (15.6), he first thought he should adopt a slave in his house as his heir (15.2f), then he tried to get an heir by his wife's slave (ch. 16), but after a final moment of doubt, when both he and his wife in turn laughed at what God was promising to do with them (chs. 17f), he became father of Isaac (ch. 21). Now strong in faith, he was prepared to sacrifice Isaac (ch. 22), but in the end arranged his marriage to Rebekah, a kinsman's son, thus ensuring that the vision and call God had given him would continue to be cherished in the family (ch. 24).

Like his father, Isaac was tempted to go to Egypt in time of famine, but the LORD stopped him from making Abraham's mistake (ch. 26) and so the vision was preserved for another generation and handed on to his son, Jacob (ch. 27). Jacob, however, was a spoiled child, with little respect for family ties or the sacredness of God's name. Thanks to his deceitful ways he became a fugitive on his uncle's farm, back where Abraham had first come from (chs. 25, 27). He betrayed no interest in the vision God had given his fathers, but as he fled from Canaan, God met with him, taught him his purposes and promised to bring him home again so that they might be fulfilled through him (ch. 28). After a lengthy exile that was exactly what happened, but when Jacob returned to Canaan he now had twelve children, who were to become the nucleus of the nation about which God had spoken to Abraham (chs. 29–35).

As the story continues we see these twelve put God's purposes in jeopardy again. Family jealousies result in one of them, Joseph, being sold into slavery in Egypt. The LORD cared for him and raised him up, but presently in time of famine his brothers left the promised land to join him in Egypt, seemingly oblivious of the hard lessons their fathers had had to learn (chs. 37–45). Jacob remembered and feared for the vision, but God reassured him that he would still fulfil his word (46.2–4).

The Genesis story is full of dramatic tension. Men now receive and then lose sight of the call and promise of God; they now show faith and then fail to stand firm in it. Abraham, Isaac and Jacob were all either tempted to, or actually did flee from Canaan in time of stress, and the story ends with the infant nation well and truly out of the promised land. So far God has made no great demands, only promises, and all he has asked for is faith, but men clearly find that difficult. Repeatedly we watch him stretch out his hand to rescue them from the muddle they get themselves into and at the end of Genesis we are left asking how he can ever restore his kingdom on earth through men like these, or indeed like ourselves today.

Fortunately the answer lies with God, not us; it is his promise and his purpose. In the closing verses of the book we see Joseph remind his brothers of that truth and encourage them to look forward in faith to the day when God will bring them back home to Canaan again (50.24).

What God was doing in those early days was choosing men through whom he would begin his redeeming work, giving them basic revelation about his plan for doing it, and showing them the kind of co-operation he wanted from them. That is, he was imparting vision and teaching the need for simple faith in him to fulfil it.

We shall see as our story progresses and other dimensions are added to the vision, that these basic ingredients remain foundational for all God will do in Israel. We shall listen to leaders, kings and prophets, just like Joseph on his death-bed, reminding the descendants of Abraham about the promise God made to their forefather, about the high calling he has given them, and about their constant need to walk in faith in that calling, vision and promise.

God's plan for the life of his holy nation – his covenant with Moses. (Exodus – Numbers)

In Egypt the Israelites multiplied until their numbers were large enough for them to become a nation. Then early in the thirteenth century God called Moses and sent him to bring them out of the life of crippling bondage into which they had fallen. Amid many miraculous signs and wonders, he led them out through the desert until they came to Mount Sinai (Exod. 1–19).

There God reminded them about his plan for them to be his 'treasured possession, a kingdom of priests and a holy nation', set apart for his work, and told them the basic principles by which they were to live if they were to be so (the Ten Commandments). After God had outlined the pattern for their social structures (the Book of the Covenant), Moses and the elders, on behalf of the people, entered into a covenant with him to be that holy people (Exod. 19–24).

Then Moses went up the mountain alone to receive instruction about building the tabernacle for worship and about instituting its priests, which he eventually was able to do, after dealing with some quite major crises in the camp (Exod. 24–40).

At the tabernacle the LORD taught them the patterns for sacrifices, priesthood, religious purification, and the like (Lev. 1–16) and gave them fairly full teaching about their life of holiness (Lev. 17–27).

Then Moses, after taking census of the tribes, arranging them and the Levites according to their divisions, and giving some further instructions about various aspects of the life they were being called to, led them north from Sinai towards Canaan where they were to live as God's people according to the patterns they had just been shown. (Num. 1–10)

However, the Israelites had already grumbled and complained about God's dealings with them more than once, and now, as they neared their destination, their grumbling intensified until finally they refused to go forward and take the land God was offering them. The outcome was that they found themselves wandering aimlessly for forty years in the wilderness south of Canaan. Because they failed to go on in faith and obedience they never entered their promised inheritance. At the end of that time it was almost entirely

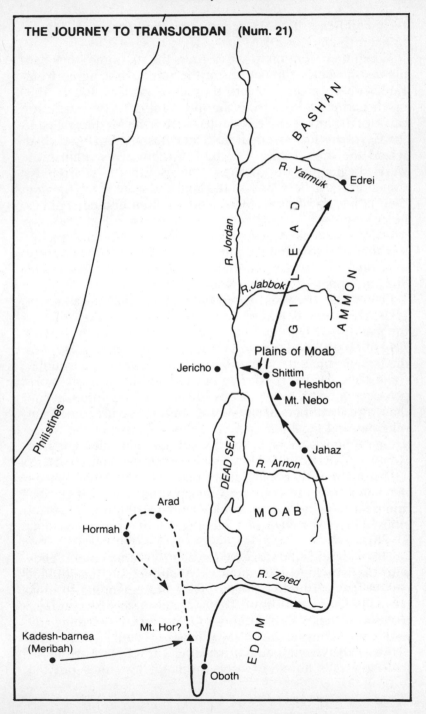

THE JOURNEY TO TRANSJORDAN (Num. 21)

their children, the next generation, that Moses led up to Canaan (Num. 10–20).

When they went up to the borders the first time, they had planned to enter the land from the south, moving up from Kadesh-barnea directly into the hill-country of Judah. But much had changed during the intervening forty years. Because of the influx of 'Sea Peoples' across the Mediterranean, the Egyptians had lost their hold on Palestine, but others had seized the opportunity to establish themselves. Philistines were beginning to occupy the southern coastlands, Canaanites still held most of the land and were strengthening their cities, and Edom, Moab and Ammon had emerged as little kingdoms in the south and east. In effect the way forward was blocked, and so the Israelites had to skirt first the territory of Edom and then the land of Moab, but eventually they pitched camp in the plains of Moab, at a place called Shittim, opposite Jericho (Num. 20–21).

From there they conquered the rest of Transjordan north of the Dead Sea, defeating Sihon, the king of the Amorites in the south, and Og, the king of Bashan in the north. Balak, king of Moab, tried in vain to halt their further progress, and the Israelites had to do battle with the Midianites, a troublesome tribe of desert rovers, but already Moses was more preoccupied with preparations for the crossing into Canaan than with the affairs of the desert. Besides giving some final religious and legal instruction, he took census of the tribes again, appointed Joshua to succeed him as leader, granted Reuben, Gad and half of Manasseh the right to occupy parts of Transjordan as their tribal inheritance after they had helped the other tribes to conquer Canaan, and made other last-minute arrangements concerning land distribution, Levitical cities, cities of refuge and inheritance of property (Num. 21–36).

That in brief is the story we traced in Volume One. It ends with the Israelites, having already conquered Transjordan, poised for entry into Canaan. They are beginning to look more like a national entity. They have laws, social structures, forms of worship and leaders – in fact almost everything any nation has. The one thing they still lack, of course, is the land on which to live out their national life. The story we are about to follow tells how they took the land, how they put the patterns God gave them into practice, how they subsequently became a kingdom, and how in the end they lost it all.

2. THE CHALLENGE OF FAITH AND OBEDIENCE (DEUTERONOMY)

Israel's call was always more than just to become a nation – it was to become God's holy nation, the expression of his own kingdom on earth. God's plan was ultimately to restore his Eden-kingdom, and Israel was to be its first planting, a kind of colony of the kingdom of heaven on earth, a base from which the rest of the world would be won back. To understand biblical history it is crucial to bear in mind that that vision of her calling was what motivated Israel to become what she did. The things God said, first to Adam, then to Abraham and thirdly to Moses, are the standard by which all her history is to be judged.

Throughout the story as told in Joshua–2 Kings there are moments, usually at the close of a great leader's lifetime, when the period just ended is reviewed in the light of that standard: the lessons to be learned from it are set forth and some advice is given for the next phase. The Book of Deuteronomy presents the first of these reviews, acting as a kind of prologue to our history by outlining the lessons Israel should have learned from her encounters with God at Sinai and in the wilderness, and drawing from them the principles on which she is to move forward into the next stage of her history. It is basically an extended sermon preached by Moses to the Israelites encamped on the east bank of the Jordan on the eve of their entry to the Promised Land to prepare them for all that lay ahead.

He recalls the main events in their story since leaving Sinai and reminds them of the need to be faithful to God once they are in the land (chs. 1–4). He then rehearses the Ten Commandments given at Sinai, and preaches a long sermon about the need for total faithfulness and dedication to God as his 'holy people' (chs. 5–11):

'Love the LORD your God with all your heart (6.5) . . . You must destroy them (pagans) totally, for they will turn your

sons away to serve other gods (7.2–4) . . . Be careful that you
do not forget the LORD your God and follow other gods
(8.11,19) . . . 'Remember what happened when you worshipped the golden calf in the wilderness! (ch. 9) . . . 'Fear the
Lord your God and serve him. Hold fast to him. He is your
God.' (10.12–22) . . . If you are faithful, God will richly bless
you in the land, but disobedience will lead to disaster (ch. 11).

In chs. 12–26 he restates many of the laws, often with short
sermons or sentences attached reminding the Israelites of the
blessings that will attend obedience and the curses that must
follow disobedience. Then in chs 27–30 he spells out the
consequences of obedience and disobedience in blessing and
curse in much fuller detail.

He then commissions Joshua, gives the Levites a copy of
the law to be read in public regularly (ch. 31), prophetically
reviews Israel's future (ch. 32), pronounces a final blessing on
the tribes (ch. 33), and ascends Mount Nebo, where, before
his death, he is granted a panoramic view of the land that
Israel will enter. The Spirit's anointing now rests on Joshua
(ch. 34).

The main theme of Deuteronomy is that God showed Israel
at Sinai the pattern of life by which his people were to live in
order to receive all the rich blessings he wanted them to have
in the land. But his call is absolute, to be holy, to be God's
people, totally dedicated to him and to his law, and so
alongside the promises stand very solemn warnings about the
disastrous consequences of disobedience. Note the concise
statement of this doctrine in 30.15–20: ' . . . I have set before
you life and death, blessings and curses. Now choose life, so
that you and your children may live . . . ' God's will, as he
had first promised to Abraham, was to bless, but two ways lay
before Israel, and only one of them would lead to blessing,
namely the way of obedience and faith. The other would most
surely lead to curse, suffering and destruction. Which road
would Israel take? And if it were to take the wrong road, what
would become of God's purpose?

To the mind of faith the answers are already known. We
have seen the pattern. Weakened by sin, man will doubtless
fall again, but God is always faithful to his word and somehow
will preserve his purpose. As Moses points out, he is merciful
and so will forgive and restore whenever Israel returns to him

in repentance (4.29–31; 30.1–10). But that will be the only means by which she will obtain her times of refreshing and restoration when she stumbles during her work of building God's kingdom.

In Summary:

In his covenant with Abraham God gave promises to be received in faith; in his covenant with Moses he gave commands to be responded to in obedience. The Genesis story is of God teaching men about his own reliability or faithfulness and about their need to become faithful in return. The Wilderness story is of God teaching them about his righteousness or holiness and about their need to become holy too.

THE CALL TO FAITH AND OBEDIENCE

THE ABRAHAMIC COVENANT
    = God's *promise*, requiring our *faith*.
  In it we learn of God's *faithfulness*.
THE MOSAIC COVENANT
    = God's *command*, requiring our *obedience*.
  In it we learn of God's *righteousness*.

The dramatic tensions remain much the same throughout. God gives his word and reveals his purpose, but repeatedly man's actions put them in jeopardy. God is patient as the centuries pass, repeatedly restoring his faltering chosen ones, sometimes with gentleness, sometimes with anger. Reviewing the story it seems a miracle in itself that we now have a nation standing on the edge of the promised land ready to enter and settle. But the question remains. Will Israel be able to meet the standards of obedience God requires, because entry to and continued possession of the land is going to depend on that? The history of the following centuries is judged in the Old Testament against the challenge of that question.

The faith message is clear, however: God's Will will somehow prevail in the end. We may ask how, but we have already seen much of his promise come to fulfilment. From one man, Abraham, we now have a people, with some understanding of what faith is and with a revelation of God's righteousness, about to take possession of their promised inheritance in Canaan.

PART TWO

FOUNDING
THE KINGDOM

1230 — 1010 BC

At each stage in Israel's history we find our attention focused on the lives of particular individuals. That is because God welcomes the co-operation of men who will walk with him in faith and lays his hand powerfully on them, with the result that they become giants among the leaders of their day. Their leadership is vastly different from that of self-made men who promote themselves into positions of prominence. God's men are generally humble people, often hesitant about accepting the role they are called to perform, commonly aware of their own inadequacy for the task, and so also very much aware of their utter dependence on God. We see the pattern clearly in the lives of men such as Abraham and Moses, and we encounter it again in Joshua and some of the judges. Just as the story of the exodus is Moses' story, so the conquest is Joshua's, the settlement Ehud's, Gideon's, Jephthah's, and the transition to monarchy Samuel's, Saul's and David's. Certainly it is also Israel's history and we meet other folk in the telling of it, but first and foremost it is the story of those who, chosen by God and anointed with his Spirit, have laid hold of the vision and faithfully pursued it. It is a story, not just about men, leaders and nations, but about men of faith.

3

Taking the Land

JOSHUA

We hear little about Joshua before his appointment to
leadership. He led Israel's fighting men against the Amalekites at Rephidim (Exod. 17.8–13), he accompanied Moses as
his personal assistant when he went up Mount Sinai (Exod.
24.13), and later stood guard over the tent of meeting (Exod.
33.11). He was puzzled by what was happening when the
Spirit came on the seventy elders in the wilderness (Num.
11.28), but he and Caleb were the only ones among the spies
to maintain the faith perspective about entering the land
(Num. 14.6–9). After the conquest of Transjordan Moses had
him commissioned to succeed him. By that time he was
already recognised as a potential leader and shepherd for the
people and one 'in whom is the Spirit.' All he now required
was the authority that came with the public recognition Moses
then gave him (Num. 27.15–23).

However, Joshua was also clearly a man who needed a lot
of encouragement and assurance. Hence Moses, just before
his death, exhorted him to be 'strong and courageous' in his
leadership, to remember that he would never be alone: 'The
LORD himself goes before you and will be with you; he will
never leave you nor forsake you. Do not be afraid; do not be
discouraged.' (Deut. 31.7f). Then after Moses' death,
Joshua's anointing was recognised by the people and they saw
he was now a man 'filled with the spirit of wisdom' (Deut.
34.9), but as we shall see, he still needed further encouragement before he could lead them into their inheritance.

His story falls neatly into four parts: Firstly we read about
how he led the people into the land, secondly how he

31

conquered it, then how he divided it among the tribes, and finally how, at the end of his life, he prepared them for settling in it. We see different qualities of leadership emerging at each stage.

1. CROSSING THE JORDAN (1.1 – 5.12)

The date must be somewhere about 1240 or 1230 BC, towards the end of Rameses II's reign in Egypt, but before 1220, when his successor, Merniptah, encountered Israel in Canaan (see p. 15).

Ch. 1: The LORD encourages Joshua to take up his leadership.

Joshua was already Israel's leader by appointment and public recognition, and the Spirit of the LORD was already on him for the job. But the man who is to lead God's people needs something more than all that – some confirming word from the LORD himself, the direct, personal word that creates complete faith. Abraham, Jacob and Moses all had it, and now God gives it to Joshua. We shall watch him question and ponder over strategies, errors and successes, but never over his calling to leadership nor the total vision and purpose behind it. The confidence for that was burnt indelibly into him right at the start – and that is always the secret of dynamic spiritual leadership. What God actually said to him added very little to what Moses and the people had already told him, but from that point on he knew he was leading because of God's call, not just because other people, however spiritually perceptive, thought it would be good to have him do so. Such knowledge makes all the difference, particularly when times of testing come.

God's opening words, 'Moses my servant is dead', may at first seem superfluous, but they are in fact very pointed. Too many leaders live in the shadow of their predecessors, bound by 'what the last man used to do'. Joshua was not to be like that. Moses had been a great man of God, one of the greatest the world was ever to see, but his task was over and done.

Joshua had different work to do; he was not called to be another Moses.

The second thing God told him was that he had called him to succeed: 'I will give you every place where you set your foot.' We can contrast the failure mentality of many church leaders, which generally results from lack or loss of confidence in their vocation. But God's call is always to bear fruit, not to fail. Of course, for Joshua, alongside that assurance went the knowledge that the land he would take was promised territory anyhow. Moses had warned the Israelites against trying to take land that was not promised to them (Deut. 2) – to do so would be to act in presumption, not faith. The principle remains the same today.

Thirdly, God urged Joshua several times, just as Moses had done, not to be afraid, but to be strong and courageous, and to know that he would always be with him. Similar boldness of faith should characterise Christian leadership (cp. Acts 4.13; 2 Tim. 1.6–8), though sadly it does not always do so.

Finally, God warned that, in order to be successful, he must live in obedience to the law of Moses, studying it daily, so that it would become automatically directive for all his actions and decisions. The same commission was given to Israel's kings (cp. Deut. 17.18–20) – and for the same reasons daily Bible-reading is still a basic requirement for successful Christian leadership.

Thus encouraged, Joshua came into his own. When he issued the order to strike camp and prepare for the crossing, the people unhesitatingly pledged him their full obedience. If Joshua had had any doubts about hearing God aright, their words must have sounded like clear confirmation, for they virtually re-echoed what God had said: 'Only may the LORD your God be with you . . . Only be strong and courageous.'

Ch. 2: Spies reconnoitre the land.

Sending out spies does not signal a lack of faith; it was necesssary strategy. Moses did the same in his day. What went wrong then was that the people fearfully heeded the negative part of the report they brought back. Joshua must have known the risk he was taking, since he had been one of Moses' spies (Num. 13–14). But what Joshua's spies now report is that the fear of Israel has already gone ahead of

them, though a few perceptive individuals, like Rahab and
her family, discern that it is the LORD they need to fear, not
just the Israelites – and it is that kind of perception that
secures salvation.

Chs 3–4: The Crossing.

God calls his leaders to take their people where others would
never dream of going, to walk in faith so that the work can be
seen to be God's. That was the nature of the trust Abraham
had been called to have, and so it was with Joshua. By Jericho
the Jordan is at its widest and at the time the Israelites were
there it was in flood. God could hardly have chosen a more
suitable time and place for testing faith and revealing his
glory. We can imagine the Levites carrying the ark to the edge
of the river, stepping faithfully, though perhaps also rather
fearfully, into the dangerous waters, when suddenly and quite
inexplicably the river simply disappeared. Once they reco-
vered from the initial astonishment, their impulse must have
been to hurry across as quickly as possible, lest the water
should just as suddenly return. But instead they had to stand
amid stream until everyone else had crossed and memorial
stones had been removed from the river-bed. Then, the
moment they stepped out on the bank the water ran in flood
again as before. When a leader goes forward in faith, his
people have to follow in obedience and faith behind him, and
for them that can often be about as testing as it is for him.

We are told that the water stopped flowing at Adam, which
is slightly less than twenty miles north of Jericho (modern Tell
ed-Damiyeh). There the Jordan is narrow with quite high,
soft limestone and clay banks which get undermined by the
water and occasionally topple into the river. In 1267 AD,
during an earthquake, the Jordan got dammed up at Adam
for sixteen hours. Something similar happened in 1906 and in
1927 the flow was stopped for just under two days. If that was
how it happened in Joshua's time, then the miracle of
earth-tremor, revelation, timing and faith is still truly asto-
nishing.

5. 1–12: The Israelites set up base camp at Gilgal.

The miracle at the Jordan had a double effect. As well as
granting the Israelites passage into the land, it caused fear to

spread among the Canaanites so that they did not attack immediately. That allowed the Israelites time to set up camp, to have themselves properly consecrated to the LORD's work by circumcision and to celebrate Passover. Passover had marked the departure from Egypt; now it marked the entry to Canaan. Their years of wandering were over.

That day the manna stopped, and they ate the fruit of the land God had originally intended them to have when he called Abraham to go and live there. That also was the LORD's provision, just as much as the manna had been, and therefore no less miraculous. It could be increased or withheld by him at any time (Deut. 28.38–42).

2. THE CONQUEST (5.13 – 11.23)

The challenges of faith and obedience were far from over now that the Israelites were in the land, as they would discover with every new step they took.

5.13 – 6.27: The fall of Jericho.
Perhaps Joshua was standing looking out over Jericho making his war plans when he was confronted by the stranger who announced that he had come neither to help nor oppose him but to take charge of his (the LORD's) army as its commander. Any other man might have reacted very differently, but Joshua was walking with God and immediately perceived the truth. The tactical advice he was given would also have seemed nothing less than ridiculous to any other military man, but again Joshua's call was to a leadership of faith, and he had only recently seen how well God honoured him when he took the seemingly ridiculous step of faith into the flooding Jordan. Once again he was to see faith vindicated as the walls of Jericho toppled and the Israelites went in and took the city.

7.1 – 8.29: The battle for Ai.
The stories we have looked at so far have spoken of the testing of faith. This story speaks about the testing of obedience. It should have required hardly any faith to take Ai, for by comparison with Jericho it was only a small village (7.3), and

MAIN SITES IN JOSHUA 1-10

yet in the initial battle Israel was thoroughly routed. Suddenly we see Joshua crumble, his confidence utterly shattered as he falls to the ground crying out to God: 'Why have you let us down?' So easily does faith vanish! But God's purpose is to sustain faith, just as he had done with Abraham, and so he orders Joshua to stand up like the leader he is supposed to be and find out why the Israelites have let him down, rather than ask faithlessly why he has let the Israelites down.

Achan's sin was blatant disobedience. His punishment may seem ruthless by our standards, but it compares almost exactly with the punishment of Ananias and Sapphira in Acts 5. At this critical phase when Israel was fighting for a first foothold in Canaan against what would under natural conditions be overwhelming odds, there was no place for men like Achan in the army.

Meantime God has to restore Joshua to his place of confidence: 'Do not be afraid; do not be discouraged' (8.1). The words echo those of his original call. Now as he leads his troops, having been taught a sharp lesson in obedience, the conquest of Ai is assured.

8.30–35: Renewing the covenant in the land.

The fall of Jericho and Ai must have allowed access to Shechem, a few miles north, in the valley between Mount Ebal and Mount Gerizim. Joshua took this early opportunity to gather the people there to renew their commitment to the covenant according to the instructions given by Moses (cp. Deut. 27).

This was a momentous occasion. Shechem was where Abraham had first stopped, where God promised: 'To your offspring I will give this land.' (Gen. 12.7). It was also where Jacob and his family, the nucleus of what was later to become Israel, first settled when they arrived in Canaan (Gen. 33.18f). And now, in the same place, Joshua celebrated the arrival of Abraham's promised offspring, the nation Jacob's family had foreshadowed. Nowhere could have been more appropriate for rededicating themselves to the God who had promised them this land.

Holding this ceremony was partly an act of faith. It declared their arrival, but also anticipated further conquest. Later, at the end of his life, after the whole land was taken and distributed among the tribes, Joshua would bring them back to Shechem to renew the covenant again (ch. 24). In the meantime, following in Abraham's and Jacob's footsteps, he set up an altar and sealed Israel's pledge of allegiance on it with sacrifice. But he also had to remind them of the blessings and curses attached to the laws God was now asking them to keep.

Ch. 9: Tricked into a treaty with the Gibeonites.

Just like Rahab the harlot, the Gibeonites saw that it was God they were up against, and like Rahab they succeeded in saving their lives. The lesson for us, however, lies not in their clever trickery, but in the Israelites' failure to detect it. Though they did take every care to check out the Gibeonites' story, men of God are required to exercise a perception that goes beyond

what is natural to other men, by seeking divine revelation as
well as making rational assessments: 'The men of Israel
sampled their provisions, but did not enquire of the LORD.'
(v. 14).

Ch. 10: The conquest of southern Palestine.

With the conquest of Jericho and Ai and the treaty with the
Gibeonites Joshua had established a strong foothold in
Canaan by driving a wedge into the centre of the land.
Surprisingly it was through the Gibeonite treaty that he was
enabled to take the southern territories, but then God can
turn all things to the fulfilling of his purposes, just as he used
Pharaoh's stubbornness to manifest his glory and used the
crucifixion to win our salvation.

The south was 'conquered in one campaign' (v. 42) and in
the middle of it Joshua's men witnessed two miracles of
nature, one of them unlike almost anything else in history.
The story of the sun standing still is a wonderful illustration of
how far God will go to honour the man who has faith in him:
'There has never been a day like it before or since, a day when
the LORD listened to a man.' (v. 14).

11.1–14: The conquest of the North.

The northern thrust, like the southern, was not something
Joshua had to plan. He was granted it when the king of Hazor
led a coalition against him.

11.15 – 12.24: 'So Joshua took the entire land.'

The secret of Joshua's success was radical obedience: 'As the
LORD commanded his servant Moses, so Moses commanded
Joshua, and Joshua did it; he left nothing undone of all that
the LORD commanded Moses.' (11.15).

The story of the conquest ends with a review of the regions
and cities taken by Moses and Joshua in Transjordan and in
Canaan, the satisfying evidence of vindicated faith.

3. THE DISTRIBUTION OF THE LAND (CHS. 12–22)

The years have rolled by and Joshua is now old. To be sure,

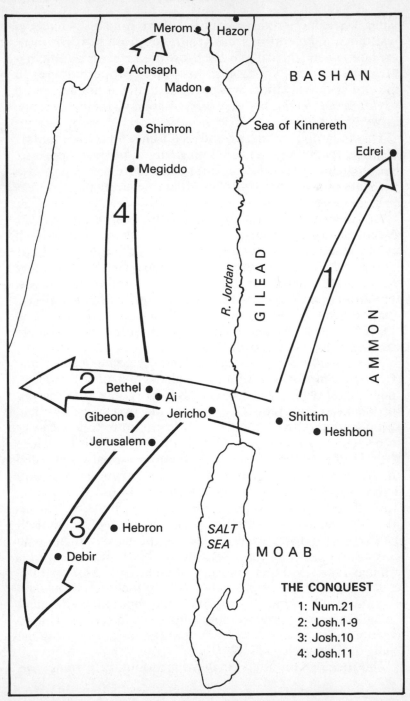

Merom • • Hazor

B A S H A N

• Achsaph

Madon •

Sea of Kinnereth

Edrei •

• Shimron

• Megiddo

4

R. Jordan

G I L E A D

1

A M M O N

2

Bethel • • Ai

Gibeon • • Jericho • Shittim

Jerusalem • • Heshbon

3 • Hebron

SALT
SEA

M O A B

• Debir

THE CONQUEST
1: Num.21
2: Josh.1-9
3: Josh.10
4: Josh.11

Israel had conquered Canaan, but there are still pockets of resistance and plenty of areas to be taken. Joshua's division of the land among the tribes is therefore undertaken in faith that they will eventually establish themselves properly there. In the end of the day there was only one that was not able to do so (Dan; see 19.47), but they were all to have their problems, as we shall see.

The geographical arrangements outlined in these chapters are most readily summarised by a glance at the map opposite, but amid the lists of towns and places there are one or two portraits of faith being vindicated and encouraged.

Chs. 13–17: Transjordan, Judah and Joseph.

After reading about the allotment for Reuben, Gad and half of Manasseh in Transjordan, land already allocated by Moses before Israel had crossed the Jordan (ch. 13), we find information relating to the settlement of the two largest territorial blocks in Canaan, Judah in the south (chs. 14–15) and Joseph, or Ephraim and the other half of Manasseh, in the centre (chs. 16–17). Politically their story will dominate the history of Israel down to the end of the monarchy.

As we read about their settlement, we come across some strikingly contrasting attitudes. Of all the men of military age, that is, over twenty when Israel left Egypt, only two survived to enter the land (cp. 5.6), namely the two spies who had stood firm in faith on the day Israel refused to follow Moses into Canaan, Joshua and Caleb (Num. 14.30). It is therefore with delight that we watch them being personally rewarded for their faithfulness with towns of their own, Joshua with Timnath Serah and Caleb with Hebron (14.6–15; 19.49f).

We have already tapped Joshua's spirit, but Caleb's was just as strong. Now eighty-five years old, he declares himself every bit as vigorous as in his youth, ready to go with enthusiasm and full confidence to do battle and secure his inheritance, a man of courage and faith (14.11). In total contrast, the Ephraimites, who were in fact 'numerous and very powerful', came bleating to Joshua about their allotment being too heavily forested and so too restrictive for them to occupy. Joshua had to drive them to the task of clearing the land for themselves (17.14–18).

The Judeans, settling as they did in mountain terrain, were

always a more rugged people than the Ephraimites living in
the richer valleys and farmlands of central Canaan.

Chs. 18–19: *The rest of the tribes*

The two main tribal blocks, Judah and Joseph, apparently
settled in their regions before the others occupied theirs.
Joshua was therefore able to set up the Tent of Meeting at a
central point in the land, at Shiloh, where it could be a focal
meeting-place for all the tribes.

The Tent, with the ark housed in it, was Israel's rallying
point. For much of the time they simply lived around it
bonded in unity by common recognition of all it symbolised
about the presence of God. But there were times when they
were called to move out from their positions and follow in
faith when it moved, as in the wilderness, or at the crossing of

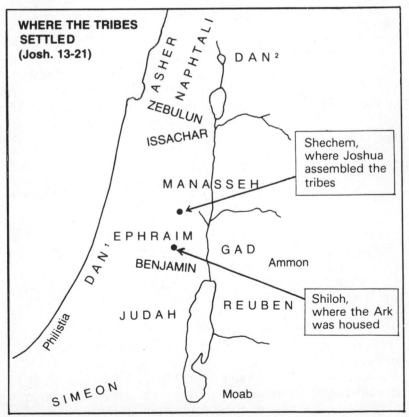

WHERE THE TRIBES
SETTLED
(Josh. 13-21)

ASHER
NAPHTALI
DAN²
ZEBULUN
ISSACHAR
MANASSEH
EPHRAIM
DAN¹
BENJAMIN
GAD
Ammon
JUDAH
REUBEN
Philistia
SIMEON
Moab

Shechem,
where Joshua
assembled the
tribes

Shiloh,
where the Ark
was housed

the Jordan (Num. 9.15–23; Josh. 3.3f). It was thus a rallying-point, not just for social intercourse and worship, but for faith, and it is in faith that Joshua now speaks to the tribes gathered around it, urging them to shake themselves out of their lethargy, to rise up and take the lands that are their allotted inheritance (18.3).

Chs. 20–21: Cities of refuge and Levitical cities.
The designation of cities of refuge, as instructed by Moses (Num. 35), was a legal necessity for maintaining justice and preventing wanton blood-vengeance between Israelite families whenever someone was killed accidentally.

The Levites were allowed no tribal territory, because they were to be free to serve the LORD as his priests and temple servants (Josh. 13.14, 33), and so were allotted various towns throughout the country to live in, again as commanded by Moses (Num. 35).

Ch. 22: Initial problems in Transjordan.
With the River Jordan dividing the land, relationship problems between east and west banks were bound to arise. It did not take long for that to happen, but when it did, it became clear that at heart both sides were united in their vision for the LORD's service.

4. JOSHUA'S REVIEW AND CHALLENGE (CHS. 23–24)

Like Moses at the end of his life, Joshua summoned a meeting of the leaders and then a national assembly, to remind them about the vision they were called to serve, about God's unfailing faithfulness in it, and about continuing need for faithfulness on their part.

Ch. 23: His address to the leaders.
As Joshua reviews the conquest he gives God all the credit for its success. But he is no starry-eyed supernaturalist. He has known the cost of leadership as well as the LORD's undergirding of it, and so he presents Israel's new leaders with the challenge of maintaining and furthering all he has won. His

admonition, 'Be very strong; be careful to obey all that is written in the Book of the Law', re-echoes his own commission so many years earlier. He has been faithful – will they be so after he is gone?

His primary purpose is, of course, to encourage them in faith and vision for their next phase, when the remaining parts of the land will have to be taken. Their greatest challenge, which was not one he had had to face, will be holding fast to God in peacetime without being drawn into the ways of pagan Canaanite neighbours. Thus he warns them: Do not associate with the people that remain, do not make alliances or intermarry with them, do not turn to their gods – hold fast to the LORD your God! If you fail to obey, God will no longer drive out the peoples before you and they will be a constant snare to you. So be men of vision and men of God!

The principles for retaining the land are essentially the same as those for winning it: hold fast to God in obedience and faith.

Ch. 24: Renewing the covenant.

Finally, Joshua calls the tribes together, repeats the challenge he has issued to their leaders and pledges them anew to be rid of all foreign gods, to serve the LORD only. That challenge means life or death. Joshua and his generation were faithful. But how will the Israelites now fare? Will they remember and obey? Or will they mess everything up again and so lose all that Joshua has won for them?

Although the ark was now housed at Shiloh, this assembly was held at Shechem, the place that since Abraham's day had been associated with covenant renewal and arrival in the land (see above, p. 37). Israel was now well and truly home where God intended her to be.

4

Settling in the Land

The Book of Judges makes disappointing reading after the faith-inspiring story of the conquest, but when we note how the hand of God continued to work amid all men's failures we can still take courage.

The means of God's operation in this period was mainly by his Spirit through the men who are called 'judges'. These were not just legal administrators, but men raised up by God and endowed with great gifts of leadership, political and military as well as legal, so that they were able to lead the people into battle against their enemies and thus restore freedom, peace, justice and religion in Israel. There are various theories about how they came to be known as judges, but the fact is that after they had won their victories and established peace, maintaining law and order, or judging, was precisely what they found themselves having to do, usually for the rest of their lives. The stories we are told about them are only the more exciting highlights of their careers, mainly the events that raised them to leadership in the first place.

In secular history the equivalent to the period of the judges in the life of a nation would be its heroic age, when knights and barons did heroic deeds, won dramatic victories and performed memorable feats that came to be remembered in folklore. These were ragged times, when central government was weak or non-existent, when strong individuals were able to make their mark, to rise up in different parts of the land and give a kind of leadership that did not last beyond their own lifetime.

However, in God's history there are some significant

differences from what we find in secular history. To begin with, Israel's judges were neither knights in shining armour nor wealthy barons, but often the most unlikely people. When we first meet them, Gideon is a frightened young man, Barak a cowardly warrior needing a woman to hold his hand, Jephthah a half-caste outlaw, Samson a man with a weakness for women. But as we follow their careers we see each one change. God did not choose the mighty, but as his Spirit worked in them they became finer persons, eventually gaining the respect of the nation.

In fact the operation of the Spirit is one of the main factors that characterises this age. The judges were first and foremost men of the Spirit, not in the same way as the prophets were to be, for they were not renowned as speakers or preachers. They were more like Joshua and Caleb, men who under the Spirit's anointing (3.10; 6.34; 11.29; 13.25; 14.6, 19; 15.14), and with the vision and enthusiasm he gave them, led Israel's armies to victory and so helped rescue and secure the land from foreign oppression. In that sense they were Israel's earliest charismatics.

Reading the biographies of the judges is in some ways like reading the early stories in Acts. Just as Joshua's strong leadership gave way to this fairly ragged age of local charismatic heroes, so Jesus' leadership was followed by a time when the charismatic ministries of individual apostles and evangelists held centre-stage in the early Church's history.

The second main factor characterising the period of the judges is apostasy and spiritual decline. The problem was the allure of the religion of the Canaanites, but since it is the history of faith we are studying here, not the history of religions, we are mercifully spared the need to know much about their gods. Their religion was bound up with agriculture and nature. Baal was the god of sky and rain; his consort, Anat (Asherah in the Old Testament), was mother earth. She only produced crops for men if the rains came in season to fertilise her soil, and so the focus of Canaanite religion was embodied in a myth in which Baal 'fertilised' Anat in an act of sexual intercourse. Correspondingly, the rituals at Canaanite temples focused on acts of intercourse between priests and priestesses representing Baal and Asherah aimed at magically persuading the gods to fulfil their part in the seasonal cycle. The purpose was to secure good harvests, but the method was, of course, an abomination in the eyes of the LORD. Nevertheless, probably for mixed reasons of sexuality and economics, Israelites were repeatedly drawn by it, and so repeatedly incurred the wrath of God. The power of the Spirit was very much needed in this age when the very fabric of faith was endangered by such enervating superstition.

Most of the battles and other events recorded in Judges were fairly localised, affecting only some of the tribes at any one time. It was an age when enthusiasm could run high, and so there were plenty of charismatic hero-tales to tell, but there was very little national co-ordination. And so, as the story progresses and social conditions deteriorate, we find leaders promoting themselves above others and inter-tribal strife breaking out. The need for strong central government – for a king – becomes increasingly apparent.

The date is roughly between 1200 and 1070. That is a much shorter time than the 450 years and more we get by adding together the periods of office of the judges, but it is not said that they all succeeded each other, only that some of them did, and since they operated locally, they must often have been contemporary with each other in different parts of the land (see map on p. 49).

Though Israel's armies had taken Canaan, much still remained to be conquered. Judges tells us about the problems the tribes had in holding on to what they had taken and in further establishing themselves in the land.

1. WHY THE PROBLEMS? (1.1 – 3.6)

Joshua had challenged Israel's leaders about two things: vision and life-style, or pressing on in faith into the fulfilment of God's purposes and obedience to the life-patterns he had shown them in the law of Moses. On both counts they failed, or at least the succeeding generations did, and repeatedly they had to be restored by God when they found themselves suffering the consequences of their failure. This was an age of many revivals, but little kingdom-building.

1.1 – 2.5: Failure to drive out the Canaanites.

Firstly, they did not press on in faith into fulfilment of the vision. Some of the tribes did, particularly in the Judean area, and were successful. The story about Caleb's inheritance is already told in Josh. 15.13–19. It demonstrates the success available to the man who goes on in faith and its inclusion again here provides an apt contrast with the stories of the other tribes that generally failed to press on and take full possession of the territories they settled in (1.21–36). As a result of this failure of faith the remaining Canaanites were to prove a perpetual snare in the land (2.1–5).

2.6 – 3.6: Failure to remain faithful to God

Secondly, the generation after Joshua did not have the same first-hand experience of God's miraculous power as Joshua's men and slowly drifted away into Baal worship. Consequently they suffered repeated reversal and had to be delivered by judges raised up by God. He therefore declared he would leave the remaining peoples in Canaan, firstly, to test Israel's allegiance and obedience, and secondly, to teach them to do battle with paganism.

The pattern outlined in this chapter forms the framework for most of the stories that follow in chs. 3–12:

Sin   – the people turn to the Baals,
Punishment – they suffer enemy oppression,
Repentance – they cry to the LORD,
Deliverance – the LORD raises up a judge
                    to deliver them.

Then the land has rest for a while and the cycle begins to repeat itself once more. The pattern is that of the two ways written into the law: obedience brings blessing and disobedience brings curse – repentance, of course, brings restoration (Deut. 30).

In most of the stories, God only raised up a judge to help after the oppression had brought the people to their knees and caused them to cry out to him (3.9, 15; 4.3; 6.7; 10.10). The message is always the same: God is faithful, but he wants his people to learn to be faithful in return, and so his punishment is discipline, not retribution.

2. JUDGES TO THE RESCUE! (3.7 – 12.15)

Charismatic biographies are popular literature in our times, as a glance along the shelves of any Christian bookshop will show. They tell about God's Spirit moving on men and women, usually in times of spiritual aridness, and transforming them into lively people of God with startling new ministries. That is basically also the nature of the stories of the judges. We shall therefore not concern ourselves too much with historical and geographical details, but more with what God was doing in their lives by his Spirit. After all, our main aim in these volumes is to tap the faith dimension relating to the way of the Spirit in Scripture. Anyhow, a glance at the map provides most of the background information we need. It is worth remembering that most of the judges operated locally, not nationally, roughly in the regions they are placed on the map.

3.7–11: Othniel.
Othniel lived at Debir in Judah, not too far from his father's home in Hebron. The details given about his victory over Cushan-Rishathaim, an invader from Aram in northern Mesopotamia, provide only a sketch outline, but they aptly summarise for us right at the start the complete pattern that we shall see worked out in the ministries of the other judges.

Every time the root of Israel's troubles is forgetting the LORD and turning to other gods, infringing the first and most basic requirement of the Mosaic covenant, namely total loyalty to God (Exod. 20.3). Paul gave the same explanation for the perversion of life among the Gentiles in his day (Rom. 1.21–32), and we still see the same effects, declining moral standards and loss of stamina, in our society today whenever the Christian voice gives way to that of atheism, humanism, superstition and so forth. Then the churches begin to decline, standards fall even further, and the need for revival becomes urgent.

And when revival does come, it also follows the patterns we find here. In every age a movement of repentance and a movement of the Spirit are both essential for any reviving work of God.

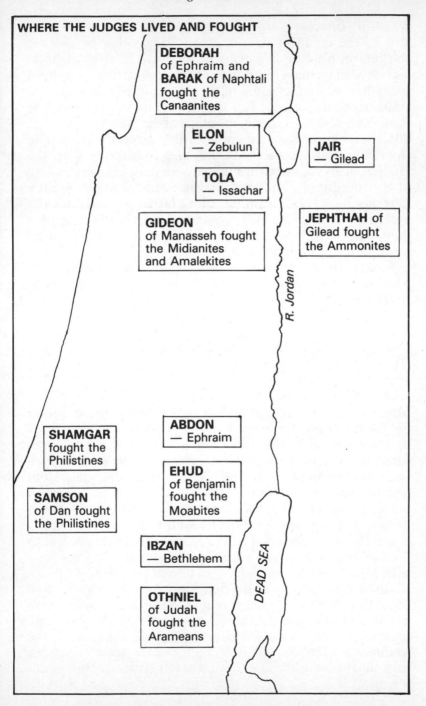

WHERE THE JUDGES LIVED AND FOUGHT

DEBORAH
of Ephraim and
BARAK of Naphtali
fought the
Canaanites

ELON
— Zebulun

JAIR
— Gilead

TOLA
— Issachar

GIDEON
of Manasseh fought
the Midianites
and Amalekites

JEPHTHAH of
Gilead fought
the Ammonites

R. Jordan

SHAMGAR
fought the
Philistines

ABDON
— Ephraim

EHUD
of Benjamin
fought the
Moabites

SAMSON
of Dan fought
the Philistines

IBZAN
— Bethlehem

DEAD SEA

OTHNIEL
of Judah
fought the
Arameans

3.12–30: Ehud.

It is to the credit of the author of Judges that he did not spiritualise his stories and paint us portraits of unrealistic piety. Men remain men and do not become unnatural super-heroes. In fact some of the details in Ehud's story are embarrassingly natural. But that is life, and life is what the Bible is all about. Certainly the ethos of the New Testament is different, but for the moment we are at an early stage in the story of the battle to restore God's kingdom. God's purposes are to remain the same throughout, but man's understanding of how they apply in life is to develop considerably over the next thousand years and more before Jesus is born. Hence the author of Hebrews is able to commend most of the judges for their faith without passing any comment on the moral perceptions of their age (Heb. 11.32).

Ehud's challenge was to deliver the Benjamites from Moabite encroachment across the Jordan into their tribal territory.

3.31: Shamgar.

One of six minor judges about whom little is known (cp. 10.1–5; 12.8–15).

Chs. 4–5: Deborah and Barak.

Most of the other judges had to deal with foreign invasion, but the challenge Barak was confronted with was a Canaanite uprising in Galilee. His story is told in ch. 4 and celebrated in song in ch. 5, though in it the glory goes to two women, Deborah, a prophetess, and Jael, a nomad's wife. Both simply used what resources they had, Jael a tent-peg and mallet to put an end to the Canaanite commander, Deborah her spiritual zeal to inspire the Israelite commander, a rather cowardly man, who even had to have her accompany him to the battlefield. (On Jael's Kenite and ancestral connections with Moses, see Exod. 2.15 – 3.1; Num. 10.29–32.)

Apart from the fact of the Spirit moving through a woman this time, the most striking revelation in these chapters is in the poem's survey of the tribes who came out to battle. Some offered themselves willingly, others did not. Presumably the southernmost tribes, Judah, Simeon and Benjamin, were not expected to come because they lived too far away. But the cry of heart-broken sadness at the failure of Reuben, Dan and Asher to send reinforcements reveals how far the vision of national unity that Joshua had engendered was now being lost.

Chs. 6–8: Gideon.

The scene shifts to central Palestine and Transjordan. The threat now comes from Midianite and other raiders from the desert fringes, thousands of them, plundering for food at the season of harvest. God's answer this time is to choose a frightened youngster trying to thresh corn in hiding down a wine-press instead of out in the open where the wind could blow the chaff away.

When we first meet him, Gideon has no sense of vision or calling, no confidence and no desire to help. But when he makes excuses, he is simply told, 'Go in the strength you have.' (6.14). And as he does so, we watch him grow in stature. He faces his first challenge, to pull down Baal's altar, with some trepidation, doing it at night for fear anyone might see him (6.27). But after the Spirit comes upon him (6.34) and he gets confirmation of his calling by exposing a fleece to the dew, he is a totally transformed man, prepared at God's behest to reduce his army to ridiculously small numbers and lead them in a clever, but foolhardy, night-time attack against the Midianites. And so, as he follows the LORD, he becomes a general not unlike the Joshua who attacked Jericho, following similar divine guidance and witnessing a similar miracle.

The people certainly recognised his potential, for they offered him the opportunity to become their king (8.22f), and his greatness is seen again as he refuses, acknowledging that God alone is king. But in the end he proved to be no new Joshua, for he made a gold ephod, which was apparently some idolatrous object that the people began to worship (8.27). Beneath the surface Gideon was still bound by his cultural background and the spirit of his age. He was therefore able to lead Israel only so far in revival, and no further.

Ch. 9: Abimelech.

Gideon's son, Abimelech, was not a judge, but a self-promoted local king of Shechem. His story need not detain us. It simply stands as a warning, contrasting sharply with the stories of the judges. His reign quickly became a horrifying fiasco and it ended in tragedy, not in the beautiful peace that followed after each of the judges' rise to power.

10.1–5: Tola and Jair.
Like Shamgar (3.31), we know next to nothing about these men.

10.6 – 12.7: Jephthah.
We now move to Transjordan where the Ammonites are exerting pressure on those living in Gilead. This time the chosen deliverer is an outcast and an outlaw, but the LORD used him mightily after he accepted his calling and the Spirit came upon him (11.29). The tale is, however, one of the most tragic in the book, because of Jephthah's thoughtless vow that leads to the death of his daughter.

The stories of the judges so far are full of accounts of wonderful deliverances, but most of them are spoiled in some way. Ehud's story was spoiled by its sheer crudeness, Deborah and Barak's by the lack of support from some of the tribes, Gideon's by his making of the ephod, and now Jephthah's by his silly vow. Certainly these men brought times of deliverance and peace to Israel, times of revival and refreshing, but clearly none of them knew God as Moses and Joshua had known him, or had the vision to give the kind of lead they had given. To be sure, the New Testament commends them for their faith, and they certainly brought Israel salvation in dire times of need, but they were not of a calibre to lead Israel in the fuller revival that was still needed.

12.8–15: Ibzan, Elon and Abdon.
Three more judges we know little about; cp. 10.1–5.

3. TROUBLE IN CENTRAL PALESTINE (CHS. 12–21)

The end of the second millennium BC was a time of industrial, as well as political, transition. Iron was beginning to replace bronze in the manufacture of metal implements, and being much stronger it afforded tactical superiority to those who could forge their weapons with it. The Israelites did not have that superiority, but those living in the plains west of Judah did (1.19).

These were the Philistines, newcomers from among the Sea Peoples, whose invasions had brought about the collapse of the Egyptian Empire. They lived in and around five cities: Gaza, Ashkelon, Ekron, Gath and Ashdod, each ruled over by its own king. Although Judah did have some initial success

CENTRAL AND SOUTHERN PALESTINE
IN SAMSON'S TIME (Judg. 13-21)

against three of their cities (1.18), they were never able to dislodge the Philistines from the plain. They must have regained whatever territories they lost quite quickly, for by Samson's time, probably in the late twelfth century, they were well and truly entrenched, beginning to unsettle the tribe of Dan on their northern border, so much so that after Samson's death the Danites were driven to seek a new home for themselves.

Chs. 13–16: Samson.

Samson was a Danite. Unlike the other judges he never led an Israelite army into battle, nor was he able to deliver his tribe from their oppressors, though he did begin a process that would ultimately have the same result many years later, in David's time (cp. 13.5).

The framework of Samson's story is different from that of the earlier judges. It certainly starts the same way, with a note that the Philistine encroachment was a direct result of Israelite apostasy (13.1), but we hear of no crying to the LORD in repentance and Samson himself is appointed to his call from conception, not at an urgent moment of distress. Indeed, when he is first introduced relations with the Philistines have not yet reached a critical stage. There is rather a state of uneasy peace. Samson is free to come and go in their towns, though the situation is tense and brittle, one that cannot last. Samson's call was to bring it to a pitch where something would have to snap, which he did most effectively as he stirred up his Philistine neighbours to anger more than once, making fools of them, slaughtering their men, burning their cornfields, and finally pulling down their temple in Gaza with much loss of life.

All of that was to be at the cost of his life, not because of his calling, but through his own folly. His parents set him apart for God as a Nazirite from birth (13.5). According to Num. 6 a Nazirite was one who took a special vow of dedication to God for a limited period of time during which he had to leave his hair uncut, abstain from wine and avoid contact with a dead body. Then at the end of his time of consecration he would seal his vow by offering sacrifice and shaving his head. Paul took such a vow at the end of his second missionary journey (Acts 18.18). Samson's Nazirite vow differed in that it was to be life-long and signified by never shaving his head, but the intention was the same: he was to be a man set apart for God.

His ungodly love-life was his undoing. Joshua had warned that relationships with pagan women would have disastrous consequences (Josh. 23.12f), and so it was with Samson. His attempt to marry a Philistine girl proved a fiasco, though God used it to stir up trouble among the Philistines (chs. 14–15), as also when he consorted with a prostitute in Gaza (16.1–3). Finally his love-affair with Delilah led to his public disgrace, though again God used it powerfully and dramatically, while Samson regained some honour in his death (15.4–31).

In Samson's personal life we see reflected the conflict between the Spirit of God and the spirit of the age that held Israel as a whole in decline. We saw similar evidences in the other judges' lives, but in Samson's they are far more exaggerated than before. Clearly, even though God was still powerfully at work, conditions generally were deteriorating in Israel as pagan influence increased among the LORD's people.

Chs. 17–18: The migration of the Danites.

God's solution to the Philistine problem, though more protracted, was in the end to be no different from his fairly simple answer to the problems the earlier judges had had to handle. He was waiting for some evidence of repentance, but things were to get a lot worse before Israel would turn to him in that way again (not until 1 Sam. 7). The reaction Samson's activities stirred up among the Philistines began to make life increasingly uncomfortable in Israel. The Danites were the first to feel the pressure, but they simply sought other territory for themselves, that is, rather than seek the LORD or stand and fight.

The story of their migration again reveals the state of moral and religious decline in the nation. The courageous faith of Joshua's conquest is replaced by the cowardly tactics of the Danites' seizure of land from a defenceless people. And on the way to their new home they forcefully kidnap an idolatrous private chaplain, whose images were made of gold that was once stolen! – and so get themselves a priest for their new sanctuary in Dan, which was later to become one of the two main centres of idolatrous worship in northern Israel where Jeroboam's golden bulls were venerated (1 Kings 12.28–30).

Chs. 19–21: The final state of the nation.

'In those days Israel had no king.' (19.1). The historian has already apologised twice for the state of the nation in these words (17.6; 18.1). He is clearly embarrassed at having to record some of the events of these days: a nauseating story of sexual perversion (ch. 19), a sorry account of civil, inter-tribal war (ch. 20), and a strange story of killing and rape to get wives for the surviving Benjamites (ch. 21). Israel has obviously sunk to a state of near anarchy. The sad comment with which the author ends the book sums it all up: 'In those days Israel had no king; everyone did as he saw fit.'

The LORD had promised, 'I will never break my covenant with you' (2.1), and sure enough he rescued Israel time and time again. There had been repentance and a turning back to God from time to time, but the overall impression is of a relentless slide into pagan ways, with a consequent loss of vision and a decline in morality and morale. The gods of Canaan were truly proving 'a snare' to Israel (2.3). Matters became progressively worse as we read through Judges. At first it was a general sort of turning away from the LORD, but later we found even the judges themselves affected: for example, Gideon led the people into idolatry, and Samson's exploits were not always highly moral, to say the least. The unsavoury flavour of the last chapters is but the logical outcome; and the contrast with the end of the Book of Joshua is remarkable. Nevertheless, God had preserved his people, wayward as they were, though clearly, if they were to continue as his people, something more was surely required of them. The need for revival was growing more urgent daily.

5

Transition to Monarchy

1 SAMUEL

By the end of the age of the judges the need for strong central government – for a king – was becoming increasingly more urgent, as the historian repeatedly comments. The people of central Palestine were acknowledging that need when they offered Gideon the opportunity to reign over them (Judg. 8.22), as were the men of Shechem when they accepted Abimelech as their king (Judg. 9.1–6), but most Israelites probably felt as Gideon did, and as Samuel was to do, that since God was Israel's king no man should hold the office (Judg. 8.23; 1 Sam. 8.6f; 12.12). Anyhow, there had been no revelation from God that it was yet time to appoint a king, though that was soon to come.

In the meantime there was a more fundamental issue to be dealt with. The power of the Philistines was increasing. They had already dislodged the Danites and presently their troops would be pressing further inland. Earlier oppression by other enemies had been dealt with when the Israelites had turned back to God and cried out for his help, but this time there was no evidence of repentance, only increasing anarchy. As both Moses and Joshua had taught, and as experience had already shown several times, God would not grant political solutions until the spiritual ill was acknowledged. Repentance and revival would have to precede any military deliverance. To bring that to pass would itself require a miracle, considering the state of national apostasy. But then, to the eyes of faith there were better grounds for expecting some such miracle than for expecting any political solution, since God's redemptive purposes, as he revealed them to Abraham, had not changed, and he had proved himself absolutely faithful to his promises so far.

1. FIRST STIRRINGS OF REVIVAL (CHS. 1–7)

The date of Samuel's birth must be about 1085 BC and the battle against the Philistines at Aphek about 1070. Israel was to sink even lower during these years before the LORD raised up Samuel and changed their fortunes.

God's way of working deliverance is usually to choose and prepare a man. So it was that he chose Abraham, Moses and Elijah; so he would send his son, Jesus; so now he prepares Samuel. In the midst of the darkest hour God searches for a man who will co-operate in his revival work. The tragedy is when he finds no one willing to do so (cp. Ezek, 22.30).

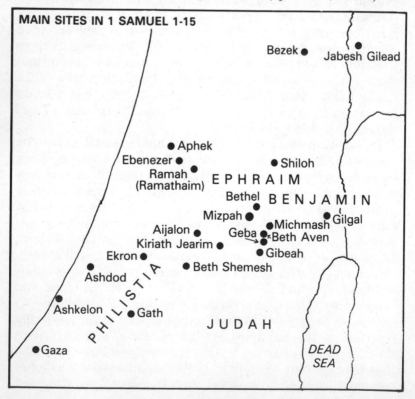

MAIN SITES IN 1 SAMUEL 1-15

Chs. 1–3: Samuel's birth, childhood and call.

Loss of political and moral fibre in a nation is usually reflected in a corresponding decline in religious standards. If we were tempted to dismiss the religious decadence of the Danites as merely an aberration at the fringe of Israelite life, then a glance at the state of the Shiloh sanctuary should immediately correct our perspective. The rot was there also, right at the very heart, in the central temple where the ark was housed. There the spectacle of drunkenness must have been very common because the old priest, Eli, readily confused prayer with it (1.12–14). His sons, who should have succeeded him, showed no reverence for the LORD, treated his sacrifices with contempt, and promiscuously slept with the women who served at the sanctuary – and he had lost all control over them (2.12–25). Conditions were in fact so bad that the LORD finally sent a prophet to announce his decision to bring Eli's priestly line to an end (2.27–36).

The child Samuel came into that darkness like a tiny ray of hope. The son of devout parents, born in answer to prayer, he was dedicated to the LORD by his grateful mother to be brought up at the sanctuary under Eli. Despite all the decadence of Shiloh, he 'continued to grow in stature and in favour with the LORD and with men', just as Jesus would also do one day (2.26; cp. Luke 2.40, 52). The LORD's hand was clearly upon him in a unique way.

The visit of the man of God who prophesied the end of Eli's line and Samuel's night vision which followed it mark the turning-point in our story. The unnamed stranger's visit changed the course of history, not simply because his message warned Eli, but rather because it prepared Samuel for what God was about to say to him. When God spoke that night, he added nothing Samuel had not already heard in the prophecy, but because of that preparation the lad was able to receive it with an understanding that might not otherwise have been possible.

God's way of working is often like that. We have already seen how, when he gave Joshua his commission, he added little to what Moses had already said to him. But before a man can speak God's word he has to hear it for himself, not just second-hand. That makes the difference between a prophet and a preacher.

And so the message of the man of God was confirmed to Samuel by the LORD and he became a prophet recognised by all Israel (3.19 – 4.1).

Chs. 4–6: The fall of Shiloh and its consequences.

In the meantime conditions continued to deteriorate in Israel. To be sure, the prophetic word was now being heard, but 'in those days the word of the LORD was rare; there were not many visions', (3.1) and there was still no evidence of the word having the kind of impact that was needed, for we read of no response in repentance.

So it was that, when the Philistine armies marched north and camped at Aphek, the Israelites were quite unable to defeat them. The account of the battle in 4.1–11 tells only a little about its effects. The slaughter of the Israelite troops, the death of Eli and his sons, and the capture of the ark were all tragic enough in themselves, but the consequences of this battle were even more far-reaching, for the Philistines were now able to push inland and take Shiloh, which they destroyed along with its temple. (The information about that is in Jer. 7.12–14; 26.6.) Of course the LORD took care of his own reputation among the Philistines, who were obliged to return the ark after a series of spectacular demonstrations of his power. But if these pagan Philistines readily recognised his hand, the Israelites were still slow to learn what he was trying to teach them about the need to return to him, and so after the battle of Aphek they found themselves living in subjection to Philistine domination throughout central Palestine for several decades.

The Philistines continued to live in their coastal plain and never occupied the whole of Canaan, but they placed garrisons at strategic points in the land (10.5; 13.3f, 23) and prevented the Israelites from manufacturing iron weapons (13.19–22), thus maintaining themselves in a position of political, economic and military dominance.

The ark was not returned to Shiloh, of course, since its temple was no longer there, but was placed in a private house at Kiriath Jearim, about eight miles west of Jerusalem where it would eventually be taken in David's time (7.1; cp. 2 Sam. 6).

Ch. 7: Revival at last!

Over the next twenty years Samuel became well known as a revival preacher, calling the nation back to God. And his ministry proved powerfully successful as people began to repent, to seek the LORD and to abandon their pagan idols. The fact that he was able to summon a national revival convention at Mizpah as an occasion for fasting and seeking the LORD shows something of the scale of his impact. The Philistines were certainly perturbed, and sent their troops to break it up, but when they did so the Israelites witnessed the first miracle of deliverance they had known since Jephthah's day. The scales at last began to tilt the other way, but it would take many years before Israel was properly re-established – there was a lot of leeway to be made up.

However, both God's promise and historical experience spell out the principle very clearly, that national revival will follow religious revival. Hence we can look forward, not to whether it will happen, but to how it will. In the meantime the mantle of judge began to fall on Samuel, who found himself having to travel around the region ministering to the LORD's people. His base was no longer the temple at Shiloh, but his home in Ramah, where he was born (= Ramathaim in 1.1).

2. ISRAEL BECOMES A KINGDOM (CHS. 8–12)

Biblical scholars believe that these chapters are drawn from a number of different sources, but even so, we may still read them as a continuous story, just as the historian intended we should. Like chs. 1–7, they are very much in the same literary style as our modern charismatic biographies, telling of the LORD's working by his Spirit through a man he raises up amid signs and wonders to perform the work to which he calls him. It is very much a story in which charismatics today will readily find themselves at home.

Samuel's ministry had the double effect of stirring Israel to repentance and of raising up a group of close prophetic followers, men of the Spirit who gathered around him to support his revival ministry in a more direct way – Israel's first charismatic movement. We meet these prophets on two occasions: on the first we read how Saul joined them and received the prophetic Spirit himself before becoming king (10.5–13), on the second how David, who had also received the Spirit, sought refuge among them when he first fled from Saul (19.18–24).

Revival did not come simply by magical wonders from heaven, but by the dedication of men prepared to face the scorn of becoming prophets or charismatics, so that, in the power of his Spirit, they could put all their energies into the work of calling the nation back to God. Behind every revival stands a man like Samuel, and he is supported by men like these. It is significant that, though their numbers seem to have been small, their impact was disproportionately extensive. They saved a nation, made and unmade its kings, but only through the power of God's Spirit working in them.

Ch. 8: The people ask for a king.

The only time the son of a judge had succeeded his father was when Abimelech became king of Shechem, and that had proved disastrous. It seems the same would have happened if Samuel's sons had followed him. Quite naturally he felt a sense of rejection when the people asked him to appoint a king, but it shows the measure of his greatness that he did not let such personal feelings control his response, but rather focused their attention on the deeper issue, that they were in danger of rejecting God in favour of a human leader. Gideon had seen the same danger in his day, but this time the LORD intervened and directed Samuel to let it be (vv. 1–9).

Though Samuel was a spiritual giant, he was also a thorough realist. The Israelites may have cherished some pipe-dream of Utopia, but he had spent too many years fighting his battle of faith amid the hard realities of political life for that. He warned the people in no uncertain terms about what they would be letting themselves in for, but in the end had to bow before the onward movement of history and agree to their request. Anyhow, the LORD's time had finally come, and Samuel knew it.

9.1 – 10.16: God chooses Saul and prepares him for his calling.

Though we read here about Saul being anointed, these

chapters do not tell the story of him becoming king, only of God preparing him for that to happen later. It is important to remember that we are not reading secular history. Before God uses a man in ministry, he has to prepare him in his spirit first. So it was with Moses, Joshua, Gideon and many others. Saul was not suddenly raised to the kingship. God did much with him in his secret heart before that happened.

The story we read here is full of wonderful 'coincidences'. It just so happens that Saul, a farmer's son out looking for stray donkeys, finds himself near Samuel's place, his servant just happens to have the right gift to offer Samuel, amazingly they happen to arrive in town just in time to catch him as he comes out to offer sacrifice, strangely Samuel knew they were coming and has a meal ready for them. By the end of that day, after Samuel had sat talking with him into the small hours of the night, Saul must have been one of the most astonished men history has ever known. Had he not simply gone looking for lost donkeys?

Next morning, when Samuel prophetically anointed him in secret to be Israel's leader, when he then began to see Samuel's more immediate prophecies fulfilling themselves as he went on his way, and finally when he found himself caught up in prophetic worship and the Spirit of the LORD coming upon him in power, his astonishment must surely have exceeded all bounds. It is little wonder he found it difficult to tell his uncle back on the farm about his strange journey. God had changed his heart (10.9), but had also given him much to come to terms with.

10.17–27: Saul is accepted at a public assembly.

The people had asked Samuel to appoint them a king, and now that he knew the LORD's man had been found and got ready, he gathered them together for the election. As he cast the lots he must have had total confidence that God's hand was on the proceedings and that Saul would be chosen.

Saul hiding behind the baggage is not just a sentimental touch to the story. It reflects the reality of spiritual struggle that many men of God experience when confronted with a call. Moses and Gideon are the best examples we have encountered hitherto of other men who sought to extricate themselves at these initial stages, and Saul was no doubt going through the same kind of crisis, hoping perhaps that Samuel had made a mistake about him in the first instance. It must therefore have shaken him when most of the people also recognised him as the right man.

However, there was not unanimity, and so for the time being Samuel simply explained some regulations of kingship and sent the people home to await further developments, to wait for God to move again.

Ch. 11: Saul is crowned king.
When Samuel first anointed Saul he advised him not to rush into anything, but to 'do whatever your hand finds to do' (10.7) and wait for God's moment. Saul had therefore returned to his farming.

God's day came when, as he was ploughing his fields, he received news that the Ammonites had set siege to Jabesh Gilead. Then, as had happened with some of the judges, the Spirit of God came upon him (v. 6) and he summoned Israel to battle. The result was two-fold: a thorough victory for Israel and the dispelling of all doubt about the choice of Saul for king.

At last Samuel was able to summon Israel to Gilgal for a ceremony of coronation at which Saul was crowned king in the presence of the LORD with great celebration.

Ch. 12: Samuel's review and challenge.
We now reach one of those turning-points in history where a review is called for. Like Moses and Joshua before him, as he hands over the reins of leadership and launches a new phase in the history of Israel, Samuel makes a last appeal for faithfulness to God. He reviews the main events of the past and draws out the lessons to be learned from it: about the blessings resulting from obedience, about the disastrous consequences of disobedience, about the continuing faithfulness of God and about repentance as the basis for revival. Looking forward to the next phase his challenge is: 'You now have a king: I may not like that very much, but never mind, the really important thing is that you and he remain faithful to God if you want to maintain this revival.'

Perhaps the best way to sum up the movement of God's Spirit through these chapters is to note again how Saul became a prophet/charismatic himself before his crowning. It was a charismatic movement that had led the battle for revival in Israel and produced its first king. The pattern is one that has repeated itself in history several times since Samuel's day and one that has implications for encouraging vision and hope in today's renewal movements.

3. THE REIGN OF KING SAUL (CHS. 13–31)

Saul was made king to do what the judges had been unable to do, to unify and establish Israel as a nation free from enemy oppression. Saul's reign was therefore almost entirely a time of war. However, it is not our purpose here to recount all the details of his campaigns, but rather to trace what spiritual forces operated in and through his kingship to give him what success he had and to cause his ultimate downfall.

Chs. 13–15: Samuel breaks with Saul.

Saul's reign started with him leading out his troops against far superior Philistine forces, miraculously defeating them at Michmash, near Bethel, and then leading a successful expedition against the Amalekites who were proving troublesome on the eastern front. But on both missions he failed to fulfil the word of the LORD through Samuel. He had excuses each time, but what the LORD was looking for in his king was a man who would obey him, not make excuses for disobedience, and so the result was rejection by both God and Samuel (15. 22f, 35).

We saw repeatedly in the tales about Joshua and the judges how God thoroughly honoured faith. Saul's first mistake was to let go of it. Right back at the time of his initial call to kingship he was told that he would one day find himself at Gilgal waiting seven days for Samuel to come to him, but in the event he was unable to hold out for the full duration and took steps to prepare for battle before Samuel arrived. That may seem a small thing in itself, but God was looking for 'a man after his own heart', a man with faith in him, who would walk in complete trust in him. And Saul had failed his first test.

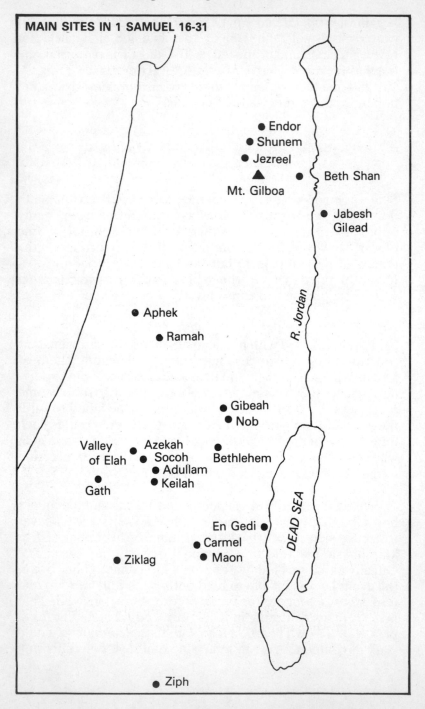

MAIN SITES IN 1 SAMUEL 16-31

Endor
Shunem
Jezreel
Mt. Gilboa
Beth Shan
Jabesh Gilead
R. Jordan
Aphek
Ramah
Gibeah
Nob
Valley of Elah
Azekah
Socoh
Bethlehem
Adullam
Keilah
Gath
En Gedi
Carmel
Maon
DEAD SEA
Ziklag
Ziph

The second test came when Samuel commissioned the slaughter of the Amalekites. Saul's apparent humanity in sparing Agag, their king, draws our sympathy more readily than Samuel's apparent ruthlessness in executing him, but reading the story in that way obscures the whole point of it. What we see in Saul's behaviour is not only disobedience, but also self-promotion and pride. He did obey God so far, but also sought glory for himself. Thus, he erected a victory monument in his own honour instead of the LORD's (15.12), and passed the blame for sparing the sheep and cattle on to his soldiers (v. 21). We can well imagine him proudly bringing home the spoils of war, revelling in his new popularity and the thought of the grand reception and celebration that would be awaiting him, leading Agag in chains as his prize trophy. But all that was suddenly shattered when Samuel appeared before him. Even after admitting his guilt, however, he is still controlled by his pride: 'I have sinned. But please honour me before the elders of my people and before Israel.' (v. 30). What the Israelites thought of him was more important to him than what God thought.

It is little wonder that Samuel was broken-hearted (v. 35). He had given everything, his whole life's work and ministry, to rescue Israel and already he was watching the very man he himself had appointed king setting his own glory above the LORD's purposes.

Chs. 16–18: The LORD chooses David and Saul becomes jealous.

The revival had gone too deep and too far for its impetus to be halted by Saul's disobedience. Samuel was not left long in his self-pity before God roused him to do something to rescue the work of the Spirit. And so David, another farmer's son, was anointed and 'the Spirit of the LORD came upon David in power.' (16.1–13).

Meantime Saul's anointing began to go sour, and David of all people was summoned with his harp to soothe him in his tempers (16.14–23).

Then we watch Saul become thoroughly jealous of this youngster when his victory over Goliath, the Philistine giant, suddenly made him the most popular person in the kingdom (17.1 – 18.11).

Saul could see clearly that the LORD was with David (18. 12), but that only made matters worse for him, since he could not then have him put away arbitrarily. So he resorted to a ruse that he hoped would bring about David's death, but that back-fired on him and resulted in David becoming his own son-in-law! (18.12–30).

In Saul we see a pattern that is unfortunately all too common today, when charismatic leaders who have known the sweet taste of success and popularity become jealous of others whose anointing seems to threaten their own. The result is always bitterness.

Chs. 19–21: David flees from Saul.

It is significant that in his moment of need David's first resort was to Samuel and his group of prophets, those with whom he must have felt the closest affinity of spirit. The way in which Saul was affected when he came into their company, 'prophesying' and falling prostrate – 'slain in the Spirit', we would say today – shows their charismatic worship could still touch a nerve in his spiritual sensitivities as in earlier times, but as the story proceeds we see that his over-riding response continued to be to his own proud and jealous spirit, rather than to God's Spirit.

After Jonathan warned David about his father's unchanged determination to be rid of him, he fled to the priests at Nob, but he knew there was little they could do besides feed him and give him Goliath's sword.

While we can appreciate why David, a deeply spiritual man himself, should have turned first to prophets and priests, it is difficult to understand why he should next have sought refuge among the Philistines at Gath. Doubtless he would have found that difficult to explain himself, for he instantly recognised what a foolish thing he had done and was quick to find a means of escape.

Chs. 22–27: David lives as a fugitive in Judah.

David was now driven to live as an outlaw, like some ancient Robin Hood, in the Judean highlands. There he gathered around him a motley band of other outlaws and discontents, but he remained true to the LORD who continually directed him by the word of his prophets, particularly one called Gad, who would later be known as 'David's seer' (22.1–5; cp. 2 Sam. 24.11).

Meantime Saul's fury knew no bounds. He had the priests at Nob killed because they had helped David and in his anger he hounded David from pillar to post, wherever he heard rumour of his presence.

In these chapters there are two well-known stories about David sparing Saul's life (chs. 24 and 26). In both of them we see how David's acts of mercy touched Saul's heart and rekindled a finer part of his spirit. Saul never became inhuman. He still had plenty of friends and carried the general support of the people. But he was a man driven by jealousy and even after David's acts of clemency, it was that spirit that continued to dominate in him, even though somewhere beneath the surface there lurked the finer person he had once been and, as these two episodes seem to suggest, could still have been again.

David recognised that truth and so, swallowing whatever pride he may have had himself, went back down to Gath and sought refuge among the Philistines once more – which surprisingly he was granted.

Chs. 28–31: Saul's last days.

As might have been expected, David's time among the Philistines proved very difficult for him, since his heart was with his own people, the Israelites, who were their enemies. But by careful forethought he survived.

Saul meantime was preparing to meet the Philistines on Mount Gilboa, in what would turn out to be his last battle, when he would be wounded and take his own life. Politically his reign had achieved something of its purpose in establishing a sense of national identity and hope, but his personal story, by contrast, has become a complete tragedy. He was a charismatic leader who failed to walk wholly with the LORD and so found himself caught in a downward spiral from which he was unable to extricate himself. At first he showed amazing potential as a man of God, but then we watched him act in disobedience and pride, lose his anointing as a consequence, become jealous of David's growing success, fall into the grip of hatred and anger, burst into mad fits, and so forth. And now, at the end he sinks to the depth of spiritual degradation by consulting a spiritualist medium, then finally commits suicide.

Saul's story cannot be read without reference to Samuel's at the beginning and David's at the end. The contrast between him and Samuel, the faithful revivalist preacher and prophet, is obvious, but David's diplomacy sometimes raises nagging questions about his integrity. For example, his conversation with the priest at Nob in ch. 21 is full of apparent lies and half-truths, as are his reports to Achish, king of Gath, in ch. 27. So why did David succeed with God and Saul fail?

The answer seems to lie in observing the same trait that we noticed in the judges, most of whom were far from perfect in their conduct – namely faith. The contrast between Saul and David on that point is probably seen most clearly by comparing the two stories in chs. 28 and 30. In the first we see Saul, finding no guidance from the prophets of the LORD, prepared to turn anywhere for help, even to a witch. In the second we see David, having lost everything in an Amalekite raid, with his own men turning against him, at that point finding strength in the LORD his God (v. 6) and so rising above his circumstances to lead them out in faith to victory. Where the one gave way in a crisis, the other stood firm in his faith in God. Saul had shown the same weakness from the beginning of his reign when he first prepared to meet the Philistines at Michmash (ch. 13); David had demonstrated the same strength from the beginning of his rise in Israel, when he faced Goliath with nothing but a few stones and unflinching faith that the battle was the LORD's (ch. 17).

Saul's story stands as a reminder that life with God's Spirit is no mere game, but a challenge to total commitment, to walking in complete faith and obedience. That was the challenge Moses and Joshua had both laid before the Israelites. We have watched the Israelites let go of it and the judges take hold of it again, Samuel live in it and Saul lose it, and now David rising up in it. It is the very challenge that underlies all kingdom building and revival.

PART THREE

THE RISE AND FALL
OF DAVID'S KINGDOM

1010 — 597 BC

If we were to trace a graph of kingdom-growth since Joshua's day, it would show gradual decline with intermittent peaks and troughs through the period of the judges, it would bottom out in Samuel's time, begin to rise in Saul's, rise steeply in David's, peak in Solomon's, and thereafter again show steady decline with intermittent rallies until the end of the kingdom in the early sixth century.

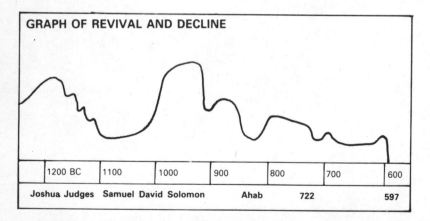

GRAPH OF REVIVAL AND DECLINE

1200 BC	1100	1000	900	800	700	600

Joshua Judges   Samuel David Solomon   Ahab   722   597

The overall pattern may have been something like that, but a closer look shows that the flow was not always quite so simple. Indeed it was often in the troughs that the most stimulating spiritual activity happened. Thus Samuel's revival began in the eleventh century trough as a prelude to the growth that ran on into the tenth, and Elijah's ministry that helped secure growth in the ninth to eighth centuries belongs in the earlier ninth century trough. Correspondingly, it is usually in the peaks that we discern the first evidences of decline. It was amid all the glories of Solomon's reign that the seeds of discontent leading to the split of the kingdom were sown, and it was amid the affluence of the early eighth century that the rot resulting in the fall of Samaria set in. The picture is never as simple as a little graph might suggest, helpful as such a visual aid might be. However, what is always possible is to trace any period of national well-being back to faithful roots and of decline back to apostasy. The principles that Moses outlined so clearly and that we have already seen operating so powerfully, of obedience and disobedience leading to blessing and curse respectively, continue to apply throughout this next phase of Israel's history.

6

David Builds the Kingdom

2 SAMUEL

David is a man about whom many books have been written. To the secular historian he was a great soldier and a shrewd diplomatist, to the eyes of religious piety he has become a paragon of humble penitence and holy godliness, but to the Old Testament writers he was neither of these, and yet in some measure both. The Bible never hides his faults nor underplays his anointing. We have already seen the mixed traits of his personality emerging in 1 Samuel, but they become more pronounced as we read on. He could be ruthless with his enemies and yet too tender-hearted with his own children. He made mistakes, some of them with dire consequences for both himself and his people, but more frequently he got it right and knew the blessing of having walked with God. We do not find evidence in him, as in Saul, of the arrogance that status can bring, but rather we see a man prepared to humble himself in repentance and weep openly before his courtiers, even at the cost of causing them to be ashamed of him and angry.

But in the end, for all his weaknesses, he went down in history as the best king Israel ever had, the model against which all others were compared. Clearly he did not earn that honour because of a flawless personality. No, it was rather because of his faith and his faithfulness. His faith kept his eye firmly fixed on the vision of kingdom-building God had given him, while his faithfulness kept him walking with God and returning to him when he stumbled. We must not read his story with the false, idealistic notions of popular pietism, but with the true measure of God's call to faith, obedience, repentance and openness to his Spirit that are the marks of a man of God.

It is also important to note that David was not called to revival ministry, but to kingdom-building. Samuel was the revivalist, the man who called the nation back to God in repentance and so set it on its spiritual feet. He had anointed Saul to build his own kingdom instead. David is therefore Samuel's true successor in the continuum of faith, but his calling is more like Joshua's than Samuel's. Just as Moses laid a foundation of faith and Joshua built a nation in Canaan on it, so Samuel called the nation back to that foundation and David constructed a kingdom on it. And therein lies the secret of his honour. He was a man who caught God's vision, a man after God's own heart, and who co-operated with him wholly in seeing that vision through to fulfilment as far as his life-span permitted him to take it.

1. DAVID'S KINGDOM IS ESTABLISHED (CHS. 1–8)

Saul's reign had done much to unify the Israelites and lift them out of their political doldrums, but the battle on Mount Gilboa gave the Philistines the upper hand once more and left Israel leaderless and in considerable disarray. The heir to the throne, Saul's son, Jonathan, had been killed in the battle. David, though once a popular hero, had settled among the Philistines themselves. Samuel was dead and no other religious leader of his stature had arisen to take his place. There was in fact no one who could immediately step into Saul's shoes, and so we enter into a time of considerable confusion, though fortunately one that was not to last long.

David had already been anointed to be the next king. But it must have been difficult for anyone, and particularly for David himself, to see how he could now become king. But then, his call, like that of every man of God, was to press on in faith. The story of his rise to power has suggested to some that he was nothing other than a cunning diplomat and opportunist, but reading it through the eyes of faith we see a man who was prepared to wait for God and to respond to his moments.

Ch. 1: David's lament over Saul and Jonathan.

David had shown nothing but loyal support for Saul as the LORD's anointed during his lifetime, but his reaction to the news of his and Jonathan's death betrays a love and respect beyond the demands of loyalty, and that in spite of all the trials he had had to endure because of Saul's jealousy. At no point had David sought to promote himself to kingship, even though Samuel had already anointed him for the position, nor was he going to do so now. David knew how to wait for God.

Chs. 2–4: David moves to Hebron and becomes king over Judah.

If David knew how to wait for God, he also knew how to move at God's bidding. When the moment came and he got the word of the LORD to go, he went without delay. The result was that he was immediately invited by his own tribesmen, the men of Judah, to become their king.

Meantime the northern tribes appointed one of Saul's sons, Ishbosheth, to be their king. They followed him for a while, until Abner, his army-commander, became disillusioned with him and went over to David. Abner was murdered in the process and then Ishbosheth was assassinated. These were muddled and uncertain times, marked by suspicion, intrigue, civil strife and bloodshed.

Ch. 5: David becomes king of all Israel.

Eventually the northern tribes invited David to be their king too and the nation was reunited. David wisely moved from Hebron and chose a neutral city on the border between the northern and southern tribal blocks for his capital, the old Jebusite stronghold of Jerusalem. He called it the city of David and somehow managed to maintain a measure of personal independence from either tribal block there.

From it he led out his first national expedition – against the Philistines, whom he thoroughly defeated, thus reversing the *status quo* at the end of Saul's reign. He did not integrate the Philistines in Israel in the same way as he did the Canaanites, but held them in subjection to himself. They proved troublesome from time to time during his reign, but they never gained mastery in the land again.

The account of this battle shows how readily he followed

the LORD's guidance in war as well as in politics. But, as we have already noted, he walked in Joshua's footsteps.

Ch. 6: David brings the ark into Jerusalem.

The greatest challenge David had to face besides the Philistine threat was that of creating unity in a nation recently torn by civil war. The ark was Israel's religious centre-piece, the one focus of unity that all the tribes acknowledged. The political value of taking it into Jerusalem is manifest. But again we should beware of reading this story as if it were only about a shrewd political move. We must also give credit for the fact that David was a profoundly religious man. His wife saw the procession enter the city, and it was his religious exuberance she scorned, not his politics.

As the story proceeds we see just how much David was governed by religious motives. He set out with joyful praise and enthusiasm, but when things did not go as he would have liked, his reaction was anger at God, which gave way to fear, which in turn brought the proceedings to a halt. Then, when he realised that his failure to continue in faith had resulted in God's blessing being diverted elsewhere, he went and finished bringing the ark into Jerusalem, and the story ends with him in the same positive, enthusiastic mood as at the beginning. Here we have a living lesson about the importance of persevering in faith and not being stopped by fear. David had to move with God, not just political decisions, though the one inevitably influenced the other.

Ch. 7: The Davidic Covenant, or God's Promise to David.

David now began to feel uneasy about having a palace for himself while the ark was housed in a tent. When he consulted the prophet Nathan, the LORD told him not to become involved in temple-building (vv. 5–7), but to concentrate on the business to which he had been called, namely kingdom-building, giving him promises about personal greatness, about times of national peace and blessing (vv. 8–11), about him becoming father of a great house (dynasty) of kings, and about his kingdom lasting 'for ever' (vv. 11–16).

The responsibility for the nation's welfare now rests largely with the king as its leader, and so God reminds him of the challenge of the two ways he had repeatedly laid before Israel through Moses and his successors, that obedience leads to blessing and disobedience to curse. Applied to the Davidic monarchy that would mean that so long as the king does right he will prosper, but if he does wrong, he must be punished. This covenant with David, however, is to last for ever, and so the king's disobedience, though it might bring him personal suffering, would not cause the dynasty to end. God's promise is quite unconditional: 'Your house and your kingdom shall endure for ever before me; your throne shall be established for ever.' (v. 16).

There are other presentations of this promise in the Old Testament that do make continuation of David's dynasty conditional on the king maintaining faithfulness in his walk with God (1 Kings 8.25; Ps. 132.12; but see 1 Chron. 17.7–14; Ps. 89.30–37, where the promise is unconditional as in 2 Sam. 7). How a promise can be both conditional and unconditional defies explanation by our systems of logic, but the fact is that at the time of the exile, precisely because the kings failed to maintain faithfulness, the Davidic succession was discontinued, and yet the promise stood and was not cancelled, for it finds fulfilment today in the eternal reign of Jesus Christ.

We shall return to this promise to David many times, because it was to form the basis for Israel's Messianic hope, as we may already see, for example, in its comparison of the king's relationship with God to that of a son with his father (v. 14). But for the moment it was simply a promise to David that one of his sons would succeed him.

Ch. 8: David's kingdom becomes an empire.

David defeated the Philistines, Moabites, Arameans, Edomites and Ammonites, all the nations around his borders, and brought them under his rule. To help him govern this little empire, he had a small group of key advisers, which interestingly included priests as well as army officers and other ministers of state (vv. 15–18). The constituent members of this cabinet had changed slightly by the end of his reign, but the pattern remained the same (20.23–25).

**THE EMPIRE OF
DAVID AND SOLOMON
(with main sites in
2 Sam. 1 – 1 Kings 11)**

PHOENICIA
Mt. Lebanon
ARAM-ZOBAH
ARAM-DAMASCUS
GESHUR

Lebo
Hamath

Sidon

Damascus

Tyre

Hazor

Lo Debar

Megiddo

Jabesh Gilead

ISRAEL

Mahanaim

Shechem

R. Jordan

R. Jabbok

AMMON

Gezer

Rabbah

Gibeon
Jerusalem

PHILISTIA

Hebron
Ziklag

Beersheba

MOAB

JUDAH

R. Zered

Wadi of Egypt

EDOM

Elath

RED SEA →

2. DAVID'S REIGN IN JERUSALEM (CHS. 9–20)

These chapters make up one continuous story told in the style of a historical novel, with a dramatic interplay of many personalities. The main characters are not the colourless names we sometimes find in historical narratives; every one of them has a living and sometimes quite complex personality. We meet Mephibosheth's deceitful servant, Ziba (or was it Mephibosheth himself who was the deceitful one?); the lustful Amnon; his beautiful, desolate sister, Tamar; the wise woman of Tekoa; the proud and ambitious Absalom; the bitter Shimei, kinsman of Saul; the clever, but proud and suicidal, Ahithophel; the ruthless, murdering Joab; the gracious old Barzillai; and several others. Then, of course, there is David himself.

David's personality is laid bare in a unique way here. No attempt is made to camouflage his weaknesses, though his greatness is equally upheld. The candidness with which his story is told is indeed nothing less than amazing, considering this was an age when court chroniclers everywhere were obliged to write only what would glorify their monarchs. However, this is sacred history, not secular, written to glorify God, not man, and nowhere else will we find such open, honest assessment of human nature as under the microscope of God's scrutiny.

The theological theme the story illustrates is summed up in one of the central statements in God's promise to David: 'When he does wrong, I will punish him with the rod of men, with floggings inflicted by men. But my love will never be taken away from him.' (7.14f). However, it is not simply a naive series of judgments following immediately on wrongdoing that we read about. Life is not often like that. Rather we watch David, by his failure to deal with wrong and his own direct involvement in it, gradually weave for himself a web of tragedy that returns upon him through his own children. The principle of God's judgement is spelled out more fully by Nathan in ch. 12, but we shall look at that in a moment.

Ch. 9: David receives Mephibosheth.
The story starts with David receiving into his care one of the

last surviving members of Saul's family, Mephibosheth, Jonathan's cripple son, along with his servant, Ziba. Whilst this was an act of kindness on David's part, it also must have helped to unify the nation further by publicly removing the last vestiges of tension between himself and the house of Saul.

Chs. 10–12: David's affair with Bathsheba.

It all happened during one of David's campaigns against the Ammonites, while his troops were besieging their capital, Rabbah. Back in Jerusalem he fell in love with Bathsheba, the wife of Uriah the Hittite, one of his chief officers (23.39). When David learned she was pregnant, he tried to cover up his mistake by recalling Uriah from the war-front and persuading him to sleep with his wife. But Uriah would not break the law that kept soldiers from women in war-time (cf. Deut. 23.9f; 1 Sam. 21.5), and so David arranged for him to be put in a fighting position where he was bound to be killed. Of course, 'the thing David had done displeased the LORD.' (11.27). He sent Nathan to confront him with his sin – and David repented. That saved his life and his crown, but not the child of the adulterous marriage.

The death of his child was only an immediate consequence of David's sin. His affair had involved seduction and murder, and so Nathan warned him that, while the LORD accepted his repentance, his action had set in motion a chain of events that would result in him seeing his sin return publicly on his own family in which there would be open rape and murder. (12.7–12).

Then, we read that a child, Solomon, was born of David's marriage to Bathsheba and surprisingly, without much further comment, we are told that 'the LORD loved him.' (v. 24).

Ch. 13: Amnon, Tamar and Absalom.

Nathan's prophecy begins to see fulfilment when David's oldest son and the natural heir to the throne, Amnon, rapes his sister and is in turn murdered by her brother, Absalom, the next in line for the throne, who as a consequence has to flee the kingdom.

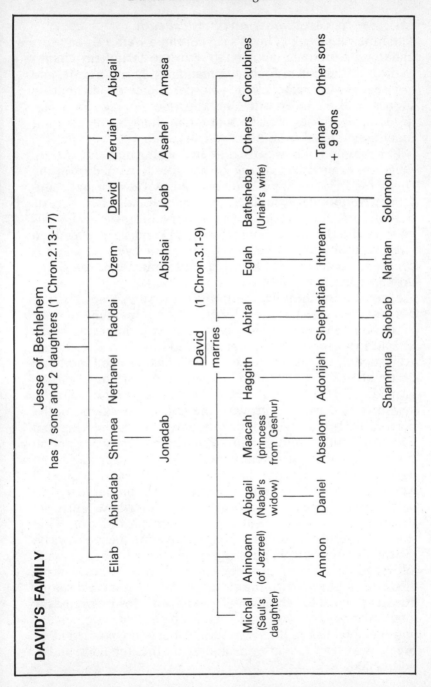

DAVID'S FAMILY

Jesse of Bethlehem
has 7 sons and 2 daughters (1 Chron.2.13-17)

Eliab | Abinadab | Shimea | Nethanel | Raddai | Ozem | David | Zeruiah | Abigail

Jonadab

Abishai | Joab | Asahel

Amasa

David (1 Chron.3.1-9)
marries

Michal (Saul's daughter) | Ahinoam (of Jezreel) | Abigail (Nabal's widow) | Maacah (princess from Geshur) | Haggith | Abital | Eglah | Bathsheba (Uriah's wife) | Others | Concubines

Amnon | Daniel | Absalom | Adonijah | Shephatiah | Ithream | Tamar + 9 sons | Other sons

Shammua | Shobab | Nathan | Solomon

Chs. 14–18: Absalom's revolt and death.

The repercussions of David's sin continue. After three years in hiding, Absalom is allowed to return to Jerusalem, thanks to the intervention of Joab, commander of David's army, and a wise woman from Tekoa, who persuades David that he should be like-minded with God who 'does not take away life; instead, he devises ways so that a banished person may not remain estranged from him.' (14.14).

But Absalom is now a discontented young man. He stirs up rebellion against David who is then forced to flee from the city. True loyalties show immediately: David's trusted counsellor, Ahithophel, who is Bathsheba's grandfather, deserts to Absalom; Ziba, Mephibosheth's servant, turns against his master; and the old jealousies against David surface again in one called Shimei, a kinsman of Saul. However, Absalom is eventually defeated and killed in battle, but David ends up a broken man.

Significantly, the point of turning in the story is not a battle, but a prayer. As David left Jerusalem with his men, he went desolate and weeping. Then came the final shattering blow: he had lost everything, it seemed, and now he was told that Ahithophel, the man who could have best advised him, had deserted. At that moment David hit rock-bottom – then he prayed (15.31). No sooner had he called to God than the answer came over the brow of the hill to meet them in the person of Hushai the Arkite, the only man in the kingdom who could outwit Ahithophel – which he presently did, and so turned the tables in David's favour. God had promised he would preserve David's kingdom, though not that David would be able to do so himself. Hence he was prepared to wait until David called on him to help, no matter how much the situation deteriorated, but the moment he did call, God answered according to his promise. Salvation must always be seen to be God's work, not ours.

Chs. 19–20: Sheba's rebellion.

David returned to Jerusalem, but was not allowed to rest for long. Absalom's revolt had stirred up the old independent national feelings of the northern tribes who now tried to break away from David's rule and so another rebellion had to be quelled.

Order was finally restored in Israel, but at considerable cost, none of which had been necessary, for as Nathan had pointed out to David: The LORD actually wanted to give and bless him abundantly, but when he tried to grab for himself, he lost it all (12.8).

3. APPENDIX TO THE REIGN OF DAVID (CHS. 21–24)

Some of the events recorded here belong to David's last years, others to earlier times. Thus, while the two songs were clearly composed at the end of his reign, the story about the Gibeonites and Saul's sons probably belongs near the beginning, before he took Mephibosheth, as the last surviving member of Saul's household, into his home (cp. 9.1).

21.1–14: The Gibeonites demand vengeance
The occasion of Saul's breach of promise with the Gibeonites is not recorded in the Old Testament, but the promise itself is (Josh. 9). Blood-vengeance may seem a cruel solution, but the principle behind it is fair justice, not excessive punishment: 'life for life, eye for eye, tooth for tooth' (Exod. 21.23f). Jesus' teaching about it in the Sermon on the Mount does not recommend that we jettison justice in favour of softness, but that we learn to temper justice with love (Matt. 5.38–42).

21.15 – 23.39: David's sons and his mighty warriors.
The account of David's reign ends with some highlights from the heroic exploits of his warriors. We need not comment on these, apart from noting a very small point that while 21.19 says one called Elhanan killed Goliath, 1 Chron. 20.5 says it was Goliath's brother, Lahmi, that he killed. That would make more sense, since we know that Goliath was killed by David (1 Sam. 17).

David's reign saw the final establishment of Israel as a kingdom, and so David gave thanks in song for his preservation and victories (ch. 22 = Ps. 18). That psalm and his 'last words' in ch. 23 remind us that there was another aspect to David's life that we have not touched on much in the stories in

1 and 2 Samuel, namely his organisation of Israel's worship and his writing of many of the psalms. We shall return to that in a moment.

Ch. 24: David at the threshing–floor of Araunah.

The story of his reign ends with a further reminder of his role in connection with Israel's worship, for his disastrous census led to him buying and offering sacrifice on the threshing floor of Araunah, which was later to become the site for Solomon's temple (2 Chron. 3.1) – a fine prophetic ending!

David's reign saw great national advances and the establishment of a small empire, but it was shot through with personal tragedy that is traced back to his sinful dealings with Bathsheba and her husband. We do not get the impression that his successes were easily gained. His early life in Saul's time was no picnic and although his armies conquered the nations round about him, tensions continued and occasionally erupted in revolt. David was a man who had to fight continuously, first to become established, and then to maintain the ground he had gained. He had to sustain his fight in the face of severe handicaps, both in the political scene and in his own personal life. But his glory rests in the fact that he fought on and did not give up till he had won through. But then, he knew it was the LORD's battle, for the LORD had promised him he would see the kingdom established. Like Joshua before him, David was a man living with a vision and he knew it was of God.

4. THE SPIRIT OF ENTHUSIASM AND PRAISE IN DAVID'S TIME (1 CHRON. 10–29)

The Chronicler's account of David's reign has a totally different tone, not because of any disagreement or contradiction, but because his interest is in aspects of the story that are scarcely touched on in 2 Samuel, particularly with respect to the organisation of worship and the priesthood. On the other hand, his interest in the historical framework of wars, diplomacy and interplay of personalities is minimal, and so he omits many of the lively stories found in 2 Samuel. The two books are helpfully complementary.

After nine chapters of genealogies and lists, that need not occupy any of our attention here, covering the time from Adam to the exile, he takes up the story with Saul's death on Mount Gilboa.

Chs. 10–12: David's rise to power.

The Chronicler makes no mention of Ishbosheth's reign or of the wars between Abner and Joab, because his sole interest is to tell us about David himself, and in doing so he portrays a sense of freshness and enthusiasm surrounding his accession. Apart from giving fuller lists of David's men, he highlights the vitality of their fighting spirit more fully, and also the zeal with which they joined him and served him.

Chs. 13–17: Jerusalem, the ark and David's kingship.

Again we find details added and subtracted, but the overall impression given here is of David successfully establishing himself in Jerusalem, building his palace, defeating the Philistines and bringing up the ark, with a few hitches, but with general joy and thanksgiving. Little is made of the incident with Michal, his wife (15.29), but much attention is given to new arrangements for the care of the ark by the Levites, and also to their worship, which now begins, for the first time in Israel's history, to be expressed in music and song (chs, 15f and 25), as well as in the sacrifices prescribed by Moses.

The introduction of music in worship clearly reflects David's own interest in song, but that in turn may be a reflection of the effects of Samuel's revival in his childhood. Apart from including one or two of his songs in the story of his life (2 Sam. 1, 22, 23), his biographer only made mention of his musical skills at the beginning, soon after he introduced us to him (1 Sam. 16). At that stage David was closely associated with Samuel and his prophets, who themselves seemed to enjoy worshipping with music (1 Sam. 10.5). Before their time there is no record of any public or corporate worship accompanied by music in the Old Testament. Certainly there were poems and songs written and sung by individuals, such as Moses or Deborah (Exod. 15; Judg. 5). Moses even composed one the Israelites had to learn by heart (Deut. 31.19; 31.30 – 32.43), but that was to help them remember God's care for them and we do not know if it was ever intended to be sung corporately in worship. The law says nothing about music in worship, and so the impression we get is that it was an innovation of David's day. It does not seem unreasonable to trace its origins further back to the outburst of prophetic praise that accompanied Samuel's revival, for every revival in history has issued in a flood of new praise songs, often to the disgust of traditionalists. If these observations are right, then the psalm-praise of the temple had its origins in charismatic revival.

One of the details worth noting in passing is that, while the ark was taken to Jerusalem, the tabernacle was left at Gibeon, about seven miles away, and there the sacrifices prescribed in the law continued to be offered (16.39–42). That explains why Solomon went to Gibeon to seek the LORD at the beginning of his reign (1 Kings 3.4). The tabernacle was eventually dismantled and brought into the temple in Jerusalem at its dedication (1 Kings 8.4).

Chs. 18–20: David's wars with his neighbours.
The details here can almost all be found in 2 Samuel, but the whole story about David and Bathsheba, and Absalom's and Sheba's revolts, is completely omitted between 20.3 and 20.4.

Chs. 21–29: David's arrangements for the worship of the temple.
The story of David's reign in 2 Samuel ended with him buying the threshing-floor of Araunah, which was to become the site for Solomon's temple. Here we are told that after he bought it, presumably right at the end of his reign, he began to make preparations for the work his son would have to undertake in the building (chs. 21f, 28f). But in the process he made many other arrangements, particularly about the ordering of priests, Levites, singers, gatekeepers and treasurers and other officials, as well as his army officers (chs. 23–27). The lists are extensive, but in the middle of them are some striking features, one of which is that the military commanders had a say in the appointment of some of the temple choirs (25.1). Presumably that was because sometimes they would have to

---

DUTIES OF THE LEVITES

In the Wilderness Tabernacle: (Num.1.47-53; 3.5-37)
  to care for the structure of the tabernacle (the Merarites).
  to care for its curtains and coverings (the Gershonites).
  to care for its furniture (the Kohathites).

In the Jerusalem Temple: (1 Chron.23-26)
  to assist the priests (1 Chron.23.28,32).
  to care for the courts, chambers, sacred vessels, etc.
      (1 Chron.23.28-32).
  as gatekeepers (1 Chron.26.1-19; cp.9.19).
  to care for the temple and palace treasuries (1 Chron.26.20-28).
  as choristers and musicians (1 Chron.25; cp.6.31f; 16.4-42).
  to help administer justice (1 Chron.23.4; 26.29-32;
      cp. 2 Chron.19.8-11).
  to teach the law (2 Chron.17.7-9; 35.3).

---

go out at the head of the army singing the LORD's praises in time of war, as in Jehoshaphat's day (2 Chron. 20.21).

Chs. 22 and 28: David's charge to Solomon.

David's reign does not end with the review and challenge to the nation we find at the end of Moses', Joshua's and Samuel's lives, but clearly their words were not forgotten, for David now passes on to his son, Solomon, the same commission to be strong in faith and careful in obedience. Even the words he uses are those of his great predecessor (see esp. 22.11–13; 28.8–10, 20). The programme may be different, but the fundamental challenge for Solomon's generation will be the same.

7

Solomon and the Challenge of Kingdom-Vision

1 KINGS 1–11

Certain patterns emerge from our study so far. For example, it is manifest that revival must precede kingdom-building to provide a good spiritual foundation for it. Thus the Israelites needed Moses' teaching before Joshua led them into the land; without that preparation it would not have been a nation that entered Canaan, only a mixed multitude. Similarly, David could not have built his kingdom without the spiritual preparation done by Samuel. Moses and Samuel were both dead before Joshua and David respectively started their work. There was potential for the two thrusts of revival and kingdom-building to overlap in Saul's day, while Samuel was still alive, but that did not work out, and so they became two distinct phases of development. And that has generally continued to be the pattern throughout history.

But after revival and building, what should come next? What should Solomon do to add to what David did? Certainly we expect to see him maintaining and consolidating David's achievements, but should there not be something new happening as well?

The answer to these questions lies in the original vision God gave through his foundational covenants, with Abraham, Moses and David, but also long before that, with Adam.

Right at the beginning, when God originally brought his kingdom on earth into being and gave man the commission to rule over it, he told man what his kingdom-work was to be: 'Be fruitful and increase in number; fill the earth and subdue it.' (Gen. 1.26–28). At that time God planted a garden-kingdom somewhere in the Middle East and from it he expected man to spread out and rule the whole earth. Now, through men like Abraham, Moses, Joshua, Samuel and David, God has replanted a colony of his kingdom in Canaan, and so we should start seeing that original commission coming into operation again. That, after all, is what the Bible is all about. It is the vision God gave Abraham when he told him his descendants would multiply to become like the stars of heaven, or the sand on the sea shore (Gen. 15.5; 22.17), and who would then mediate blessing to all peoples on earth (Gen. 12.3). The same vision underlies the themes of multiplication, possession of the land, and victory over all enemies in both the Mosaic and Davidic Covenants (Deut. 11.22–25; 2 Sam. 7.8–11). God's purpose was not simply to build a little kingdom-unit in Canaan and leave it at that, but to recapture or redeem the whole earth for himself.

Hence the fuller pattern we look for is revival leading to kingdom-building leading to growth. And as we read of Solomon's reign, that is exactly what we find – at least, to begin with. But then things start to go wrong and we watch other patterns and principles come into operation.

While growth is always God's desire, and so is bound to happen in the end, in his purposes it is not simply achieved by good government, military strength, economic strategy, or any human means. These things are important, but in the end of the day it is his kingdom, not man's, and so its growth results only from man's co-operation with his plan for building it, that is, as we have so often seen already, by faith and obedience. In each generation there is therefore the potential danger of losing what was gained in the last, or some of it. And that is exactly what we find happened in Solomon's time.

1. SOLOMON CONSOLIDATES DAVID'S WORK (CHS. 1–8)

This is not a commentary in which we should get caught up in the details of political intrigues and temple structures. What we are looking for is the movement of God that explains why things happened as they did. Why was it that Samuel's revival and David's kingdom collapsed? The question is akin to one people still ask about revivals today: Why is it that so many of them, both national and local, fail to last, or even turn sour?

Chs. 1–2: Solomon becomes king.

The date is about 970. David is dying. Adonijah, the natural heir, tries to secure the throne for himself by a coup, but David nominates Solomon to be his successor. After David's death, Adonijah and his followers are executed or exiled and Solomon is firmly established as king.

Some of the acts surrounding Solomon's accession have an unpleasant flavour about them, such as the murder of Adonijah (2.13–25), the killing of Joab at the altar (2.28–35), the execution of Shimei (2.36–46), and even the apparent intrigue that helped raise Solomon to the throne in the first place (1.11–27). But all of them were executions of justice and so their effect was simply that 'the kingdom was now firmly established in Solomon's hands.' (2.46).

Some of them were actually commissioned by David (2.5–9), but he was well aware that political manoeuvring, whilst necessary, was not what would govern the long-term flow of God's kingdom purposes, and so his last charge to Solomon began with the really crucial reminder to 'be strong . . . observe what the LORD your God requires . . . keep his decrees . . .' (2.2–4). That was the rock on which Solomon would either build for God, or stumble.

Chs. 3–4: A glimpse of Paradise.

Solomon began his reign with a good heart, dedicating himself to the LORD and seeking wisdom for the task, and the LORD honoured his dedication, promising to bless him with abundance as well. He quickly gained the reputation of a wise and just king (ch. 3). On Gibeon in 3.4 see page 88.

His reign was also a time of peace, and so he was able to give attention to the internal, governmental structures of the state in a way his father had not been able to do because of his constant wars (4.1–28). In addition, culture and learning began to flourish in Jerusalem, Solomon himself being its chief patron and so gaining an international reputation for his wisdom (4.29–34).

Indeed, the historian's impression of this age is that it was a time when Israel came very near to seeing fulfilment of God's promise to Abraham:

*The people of Judah and Israel were as numerous as the sand
on the seashore; they ate, they drank and they were happy.
And Solomon ruled over all the kingdoms from the River to
the land of the Philistines, as far as the border of Egypt.*
(4.20f; cp. Gen. 15.18; 22.17)

Chs. 5–8: Solomon's building projects.
Perhaps the most concrete evidences of the new wealth
flowing into Israel at this time were in the new buildings rising
in the city. Solomon traded with Hiram, king of Tyre, for
wood, materials, labour and craftsmen for building his
palace, a palace for his Egyptian wife, an audience hall for
state occasions, a judgement hall and the temple – the last, of
course, being described in the greatest detail. Its basic plan
was the same as that of the wilderness tabernacle, though it
naturally had many additional features and refinements.

In the middle of all the building work, he was reminded that
the LORD was still looking for faithfulness from him, that no
temple could ever become a substitute for that basic requirement (6.11–13). The way the LORD's glory filled the temple
on the day the ark was brought into it showed clearly how
much God still approved of all he was doing, and his prayers
of dedication reveal a heart that was as right with God as
anyone's could be. He was well aware that his temple would
not automatically or magically secure God's presence in
Jerusalem. God was far too big for that. Solomon certainly
did not build the temple as a house for God to live in, but
rather as the place where God, he prayed, would put his
Name and where men could come to pray for forgiveness and
mercy (8.27–30).

When God's glory came to dwell in the sanctuary, the same
thing was happening as at Mount Sinai when his glory filled
the wilderness tabernacle (Exod. 40.34f). Similarly, Ezekiel
and Haggai both told how his glory would again fill the temple
once it was rebuilt after the exile (Ezek. 43.1–5; Hag. 2.6–9).
God's glory was the symbol of his presence with his people
and the tabernacle/temple his appointed place where he
would meet with them, as he did with Isaiah (Isa. 6). Since
New Testament times, after the sacrifice of Christ rendered
the temple and its systems obsolete, God's glory has come to
dwell with his people in a different, more intimate and

SOLOMON'S TEMPLE

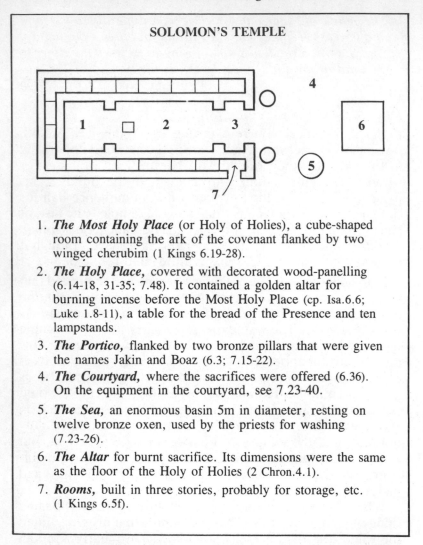

1. *The Most Holy Place* (or Holy of Holies), a cube-shaped room containing the ark of the covenant flanked by two winged cherubim (1 Kings 6.19-28).

2. *The Holy Place,* covered with decorated wood-panelling (6.14-18, 31-35; 7.48). It contained a golden altar for burning incense before the Most Holy Place (cp. Isa.6.6; Luke 1.8-11), a table for the bread of the Presence and ten lampstands.

3. *The Portico,* flanked by two bronze pillars that were given the names Jakin and Boaz (6.3; 7.15-22).

4. *The Courtyard,* where the sacrifices were offered (6.36). On the equipment in the courtyard, see 7.23-40.

5. *The Sea,* an enormous basin 5m in diameter, resting on twelve bronze oxen, used by the priests for washing (7.23-26).

6. *The Altar* for burnt sacrifice. Its dimensions were the same as the floor of the Holy of Holies (2 Chron.4.1).

7. *Rooms,* built in three stories, probably for storage, etc. (1 Kings 6.5f).

personal way, namely by his Spirit in the fellowship of believers and in our bodies, which have now become the Lord's temple (1 Cor. 3.16; 6.19), purified and made ready to receive him by the blood of Jesus. It is therefore not at all surprising that the temple did not survive long after Christ's death.

2. THE BEGINNING OF DECLINE (CHS. 9–11; 2 CHRON. 1–9)

The dedication of the temple marked the height of Solomon's reign. The political and social climate changed little in its latter half, but the spiritual climate did, and after his death everything else changed too – very dramatically. The rot, it seems, started soon after the temple was completed.

9.1–9: God's second charge to Solomon.

This second half of Solomon's reign, like the first, began with God speaking to him, firstly to acknowledge his work on the temple, but also to remind him, and that very forcefully, of the need for continued obedience, if David's achievements were not to be lost and his magnificent new temple was not to become a symbol of disgrace.

The really telling statement is in v. 1: Solomon 'had achieved all he had desired to do.' The account of his reign in 2 Chron. 1–9 gives the impression that most of what he did was what David had suggested he should do anyhow, but irrespective of the amount of personal initiative in his various enterprises, it seems he had reached a point either where he felt he had done enough, or else where his vision for further expansion of the LORD's work ran out. When that happens in anyone's ministry, danger-point has been reached, as Joshua foresaw in his day, and as the period of the judges vividly illustrated. The moment the LORD's people let go of the challenge of faith and cease to press forward in kingdom-work, the wrong things begin to distract them and lead them away from God and his call on their lives. And so it was with Solomon.

9.10 – 10.29: The splendour of Solomon's kingdom.

In the meantime, the expansive growth we expected to follow David's reign had in fact been happening. Israel was now a little empire of some standing in the ancient Near East. Solomon had already established treaty-relations with Egypt and had sealed that alliance by marrying Pharaoh's daughter and building her a palace in Jerusalem (3.1; 7.8). On the northern front he had made a trading agreement with Hiram, king of Tyre, and that had secured his supplies of timber and craftsmen for the work of the temple (ch. 5).

Besides maintaining these relationships, Solomon also exploited the fact that he was geographically the middle-man on the trade-routes between Egypt and Kue (= Cilicia, in Asia Minor), and presently found himself being paid a court visit by the ruler of another great trading power, the Queen of Sheba (= Sabea in S. W. Arabia). In addition to over-land trading, with Phoenician help he also ventured into sea-trading in the Red Sea down the coast of Africa and possibly round southern Arabia to India. Wealth and luxury-goods flowed into Israel from every direction, so much so that it was said that Solomon had 'made silver as common in Jerusalem as stones.' (10.27).

Ch. 11: The cost of Solomon's splendour.
While Solomon's wealth and wisdom attracted international attention, it was not gained without political cost. Apart from having to give Hiram twenty Galilean towns to clear his debt to him (9.11), and having to deal with revolts in Edom and Damascus (11.14–25), he was also faced with the threat of rebellion at home (11.26–40). The problem was slave-labour. Though Solomon mainly used the old inhabitants of the land on his building projects (9.15–23), he was also compelled to conscript forced labour from among native Israelites (5.13f), and it was over that issue that the kingdom finally split (ch. 12).

But the causes of discontent went much deeper. Solomon's international trading alliances had been consolidated by a number of diplomatic marriages, such as his marriage with Pharaoh's daughter (3.1; 11.1). The result was an influx of foreign gods under his own royal patronage, which began to promote national apostasy and erode the very faith his kingship was supposed to represent and uphold. God's response was to warn Solomon personally of the consequences of his behaviour and send a prophet to the dissident Jeroboam son of Nebat, who, paradoxically, was one of the most promising young officers in charge of Solomon's slave-labour work-force, commissioning him to lead out the northern tribes in rebellion – which he was to do after Solomon's death.

'So near and yet so far' must be the verdict on Solomon's

reign. It started with such clear hope for fulfilment of the promises to Israel's forefathers, and yet it ended in disaster. The pattern is a repeating one in Israel's history: the joy of Eden was followed by the fall, the flood and the confusion of Babel; the thrill of God's promise to Abraham vanished in the slavery of Egypt; the glory of the Exodus was spoiled by the forty years of wilderness wandering; the triumph of the conquest was lost in the depression of the period of the judges; Samuel's revival was sullied by Saul's madness; David's empire was ruined by the time of Solomon's death. And the reason was always the same – failure to walk in faithfulness with God.

2 Chronicles 1–9.

The account of Solomon's reign in Chronicles is fundamentally the same as in Kings, with a few small additions and subtractions. The main difference between the two, as we have already noted, is that the Chronicler gives the impression that Solomon's vision was not entirely his own, but much of it executed in obedience to his father's will. He also says nothing about apostasy or the discontent that was growing during Solomon's time, though in ch. 10, when he tells how his son, Rehoboam, lost the allegiance of the northern tribes, he acknowledges that the problem was already there.

Apart from observing these minor differences, it would add little to this present study to discuss 2 Chron. 1–9 in greater detail.

8

The Decline and Fall of the Kingdom

1 KINGS 12 – 2 KINGS 25

After Solomon the Davidic monarchy continued in Jerusalem for more than 300 years, but it never attained anything like the same splendour again. The split between north and south proved final and decisive. At one level that does not surprise us at all, for the relationship between the two had always been brittle. At the start of David's reign the north had separately followed Saul's son, Ishbosheth, and towards the end of it Sheba had been able to lead them out in revolt again. Perhaps the tensions ran even deeper, back through the period of the judges, but both were the LORD's people and while they walked together with him they remained one. The vision of reunion under Davidic rule was therefore never lost and it became part of Israel's prophetic expectation (e.g. Jer. 30–31; Ezek. 37), but it was never to materialise in Old Testament times.

As we read the stories of the divided kingdoms, we become conscious of another shift of emphasis. In the wilderness and in the days of the judges the LORD spoke through his leaders to the people as a whole and national well-being depended on their corporate response. But now the responsibility for the nation's welfare is almost entirely the kings'. They stand, as it were, between God and the people, and when they are faithful or unfaithful, they influence the whole mood of the nation correspondingly, with the result that God either gives or withholds his blessings. Their calling was not just to political leadership, but to spiritual also. The power of growth or decline, revival or death, prosperity or poverty was very much in their hands. That is why the only law of kingship in the Bible insists so strongly that they be men soaked in the Word of God (Deut. 17.14–20), and why Samuel had the kings he appointed endued with God's Spirit first (1 Sam. 10 and 16). Above all else they had to be men of God. But then, it was not just a nation they were leading – it was God's people.

It is thus important to remind ourselves, before we start reading about kings whose reigns are judged almost exclusively by that standard, that we are not handling secular history, but the story of a people called by God to build his kingdom and reflect his glory on earth. Some of the 'bad' kings were, in fact, quite successful by the world's standards, but the Bible does not assess them by their military, cultural or political successes, rather by their influence for God among men.

The Judean kings are constantly compared with David. It is either said that their heart was or was not wholly devoted to the LORD like David's, or that they did or did not do right in the eyes of the LORD as David had done. We have seen that David was certainly not a perfect king, but equally that he did live by his faith and did return to God in obedience when he strayed from it. The LORD's people have not idealised his memory; if they had, the stories about him in 1 and 2 Samuel would not have survived. What they did cherish was the memory of his faithfulness in holding to the calling he had been given, to build the kingdom for God. However, most of his successors proved half-hearted about that calling, and so as the years passed, men began to look forward to a day when God would send them a king fully after David's heart, one truly anointed with God's Spirit, one who would rule on David's throne as the LORD intended the Davidic kings should rule, one they would call Messiah or Christ.

A few of the kings, however, did recapture something of the vision and called the people back to God, who then granted times of refreshing. These are the times we shall highlight as we skim through the story. Their circumstances vary and revival is not always the best term to describe them – hence the headings for the chapter-sections that follow: 'Revival and . . .' The Chronicler generally describes them in greater detail in his account, which we shall therefore use more fully in this section.

1. THE FIRST FIFTY YEARS – REVIVAL AND RECOVERY
(1 KINGS 12–15; 2 CHRON. 10–16)

1 Kings 12.1–24: The northern tribes separate from Rehoboam.

On the surface it might seem that the split was the result of a political blunder by a young and inexperienced ruler. Jeroboam did not come demanding separation, nor did he present himself as a political rival. At first he was only a dissident voice asking better conditions for the people, but Rehoboam heeded the wrong advice and made a disastrous diplomatic mistake that drove him to extreme action.

That is the gist of the matter viewed from the politician's angle, but we need to reckon with the hand of God as well, and the historian aptly remarks that 'this turn of events was from the LORD, to fulfil the word the LORD had spoken . . . ' (v. 15). And so once more we are confronted with that strange interplay of God's purposes and politics we have encountered several times in this study. God had already spoken to Jeroboam through Ahijah the prophet, but just as David had had to bide his time for the political opportunity to take up his kingship, so Jeroboam had to wait too. God had told him he would not take Rehoboam's throne from him because his purpose was for David's descendants to continue in Jerusalem, but even the promise of rule over the northern tribes must have seemed a bit like a pipe-dream to Jeroboam when he had fled from Solomon to seek refuge in Egypt (11.37–40). When he returned from his exile, he knew what God had promised him, but he still had to wait for the invitation to come from the Israelites before he could become their king (12.20).

However, it was not just Jeroboam who recognised God's hand in this turn of events. A prophet called Shemaiah did too, and when he spoke to Rehoboam, even he recognised it was God's doing, and so gave up all his plans to regain the lost territories.

12.25 – 14.20: Apostasy in the North.

God told Jeroboam he could have a dynasty of his own in the north just as lasting as David's was to be in the south (11.38), but as soon as he became king he went off the rails, instituting

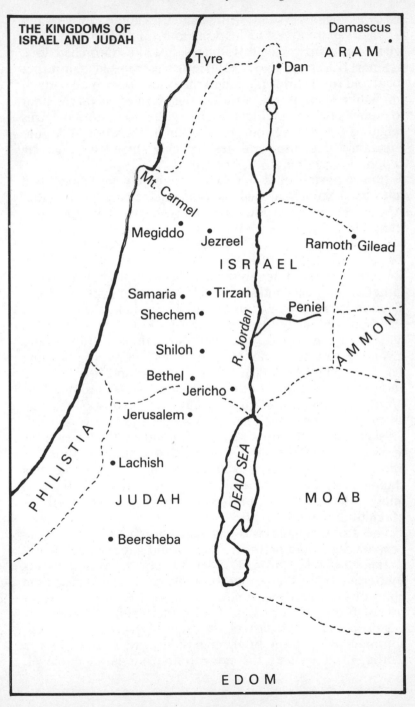

THE KINGDOMS OF
ISRAEL AND JUDAH

Damascus

A R A M

Tyre

Dan

Mt. Carmel

Megiddo

Jezreel

Ramoth Gilead

I S R A E L

Samaria

Tirzah

Shechem

Peniel

R. Jordan

AMMON

Shiloh

Bethel

Jericho

Jerusalem

PHILISTIA

Lachish

DEAD SEA

J U D A H

M O A B

Beersheba

E D O M

his own religious system, with sanctuaries at the southern and northern extremities of his kingdom, in Bethel and Dan, where he set up golden calf-images, just like Aaron had done at Sinai (12.28f; cp. Exod. 32). He also patronised many other local and rural shrines, opened the priesthood to all sorts of unqualified people, and adjusted the Mosaic festival calendar to suit his own political ideals (12.25–33; 13.33). This religious free-for-all soon resulted in a wholesale slide into Canaanite paganism and very quickly stirred up a strong prophetic reaction (13.1 – 14.18).

It must have been with a sadness akin to what Samuel had felt when he told Saul the LORD had rejected him as king, that Ahijah the prophet now told Jeroboam virtually the same thing (14.7–16).

14.21 – 15.8: Meantime in Judah.

Rehoboam did nothing to reverse the religious policies of his father's later years and so the slide into paganism continued. Then in his fifth year disaster struck. Shishak, the Egyptian Pharaoh who succeeded the one whose daughter Solomon had married, had broken off friendly relations with Judah and given asylum to some of Solomon's enemies, including Jeroboam (11.18–22, 40). When the kingdoms of Israel and Judah separated, most of the dependent states around their borders must have broken free, leaving them unsupported by allies, however unwilling, as well as internally divided. Shishak seized the opportunity afforded by their weakness and invaded with terrible force. Shishak (called Sheshonk or Shoshenk by the Egyptians) has left us his own record of this campaign which claims he took, not only Jerusalem, but also many other Judean and Israelite towns as far north as Megiddo, over 150 in all.

The LORD's hand was discerned in these events. The prophet Shemaiah predicted they would happen and clearly explained why (2 Chron. 12.5–8). The cost to Jerusalem was shattering, but it seems that Rehoboam again recognised the hand of God and this time reacted with some measure of repentance (2 Chron. 12.12), with the result that recovery began in the latter part of his reign (1 Kings 14.27f) and continued on into the brief reign of his son, Abijah (15.4; 2 Chron. 13). However, this was certainly not national revival.

There was no call to repentance, no proper change in religious policy, and so there was never peace in either Rehoboam's or Abijah's time. Instead there was constant border-feuding between them and Jeroboam until Asa became king.

15.9–24: Revival in Asa's time.

The account of Asa's reign in Kings is very brief and blunt: it started with him purging the temple of the pagan abuses that had crept into it; then he found himself at war with the North, but by making an alliance with Damascus he quickly got the upper hand; and finally he ended his life suffering with diseased feet. The only comments the historian makes are that he 'did what was right in the eyes of the LORD, as his father David had done', and that his 'heart was fully committed to the LORD all his life.' (vv. 11 & 14).

The Chronicler gives much fuller details, painting for us a picture of full-blown revival. His reforms were not just a purge, but were accompanied by a summons to Judah to seek the LORD and return to his law (2 Chron. 14.4). We see Asa early in his reign stirring the people to faith and vision (14.7) and being rewarded by the LORD with a resounding victory over invaders from the south (14.8–15). We watch him heed the voice of the LORD's prophet, continue with his reforms and seal them by summoning his people to a national rededication festival – and the LORD blessed him with peace through most of his long reign (ch. 15).

But towards its end he let go of his high faith, with disastrous results. It was then that the old hostilities between North and South erupted again, when Asa called on the Arameans for help. A certain Hanani confronted him about doing that without first consulting the LORD, whereupon Asa, in total contrast with his response to the prophet who spoke to him at the beginning of his reign, had Hanani put in prison. The picture of Asa in his last years is one of an angry, oppressive ruler, suffering with his diseased feet, surrounded by doctors, but stubbornly refusing to seek help from the LORD (16.10 – 13). In his life-story we find echoes of patterns we saw in the lives of Saul and Solomon, both of them men who had walked with God and saw tremendous revival blessings, but then went astray and lost so much of the further blessings that could have been theirs. The message is clear and needs no comment more than Hanani's in 2 Chron. 16.7–9:

> *When you relied on the LORD, he delivered them* (your enemies) *into your hand. For the eyes of the LORD range throughout the earth to strengthen those whose hearts are fully committed to him. You have done a foolish thing . . .'*

2. REVIVAL AND REVOLUTION IN ISRAEL
(1 KINGS 15.25 – 2 KINGS 13)

Whereas the southern kings are constantly compared with David, the northern ones are measured by the standard of Jeroboam, and virtually all of them are condemned for not abolishing his golden calf-images. These remained until the

THE FIRST FIFTY YEARS OF THE DIVIDED MONARCHY		
JUDAH	DATE	ISRAEL
Rehoboam 931-14 Pharaoh Shishak invades Palestine in 926.	931	Jeroboam I 931-10 Encouraged by Ahijah the prophet he leads the northern tribes to independence.
National recovery begins at the end of his reign. Abijah 914-11 National recovery continues. Asa 911-870	920	He makes Shechem, then Peniel, his capital and Bethel and Dan his sanctuary towns.
R His reign starts with E reforms leading to revival.	910	Nadab 910-09, assassinated.
V I V Later he allies with A Damascus against Baasha. L	900	Baasha 910-886 The capital moves to Tirzah. Baasha continues hostilities towards Judah.
Towards the end of his reign he develops disease in his feet and his faith grows cold	890	Elah 886-5, assassinated Zimri 885, assassinated
	880	Omri 885-74

destruction of the kingdom in 722 and are frequently referred to as 'the sin of Jeroboam son of Nebat which he caused Israel to commit'. To the biblical historian, the fact that individual kings did nothing to remove them seems to outweigh almost everything else that might have been said in their favour.

We shall not examine the northern story in much detail, partly because it is also studied in Volume Three of this series, and partly because our main interest here is in the Davidic kings in whose succession Jesus stands.

15.25 – 16.34: The slide into paganism.

When Jeroboam seceded from Judah he made Shechem his capital at first, though later he moved to Peniel in Transjordan (1 Kings 12.25). The northern capital was moved again to Tirzah (15.33) before it was finally established in Samaria (16.23f). These movements simply reflect the political unsettlement that is Israel's history before the reign of Omri began in 885 BC. During these first forty-five years or so the throne changed hands five times, three of them by assassinations. Jeroboam's dynasty ended abruptly when his son, Nadab, was killed in his second year. Baasha, his successor, reigned for twenty-four years, but his dynasty ended in the same way as Jeroboam's when his son, Elah, was murdered, also in his second year. Elah's assassin only lasted a week, until he was removed by Omri.

Though he only ruled for twelve years, Omri proved to be one of the strongest political leaders the north ever had. He established Israel as a kingdom of international repute which more than 150 years after his death the Assyrians were still calling 'the House of Omri'. It was he who built Samaria to be the state capital. However, our biblical historian tells very little about him, because his main concern is with what men did or did not do for God, and in his estimation Omri's reign was a disaster. It marked the beginning of a full-scale slide into Canaanite religion, which was precipitated when his son, Ahab, married Jezebel, a Sidonian princess, and built a temple for her gods in Samaria. She proved to be a militant protagonist of paganism and soon Israel's faith was faced with the most serious challenge of its history.

1 Kings 17 – 2 Kings 8: Elijah and Elisha lead the nation in revival.

Behind every revival stand men of the Spirit who are prepared to speak God's word. The Old Testament calls them prophets; today we more commonly call them charismatics. We saw them active in Samuel's day, and again in Asa's, but the stories of Elijah and Elisha give us by far the fullest account of a prophetic thrust in national revival in all the Old Testament histories. A fuller study of their story will be found in Volume Three, but here we can at least note in passing some of the patterns that must by now be becoming quite familiar:

— the general context of decadent religion is obvious;

— the corresponding decadence in national morality is reflected, for example, in the king's seizure of Naboth's vineyard (1 Kings 21);

— God's choice of a man to lead the revival brings first Elijah, then Elisha, to prominence;

— the powerful effectiveness of their word calling for repentance and a return to God is evidenced repeatedly, but perhaps most vividly and memorably in Elijah's challenge to the Israelites on Mount Carmel and to the king in connection with Naboth's vineyard (1 Kings 18, 21);

— the openness to the Spirit is manifest, particularly in the miracles they performed, but also in the boldness with which they approached the king (cp. again 1 Kings 18, 21).

The reviving power of their preaching is reflected partly in the fact that the Israelites did not in the end jettison their faith for Baalism, and partly in the growth of a new movement of prophetic men supporting their ministry (2 Kings 2–8). We do not get the impression that these prophets were very numerous, but they certainly had a powerful impact. Within a space of about thirty years after Ahab's accession their revival work reached a stage where Elisha was able, like Samuel before him, to anoint a king to consolidate their work and build a new kingdom of faith in Israel (2 Kings 9).

There is, however, one major difference between them and other charismatic revivalists in Old Testament times, and that is seen in the number of miracle stories preserved about them. Samuel did witness miracles in his ministry, but not of the same nature as Elijah's and Elisha's, nor with the same concentration. In fact this period is noted as one of only three in Biblical times that was marked for such intensive miraculous activity, the other two being the ages of Moses and Jesus. All three were times of revival, but they were also times of open warfare against external forces that sought to destroy the work of God. Pharaoh tried to break the nation through slavery, Jezebel tried to eradicate its faith, and Satan tried to stop the redeeming work of Christ. These were all times when something more than revival preaching was called for, when the power of God performing wonders through his Spirit was also needed. It is not without reason that it was Moses and Elijah, rather than Samuel and David, for example, who were allowed to encourage Jesus on the Mount of Transfiguration. They had fought the same kind of battle before him and could appreciate the challenges he was facing better than any other men in history.

In our own century the onslaught against Christian faith throughout the world has been with a fury quite unparalleled for well over a thousand years, and we have again witnessed a remarkable increase in miraculous activity. We may call the enemy by a different name, but the nature of the warfare is much the same as in Elijah's day, and as then, so now God does not leave his work undefended. Again he has been raising up the same kind of troops to fight his battle, men filled with his Spirit and power.

Towards the end of his reign the prophetic word started to make some impact on Ahab (21.27–29). Had he lived longer, he might have come to full repentance, but his life was prematurely cut short when he fell in a battle he ought never to have fought, if only he had heeded Micaiah, another of the LORD's prophets (1 Kings 22).

His son, Ahaziah, was a thorough pagan, but his reign was brief, for he died from a fall in his second year, shortly after trying to get help from Baal-Zebub, the Philistine god of Ekron (2 Kings 1).

His successor, Joram (or Jehoram), by contrast, began to show signs of willingness to reform when he got rid of some of the trappings of Baal (2 Kings 3.1f). He also showed more openness to Elisha than his fathers had shown to Elijah (3.11–14; 5.8f; 6.21f; 8.1–6), but Jezebel was still very much the power behind the throne and until she was dealt with,

Elisha realised, there could never be full restoration of faith in Israel.

Chs. 9–10: Jehu overthrows the house of Ahab.

In obedience to a commission Elijah must have passed on to him (cf. 1 Kings 19.16f), Elisha had an army officer, called Jehu, anointed to take the throne. His coup, however, became something of a blood-bath, in which Jehoram and the king of Judah were both killed, as also were Jezebel, seventy sons of the house of Ahab, and all the ministers of Baal in Samaria – hardly the way we would want revival to be consolidated today, though it clearly had the initial support of Elisha and his prophets, and also of Jonadab son of Rechab, the leader of another enthusiastic group, the Rechabites, who were totally dedicated to the LORD's work too (10.15f; cp. Jer. 35). Nevertheless, Jehu's excesses were not allowed to pass uncriticised by later prophets (Hos. 1.4f).

And so, the battle for the faith, that had been spear-headed by the prophets, was finally won by the sword of a man, who like Saul, David and Jeroboam, had been roused to the task by the prophets themselves. This was, however, to be the last occasion in biblical times, though not the last in history, that a prophetic movement would advocate the use of military force for the defence of faith.

3. REVIVAL AND RESTORATION IN JUDAH
(1 KINGS 22 – 2 KINGS 14; 2 CHRON. 17–24)

Judah's story in the ninth century is inextricably bound up with Israel's. Asa's son, Jehoshaphat, became king after Omri had made the North a strong kingdom and both he and his son, Jehoram, lived somewhat in the shadow of Israel. Indeed Jehoram (his northern contemporary had the same name) even married Ahab's daughter, Athaliah, and that, of course, brought Baalism right into Jerusalem. However, Jehoshaphat's reign did not start on that note.

1 Kings 22: Jehoshaphat continues Asa's reforms (2 Chron. 17–20).

We are not told much about Jehoshaphat in 1 Kings, except

JUDAH	DATE	ISRAEL
THE NINTH CENTURY BC		
Asa 911-870	880	Omri 885-74 Builds Samaria and makes Israel politically strong. Ahab 874-53
Jehoshaphat 870-48 Continues and consolidates Asa's reforms. Judah prospers in his time. He lived at peace with Ahab.	870	Marries Jezebel and allows her to popularise Baalism. Almost all Elijah's ministry was during his reign.
	860	
		R E Ahab is killed in battle at Jabesh-Gilead. Ahaziah 853-52 Jehoram 852-41
Jehoram 848-41 Ahaziah 841, killed by Jehu. Athaliah 841-35 Pagan daughter of Jezebel, deposed in a palace coup.	850	V I V Elisha continues Elijah's revival ministry.
	840	Jehu 841-14 A L An army officer anointed by Elisha to overthrow the house of Omri and purge the land of Baalism.
Joash 835-796 R E V I V A L Boy-king whose reforms restored faith in Judah. Elijah's revival was now spilling over into the southern kingdom.	830	Continuing war with Syria.
	820	Period of weakness in Israel.
	810	Jehoahaz 814-798
Joash's own faith declined at the end of his reign.	800	

that he fought alongside Ahab in the battle against the Arameans in which Ahab was killed, that he continued to pursue his father's reforming policies and that a fleet of trading ships he built was wrecked before it ever set sail.

The Chronicler gives much fuller details. In his reckoning Jehoshaphat was one of Israel's best kings, one who from his early years 'strengthened himself' and 'sought the God of his father and followed his commands.' (17.1, 4). In addition to furthering Asa's purge of paganism, he sent trained officials and Levites through the land to instruct the people in the law

(17.5–9), and the LORD blessed him with prosperity and national security (17.10–19). He was rebuked by a prophet called Jehu for helping the apostate Ahab in his battle with the Arameans, but even then the prophet found he could not be too hard on him because his heart was good with the LORD (18.1 – 19.3). Even the judges and other legal officers he appointed in the land were commanded to administer justice in the name of the LORD and to call the people back to God in repentance (19.4–11).

The truly memorable occasion when God vindicated his faith was when a coalition of Moabites and others marched into Judah. Jehoshaphat called his people to prayer and was given a prophetic promise that God would fight for them. In the strength of that word he spoke faith to his troops, who, thus inspired, marched out to battle led by a choir praising God for the anticipated victory. In the event they never had to do battle, for the enemy was thrown into sudden confusion and ended up fighting among themselves. The story is well known and is told to God's glory. It is encased in praise from beginning to end and illustrates the kind of faith that calls forth miracles (20.1–30).

Jehoshaphat's reign is thus remembered as a remarkable time of refreshing in Judah. The principles undergirding it are clear: living in repentance and obedience, heeding the word of the LORD, and going forward in faith. These are the same principles as we have seen necessary for revival and kingdom-building, but Jehoshaphat's work was neither of these. The kingdom did not grow under him, but it lived under God's protection; he introduced no revival (Asa had done that), but he lived in the continuing good of it. However, from this account of his reign we learn how important our basic revival and kingdom-building principles are for sustaining the LORD's work as well as encouraging new birth or growth.

Jehoshaphat is certainly not idealised as a figure of perfection. He made his mistakes, and would make more before his end (20.31–37), but at least his heart was after God.

2 Kings 8–12: Decline and revival (2 Chron. 21–24).

Jehoram's marriage to Ahab's daughter brought royal patronage of Baalism into Jerusalem and brought Judean religious policy into alignment with Ahab's. The decline of faith and morale that followed had disastrous consequences. Jehoram found himself being assailed along his borders on every side and after eight years died of a painful bowel disease. Few lamented his passing (2 Kings 8.16–23; 2 Chron. 21).

His son, Ahaziah, only lasted one year. His friendship with the house of Ahab resulted in premature death, for he was assassinated along with Jehoram of Israel, whom he was visiting at the time Jehu rose up in revolt (2 Kings 8.24 – 9.29; 2 Chron. 22).

That left Ahab's daughter, Athaliah, in control in Jerusalem. She set about systematically getting rid of the Davidic royal family, but one son, Joash (Jehoash) was rescued by his aunt and for six years he was kept hidden at the temple where he grew up under the tutelage of the high priest, Jehoiada (2 Kings 11.1–3; 2 Chron. 22.10–12). Then when the boy was old enough, Jehoiada organised a coup that put him on the throne and got rid of both Athaliah and her Baalism (2 Kings 11; 2 Chron. 23).

It was seven years since Jehu had started to purge Israel of paganism when the reforms in Judah got under way. This time it is not so much revival that we read about, but rather reformation, throwing out idols and refurbishing the temple. But that is because the revival work had already been done up north by Elijah and Elisha, and Joash's and Jehoiada's work represents the rebuilding that had to take place after it.

Joash slid away from faith after Jehoiada, his faithful chaplain and tutor, died, and so his reign ended on a sadder note. Powerful as the impact of revival can be, as we have seen over and again, its gains can so easily be lost unless it is followed by consistent and faithful kingdom-building.

4. ISRAEL FALLS – REVIVAL AND RESISTANCE IN JUDAH
(2 KINGS 13–20; 2 CHRON. 25–32)

As we leave the age of the house of Ahab and the revival work of Elijah and Elisha behind, we move forward into a completely different phase of Israel's history. Hitherto it was mainly small nations around their borders, nations about the same size as themselves, that the two kingdoms had had to contend with, but about 900 BC, in northern Mesopotamia, the Assyrians began to expand their frontiers. In 853, towards the end of Ahab's reign, they engaged a coalition of Palestinian forces at Qarqar on the River Orontes, and in 841 Jehu, almost immediately after becoming king of Israel, was obliged to pay them tribute (both events are known only from Assyrian records and are not mentioned in the Bible), but they were not ready at that time to build their empire in the west and so did not bother the Palestinian states again for a century.

For much of those hundred years Israel was occupied in prolonged wars with Syria (Aram; 2 Kings 13). The revival that set Jehu on the throne was at first followed by political decline rather than resurgence, but it put fibre back into the nation's muscle, and, with the prophets (who included Jonah; 14.25) still encouraging them, Jehu's successors eventually led Israel forward into an age of considerable wealth and security during the reign of Jeroboam II (782–53 BC; 2 Kings 14.22–29). It was in his time that Amos and Hosea prophesied, but their warnings went largely unheeded by the people of Israel. In 732 the Assyrians took Damascus, and then finally in 722 they took Samaria, deported its inhabitants and brought the history of Northern Israel to an end, just as both prophets foretold would happen.

The story of Israel's last years need not occupy our attention here. It is told in 2 Kings 15 and 17. They were years of turmoil, very much in contrast with the peace and affluence of Jeroboam's reign. In the thirty years between his death and the fall of Samaria in 722 Israel had six kings, four of them coming to power by assassination. And the voice of the prophets went largely unheeded (2 Kings 17.13f). The historian has no doubt about the root causes of the disaster. On the surface it looked just like a growing empire swallowing up a small kingdom, but underneath there lay a continuous record of disobedience and unfaithfulness. Israel's fall was no mere accident of history. It was the effect of the LORD's hand descending in judgement (2 Kings 17).

THE LAST YEARS OF THE NORTHERN KINGDOM			
JUDAH	DATE	ISRAEL	ASSYRIA
Uzziah 767-42 Age of peace with Israel.	770 760	Jeroboam II 782-53 Time of security and wealth in Israel.	No immediate threat to the West from Assyria.
	750	Zechariah 753-52 Shallum 752 Menahem 752-42	
Jotham 742-35	740	Pekahiah 742-40 Pekah 740-32	Tiglath-Pileser III 745-27 Leads the Assyrian armies west.
Ahaz 735-15	730 720	Hoshea 732-22 Vassal of Assyria after fall of Damascus. FALL OF SAMARIA ——— 722 ———	Takes Damascus in 732 Shalmaneser V 726-22 Takes Samaria in 722.

According to 2 Kings 15.27, Pekah reigned for 20 years. Presumably that was as a rival king for about 14 years, until he assassinated Pekahiah and became sole ruler. These were turbulent years.

2 Kings 17.4 suggests that Shalmaneser managed to arrest Hoshea before he laid siege to Samaria in 724.

It may seem strange that Judah was able to retain a measure of independence and in the end survive the age of Assyrian domination, but then we need to remind ourselves that we are reading, not just a history of nations, but a history of God's purposes, and he had a separate destiny for Judah that was intimately related to his promise to David. That can only be fully appreciated when the history is read in connection with the teaching of the prophets, as we do in Volume Three, but for the present we must adhere to our aim of tracing the various moves of revival as recorded by the historians.

Judah enjoyed the same fruits of peace and prosperity as Israel in the early half of the eighth century, when Amaziah and then Uzziah (= Azariah) ruled. By the time Jotham became king the mood had begun to change, but it is only with Ahaz's reign that we need to take up the story.

Ch. 16: Ahaz leads the nation into apostasy (2 Chron. 28).

Ahaz became king in 735 and almost immediately found himself besieged in Jerusalem by the joint forces of Israel and Aram. Their aim was apparently to have him replaced with a puppet-king, called Ben-Tabeel (Isa. 7.6). Isaiah tried to encourage Ahaz to put his faith in God's promises to David, but to no avail (Isa. 7). He sent for help to Tiglath-Pileser of Assyria, who needed no second invitation to extend his imperial hand into Palestine. Damascus fell to him in 732, Samaria became his vassal, and Ahaz had to pay him tribute.

In the face of these international pressures Ahaz crumbled spiritually as well as politically. Having rejected Isaiah's invitation to faith, he quickly turned to other gods. A new altar appeared in the temple, copied from one he saw in Damascus, and before long Jerusalem was riddled with paganism and superstition, to the utter disgust of both our historians. Apparently he even closed the temple altogether in the end (2 Chron. 28.24).

Chs. 18–20: Hezekiah leads the nation back to God (2 Chron. 29–32).

These were unusually traumatic times for the LORD's people. The Assyrians were now right at Jerusalem's doorstep and were later to press on south through Judah into Egypt. Fortunately Ahaz was succeeded by Hezekiah in 715, just before Jerusalem's own hour of crisis came.

The story of how immediately he became king he led Judah in reform and revival is best followed from the Chronicler's fuller account. His first act was to reform and restore the temple. He had the Levites reconsecrate themselves and in just over a fortnight they had the temple purged and restored. Then he summoned the people of the land to a national Passover celebration (chs. 29f). While these acts are important in themselves, the mood they generated in the community at every level is even more important, for at every stage we sense a new movement of enthusiasm and praise. Indeed, the

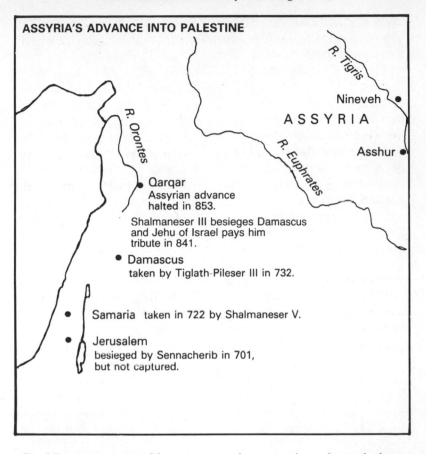

ASSYRIA'S ADVANCE INTO PALESTINE

ASSYRIA

Nineveh

Asshur

R. Tigris

R. Euphrates

R. Orontes

Qarqar
Assyrian advance
halted in 853.

Shalmaneser III besieges Damascus
and Jehu of Israel pays him
tribute in 841.

Damascus
taken by Tiglath-Pileser III in 732.

Samaria taken in 722 by Shalmaneser V.

Jerusalem
besieged by Sennacherib in 701,
but not captured.

final Passover turned into an amazing occasion of conviction, re-dedication and joy. And the result was that revival spilled out into the rest of the country and men gave themselves and their dues to God. The morale of the state rose beyond measure (ch. 31).

What we have here is not just temple reform, but a full-scale revival of faith, vision and hope. And that was certainly needed to prepare for what lay ahead. When the Assyrians did eventually march on Jerusalem, they found walls that had been fortified, citizens who would not readily bow in fear, and a city that could not easily be taken (ch. 32).

In 711 some Judean and Philistine cities tried to persuade Hezekiah to join them by allying with Egypt in revolt against Assyria. Isaiah warned him against doing so (Isa. 20) and

Hezekiah, unlike Ahaz before him, heeded the prophet, with the result that Jerusalem escaped the wrath of Assyria when the rebels were crushed.

The real crisis came in 701. By then Hezekiah had completed his religious reforms (2 Kings 18.1–8) and strengthened Jerusalem's fortifications, which included digging a new tunnel to bring the water-supply from the spring outside the walls into the city (2 Chron. 32.30; it is still possible to walk through this tunnel in Jerusalem today). When Sargon of Assyria died in 705, rebellion broke out in the empire. Hezekiah became ringleader of a revolt in Palestine, but Sargon's successor, Sennacherib, systematically crushed the participating cities and set siege to Jerusalem. Hezekiah tried to buy him off, but to no avail (2 Kings 18.13–16). He knew extreme anguish before the boasting might of Assyria (18.17– 19.13), but he turned to God in prayer (19.14–19), was answered first by an encouraging prophecy from Isaiah (19.20-34) and then by a miracle of deliverance that still leaves us as astounded as both the Israelites and the Assyrians must have been when it originally happened (19.35f)

THE AGE OF ASSYRIAN INVASION				
DATE	JUDAH	ISRAEL	ARAM	ASSYRIA
740	Jotham 742-35			Tiglath-Pileser III 745-27
730	Ahaz 735-15 Faithfully paid tribute to Assyria after 732, but led Judah into paganism.		FALL OF DAMASCUS ← 732	← 734
		FALL OF SAMARIA ← 722		Shalmaneser V 726-22
720				← 724 Sargon II 721-05
710	Hezekiah 715-687 [R E V I V A L] Reforms leading to revival. Revolt of Judean towns quelled (Hezekiah did not participate).			← 711
700	Hezekiah leads a revolt against Assyria. Jerusalem is besieged and is miraculously delivered.			Sennacherib 704-681 ← 701

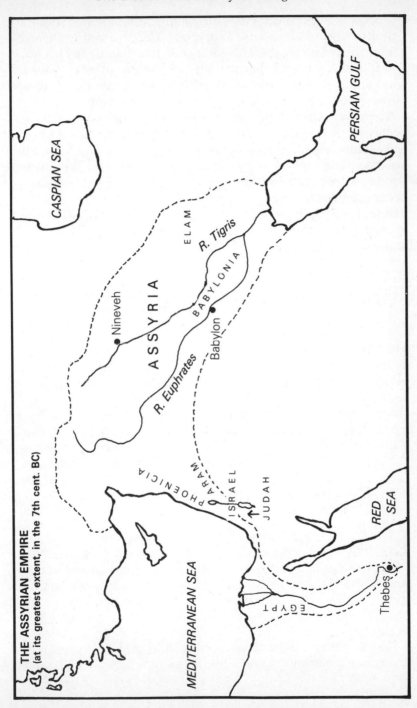

THE ASSYRIAN EMPIRE
(at its greatest extent, in the 7th cent. BC)

At the height of the crisis king and prophet stood side by side in prayer before God (2 Chron. 32.20) – and he heard them. Such was Hezekiah's faith, just like Samuel's (1 Sam. 7), Jehoshaphat's (2 Chron. 20), and many others', whom God vindicated in the most startling ways. Truly he rewards those who walk in faith and obedience with him.

However, after all the encouragement to faith he must have received through the relief of Jerusalem, and later when miraculously healed of a serious illness and granted a most spectacular prophetic sign (2 Kings 20.1–11), Hezekiah was tempted to pride and disappointed Isaiah by befriending some Babylonian envoys who came to visit him (20.12–19). His faith should have led him to trust in God alone, not in any foreign friendships, for his call was to build God's kingdom, not just a political state in alliance with other worldly powers.

5. REVIVAL AND REFORMATION – THEN EXILE (2 KINGS 21–25; 2 CHRON. 33–36)

Hezekiah was succeeded by Manasseh whose long reign saw a reversal of everything his father had achieved. Manasseh reverted to Ahaz's ways, and if anything, outdid his grand-father in encouraging the proliferation of pagan and supersti-tious practices. Some prophets did speak out against him, but he effectively silenced their protests. According to the Chronicler, he showed some signs of repentance later in his reign, but whatever reforms he might have instituted must have been very sparse, for after the brief two-year reign of his son, Amon, there was still plenty of paganism for Josiah to get rid of in his purges.

Chs. 22 – 23: Josiah's reforms (2 Chron. 34f).
Like Joash two centuries earlier, Josiah was a boy when he became king, and also like Joash, his reforming activities are associated with repairs to the temple. But there is one major difference, for this time the reforms were not sparked off by revolutionary zeal, but by a rediscovery of the word of God in Scripture.

The fact that 'the Book of the Law' had been so completely abandoned during Manasseh's reign that it was well nigh

THE LAST YEARS OF DAVID'S KINGDOM			
DATE	JUDAH	MESOPOTAMIA	
650	Manasseh 687-42 A faithful Assyrian vassal. Age of religious apostasy.	Ashurbanipal 668–27 Height of	A S S Y
640	Amon 642-40 Josiah 640-09	Assyrian power	R I A N
630		Sinsharishkun 629-12 Assyria's decline begins.	E M P
620	Josiah's reforms 622 REVIVAL		I R E
		FALL OF NINEVEH 612	
610	Jehoahaz 609 Jehoiakim 609-597 Egypt's vassal until 604/3 when he goes over to the Babylonians.	Nebuchadnezzar 605-562	B A B Y L
600	Rebels against Babylon 600. Jehoiachin 597 JERUSALEM FALLS 597 ←	Takes Jerusalem 597. First deportation.	O N I
590	Zedekiah 597-87 Appointed by Nebuchadnezzar Rebels against Babylon 589. JERUSALEM ← DESTROYED 587*.	Destroys Jerusalem 587. Second deportation.	A N E M
580	THE EXILE (Usually dated from the first deportation in 597).		P I R E

* Or 586 according to a different method of calendar reckoning.

forgotten is startling enough in itself, but the impact that reading it made on the king is even more startling. This is the first time that we hear of revival sparked off by a simple reading of the Bible, but it was certainly not to be the last (cp. Neh. 8).

The prophetic voice was also active in encouraging Josiah's reforms. Besides the prophetess Huldah mentioned in ch. 22 it seems that Jeremiah and Zephaniah were also both preaching repentance before the reforms.

The reforms themselves began with a purge of the temple, but quickly spread to the rest of Jerusalem and the villages of Judah, even spilling over into the old Northern Kingdom where Jeroboam's apostate sanctuary at Bethel was finally desecrated. Mediums, spiritists and all sorts of superstitious paraphernalia were outlawed. The purges seem to have been very thorough.

But these were more than reforms. A new mood was in the air. On the international scene Assyria was declining, though certainly not yet dead. That in itself must have engendered optimism, but it does not explain the positive revival atmosphere that accompanied Josiah's reforms. When Passover was celebrated, the historian comments, nothing quite like it had been seen in Israel since the days of the judges. That is not just political optimism – that is revival. The Chronicler again gives fuller details, but in essence adds little to the portrait of enthusiasm so vividly captured in 2 Kings.

However, as our historian sadly notes, it all came too late to save Judah (2 Kings 23.26f). The accumulation of wrong from earlier times had so permeated the fabric of society that no sooner was Josiah dead than paganism flooded the land once more, particularly during the reign of Jehoiakim. (The most vivid account of the paganism of these last years is found in Ezek. 8.)

Chs. 24–25: Jerusalem's last days (2 Chron. 36).

From this point on the author of Kings concentrates primarily on the sequence of events that led to the fall of Jerusalem to the Babylonians and tells us very little about religious affairs in these last years. These things probably seemed no longer relevant to him anyhow. Though there were prophets who were still very active, particularly Jeremiah and Ezekiel, but also others as well, they were not much heeded any more. This was certainly not an age of revival zeal and so the momentum towards final destruction became irreversible. All that was therefore left for the historian to do was tell the story of how the end came. The Chronicler is less concerned to recount all the details, but even his more religious comments add little to what we have already noted here.

As we cast our eye over the course of history from the days

of Moses and Joshua, it seems to be littered with lost promises and failed hopes. Certainly there was progress, for Israel did become a settled nation and a kingdom. There were also moments of great faith-expectation, especially when the empire began to take shape and Solomon ruled over a happy and prosperous kingdom. But that too came to naught, and always it was the same problem – a basic inability to remain faithful to God. The final picture is far from encouraging.

However, there was always a faithful remnant who rose up from time to time and fought for the faith. They were mainly prophets, or kings who heeded the prophets, and they led the nation in revival more than once. Through all Israel's political ups and downs it was these men of the Spirit who provided the steadying undercurrent of faith and vision. The charismatic vocation is still the same today!

PART FOUR

THE ADVENT OF CHRIST'S
KINGDOM

597 BC — 46 AD

To many Jews (as the LORD's people came to be called after the exile) the destruction of Jerusalem and the removal of her kings must have seemed like the end of God's promise to David. However, he had prepared them well for this hour. Their prophets had been warning them about it for over a century and those who had paid even the slightest attention to them could not have been taken entirely by surprise. But as well as foretelling judgement and exile, they had also laid a foundation for hope that would ensure continued faith in God's purposes, for they had already seen beyond the exile to a day when God would not only restore the nation to its land, but also the kingship to David's line. Even more than that, they had seen that the coming king would effectively establish the kingdom according to his original plan in a way that none of David's descendants had hitherto been able to do.

The exile was neither a set-back nor a disaster from God's perspective, but his way of preparing his people for the next stage in the unfolding of his purposes, his means of teaching them the cost of disobedience. Indeed the experience of God's judgement in the humiliation of seeing their kingdoms crushed and of undergoing the suffering of exile, proved to be a most effective refining process. Those who returned were in many ways a changed people, unique in ancient times. They were only a remnant of what Israel had been, but they now knew the uniqueness of God, they recognised his call to righteousness, and they believed there would be a day when all his promises would be fulfilled, when the expected Son of David would be born and the kingdom would be established by his hand. They were basically a more faithful people, but also a waiting people.

9

Rebuilding and Waiting for the King

THE EXILE TO CHRIST

The story of the post-exilic community belongs to Volume Four of this series, but for the sake of continuity in our historical survey we need to review it briefly here. The Jews who returned, though not very numerous, were men with a strong sense of purpose. The fact that the exile had happened as the prophets foretold taught them to respect and cherish their teaching, and so, inspired by their further vision of Israel as the base from which God would establish his world-kingdom, they returned full of enthusiasm to rebuild in and around Jerusalem.

Their story is also relevant here because it includes accounts of two major times of refreshing, one associated with the rebuilding of the temple and the prophetic ministries of Haggai and Zechariah, the other with the rebuilding of the city walls and the establishment of the law, inspired by the teaching of Malachi, the prophet, and Ezra, the scribe.

1. REVIVAL AND REBUILDING (EZRA AND NEHEMIAH)

Ezra 1 – 6: The exiles return and rebuild the temple.
Soon after Cyrus took Babylon in 539 he issued an edict encouraging exiles to return to their homelands. One called Sheshbazzar was appointed governor of Judah and he led the first Jewish returning party. They brought treasures from the old temple with them and some of their leaders gave contributions towards building a new one. That autumn (537)

125

they rebuilt the altar and restarted sacrificial worship (1.1 – 3.6). Preparatory work was also begun on the temple and the following spring the foundation was laid (3.7–13), but opposition from some of the people in the land brought everything to a standstill and work was abandoned for the next fifteen years (ch. 4).

Judging by some of the comments made by Haggai in particular, it seems the general mood quickly degenerated into depression (Hag. 1.2–11), but in 520 he and his fellow-prophet, Zechariah, encouraged the new governor, Zerubbabel, and the priest, Joshua, to restart the work, and thanks to their enthusiasm the mood swung to one of revival. Then a surprising thing happened: As might have been expected, there was renewed opposition, but that led to a search which uncovered a decree of Cyrus authorising the rebuilding and enjoining that costs be met from the royal treasury – which effectively meant out of the pockets of those senior officials who were trying to stop the work! (chs. 5–6).

The work now moved rapidly to completion. The new temple was dedicated and Passover celebrated in it for the first time in the spring of 515 BC amid great rejoicing, particularly over the miraculous provision from the royal treasury!

Neh. 1–7, 11–13: Nehemiah rebuilds Jerusalem's walls.

We now move forward about seventy years. From the book of Malachi we learn that the fresh, revival enthusiasm of the early days had not lasted. Priests and people alike had grown careless about the service of God. Reform and revival were again badly needed.

In 445 Nehemiah, a Jew of high standing at the court of Artaxerxes, was appointed Governor of Judah. He came with permission to resume the work of rebuilding Jerusalem and its walls, halted some forty years earlier (see Ezra 4.6–23). The old opposition was still there and active (Neh. 2.10, 19), but Nehemiah was unshaken and after a brief tour of inspection, he set the people to work on the walls. His zeal stirred up vehement anger, particularly among the Samaritans, who did all they could to have the work stopped. However, in Nehemiah they met a man of strong faith, unshakable determination and careful strategy. Within only fifty-two days the walls were complete.

Steps were then taken to have the city repopulated, and the walls were dedicated in an official, but joyous ceremony (chs. 11f). It must have been a satisfied Nehemiah who, after twelve years as governor, went back to report to Artaxerxes, for the city was now strongly established (13.6).

Ezra 7–10, Neh. 8–10: Ezra brings reform and revival.

Ezra 7–10 takes us back to 458, thirteen years before Nehemiah's visit (7.8), when the Persian king, Artaxerxes, was concerned about religious apathy in Jerusalem. Fearing lest the God of the Jews should become angry and 'there be wrath against the realm of the king and of his sons' (7.23), he sent Ezra, a priest and teacher of the Law of Moses, with orders to execute reform and encourage revival. God moves in mysterious ways!

Ezra's main challenge was the appalling effect of mixed marriages in drawing Jews away into unfaithfulness. He tackled the problem with prayer and fasting and as he did so the LORD moved in power among the people. Though it was mid-winter and raining heavily when they came together, they fell under such conviction as he spoke that they agreed to rectify the problem. Only four opposed him!

With Neh. 8–10 we move forward again to Nehemiah's time, and there we see just how much Ezra's burning passion was for the Law. When the people assembled in the autumn to celebrate Tabernacles, he read it aloud to them 'from daybreak till noon' (8.3) and got Levites to translate or interpret as he read. Every day of that week-long festival he read it to them. Apparently it was a forgotten book, but the people found much joy in re-discovering it. A fortnight later he was reading it to them again, this time along with prayer and confession of sins; and that led to the leaders, Levites and priests signing an agreement to keep the law henceforth. This was now the second time that Scripture reading had led to revival (cp. 2 Kings 22f).

Nehemiah's achievement was to build walls and faith, Ezra's was to establish the Jews as the people of the Law, thus giving Judaism its peculiar flavour that has lasted down to

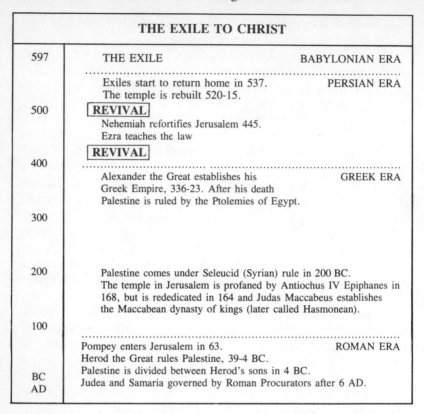

	THE EXILE TO CHRIST	
597	THE EXILE	BABYLONIAN ERA
	Exiles start to return home in 537.	PERSIAN ERA
	The temple is rebuilt 520-15.	
500	REVIVAL	
	Nehemiah refortifies Jerusalem 445.	
	Ezra teaches the law	
	REVIVAL	
400		
	Alexander the Great establishes his	GREEK ERA
	Greek Empire, 336-23. After his death	
	Palestine is ruled by the Ptolemies of Egypt.	
300		
200	Palestine comes under Seleucid (Syrian) rule in 200 BC.	
	The temple in Jerusalem is profaned by Antiochus IV Epiphanes in 168, but is rededicated in 164 and Judas Maccabeus establishes the Maccabean dynasty of kings (later called Hasmonean).	
100		
	Pompey enters Jerusalem in 63.	ROMAN ERA
	Herod the Great rules Palestine, 39-4 BC.	
BC	Palestine is divided between Herod's sons in 4 BC.	
AD	Judea and Samaria governed by Roman Procurators after 6 AD.	

today. It is doubtful that Ezra would have foreseen the legalism of Jesus' day, for his intention was simply to bring reform and encourage revival, and in that he seems to have largely succeeded.

2. FROM EZRA TO CHRIST

Post-exilic history is almost entirely governed by changes of empire – from Babylonian to Persian to Greek to Roman. The Old Testament histories only take us into the Persian era, though Daniel's visions carry us forward into the Greek. The details of these years need not concern us here, though it is important to note some of the main changes that happened during them.

Alexander the Great's campaigns in 336–23 brought the

Persian empire under Greek control, stretching south into Egypt and east into India. When he died in 323, his empire was divided between his generals. Palestine was first taken under the rule of the Egyptian Ptolemies, but in 200 it passed to the Syrian Seleucids.

One of Alexander's great aims had been to establish Hellenistic (Greek) language and culture uniformly throughout his conquered territories. That vision led to Greek ways becoming established everywhere, including Judah. Whilst there were benefits associated with a common international language and culture, it meant that the LORD's people had sometimes to struggle to retain their Jewish identity. However, that only became a serious problem in 168 BC when their Seleucid overlord, Antiochus Epiphanes, abolished Jewish religion, instituted pagan sacrifices and set up an idol of the Greek god Zeus in the temple ('the abomination of desolation', cp. Dan. 11.31).

Jewish resistance became militant when a priest called Mattathias refused to offer pagan sacrifice and slew an officer trying to enforce it. He and his five sons fled to the hills and began a guerrilla war under the leadership of one of them, Judas Maccabeus ('The Hammer'). Their rebellion was amazingly successful. The temple was rededicated in December 164 (still celebrated by Jews in the feast of Hanukkah) and Judas established himself as king of what became virtually an independent state. It reached its zenith shortly before 100 BC, when Galilee and other neighbouring territories were annexed, restoring the kingdom to something like its old Davidic boundaries and it lasted until the Roman general, Pompey, took Jerusalem in 63 BC.

The Romans allowed self-government to continue. Herod the Great (39–4 BC), though he was disliked by the Jews, did much to establish them in cultural and political strength. Besides building new cities (e.g. Caesarea), palaces and fortresses, he set about rebuilding the temple in Jerusalem to more splendid proportions than ever before. On his death his kingdom was divided between three sons: Archelaus received Judea and Samaria, Herod Antipas (Luke 23) Galilee and Perea, and Philip Iturea and Traconitis (see map on p. 141). In 6 AD Archelaus was exiled and his lands came under the direct governorship of Roman procurators, the fifth of whom was Pontius Pilate (Matt. 27).

For a brief period Philip's son, Herod Agrippa, ruled over all his grandfather's territories, but he died suddenly in 44, during his persecution of the Church (Acts 12), and authority passed back into the hands of the procurators. Hence in Paul's day the picture was roughly as in Jesus', though the names had changed, of course. At his trial we meet Felix and Festus (Acts 24f) instead of Pilate, and Herod Agrippa II (Acts 25f) instead of Herod Antipas.

Whilst there were no great moves of revival inspired by Spirit or Word during these 400 years after Ezra, God was far from inactive. While Israel waited, he was arranging the international scene like some master chess-player preparing for his final, decisive move. The Roman Empire brought

RULERS OF PALESTINE IN NEW TESTAMENT TIMES			
DATE	JUDEA & SAMARIA	GALILEE & PEREA	ITUREA & TRACONITIS
BC AD	Herod the Great 39-4 BC (Matt.2.1.)		
	Archelaus − 6 AD (Matt.2.22)	Herod Antipas − 39 AD (Luke 3.1; 23.6-12)	Philip −34 AD (Luke 3.1)
10	Roman province rule by procurators 6 AD.		
20			
30	Pontius Pilate 26-36 (Matt.27)		Herod Agrippa 34-44 (Acts 12)
40		Added to Agrippa 39	
	Added Agrippa 41		
50	Governed by Roman Procurators 44−		
	Felix 52-60 (Acts 24)	Herod Agrippa II 53-90 (Acts 25-26)	
60	Festus 60-62 (Acts 25)		
70			

peace to the ancient world making travel safer than at any
time before, and in the early first century AD there was
religious toleration. The Greeks had given the world a
common language and culture enabling communication
across national borders. The Persians had encouraged the
rebuilding of Jerusalem and the establishment of the Jewish
state. And thanks to the Babylonians, there were now Jews in
every land and in every main city waiting for their Messiah.
The time was ripe as never before for Christ to come. God's
preparation was complete.

3. CHANGES IN JUDAISM AND THE PROGRESS OF KINGDOM HOPE

Alongside the political changes there were also many religious and cultural shifts that occurred after the exile and
crystallised during the four hundred years after Ezra.

Israel was no longer just a Palestinian state, but a people
dispersed through every country in the ancient world. They
still looked on *Jerusalem* as their faith-centre and by New
Testament times it had become a place of pilgrimage, but its
centrality was more religious than political. Whereas old
Israel had been a nation, Judaism became a world faith,
though preserving a longing for restoration of national,
political status as 'Israel'.

Though *the temple* stood in Jerusalem again, for the
scattered Jews it could not be a place of regular meeting.
Synagogues began to appear locally as places of assembly,
Scripture-reading, teaching and prayer, though not of sacrificial worship. For that a pilgrimage to Jerusalem was necessary.

The Law became more central to Jewish life, partly
because it offered a basis for common cultural identity to the
scattered people. Some laws became especially important
since they provided, as it were, distinctive badges of Judaism,
particularly circumcision, Sabbath-observance and the food-
laws. This new emphasis on the Law gradually made many
Jews more legalistic and ritualistic in their faith. Jesus found
the Pharisees particularly so.

Meantime in Jerusalem *the priests* found themselves with a new status and authority now that there were no kings. The power they attained is clearly seen in the story of Jesus' trial. Also particularly powerful were *the parties* that began to appear. By New Testament times we find:

— *Pharisees*, spiritually-minded men, ardent believers in righteousness, with a strict and legalistic attitude to the Law. Many became Christians (including Paul):

— *Sadducees*, religious conservatives, having little time for personal spiritual matters (Matt. 22.23; Acts 23.8), mainly drawn from priestly and aristocratic families.

— *Essenes*, living a communal life withdrawn from society, mostly in semi-monastic settlements of which the Qumran Community by the Dead Sea may have been one. They are not mentioned in the New Testament.

— *Zealots*, political militants who believed God, not Caesar, was Israel's true King. They were active throughout the Jewish revolt of 66–73 AD. Their last stronghold, Masada, fell in May 74.

— *Samaritans*, descendants of peoples resettled by the Assyrians around Samaria after 722 BC. There was never much love lost between them and other Jews who always regarded them as unorthodox.

On the more spiritual side, the exile confirmed the truth of *the prophets' message* about sin bringing judgment, and so we find a new emphasis on sin, penitence, lamentation, fasting and atonement. *The Feast of Atonement* became one of the most important annual festivals. But the focus of sin-consciousness was no longer the apostasy the prophets had opposed in pre-exilic times. Through the judgment of exile the battle for *monotheism* had been well and truly won among the Jews and by Jesus' time it was no longer a living issue.

Then finally, *Messianic hope* became much stronger in post-exilic times. Since there was no longer a king on the throne, the promise of eternal rule to David took on new significance as Jews set themselves to wait for the coming Son of David who would restore their kingdom.

The portrait the prophets and the psalms draw of the Messiah is basically a description of all that the Davidic kings ought to have been but never were, though it also goes beyond that:

— he is to be filled with the Spirit of God and is to be the embodiment of righteousness and justice (Isa. 11.1–5).

— His reign is to bring peace and a restoring of the harmony in nature that once prevailed in the Garden of Eden (Isa. 9.2–7; 11.6–9).

— His ministry is to be marked by comfort, release, healing, good news and great joy (Isa. 61.1–3).

— His coming will be in fulfilment of God's covenant with David, and will also lead to fulfilment of his promise to Abraham about descendants 'as countless as the stars of the sky and as measureless as the sand on the seashore.' (Jer. 33.14–26).

— He will exercise the authoritative kingship promised to David, but more than that, will rule over the whole world, just as God originally intended Adam should do (Ps. 2; 110).

— But he will exercise that authority with a gentleness and humility that is not characteristic of earthly rulers (Isa. 42.1–4; Zech. 9.9f).

— He is to be priest as well as king, for his function is also to be sacrificial, to remove his people's sin (Ps. 110.4; Zech. 3.8f; cf. Heb. 4.14 – 10.18).

— He will see suffering and death for his people's sins, but he will also see resurrection victory. (Isa. 53 – Jews do not view this passage as Messianic, though Jesus did himself.)

— He is to be God's son (Ps. 2.7).

There is much more than that said about the coming Davidic king in the Old Testament, and some of the points we have noted are open to some measure of interpretation, but the general picture is clear.

The returning exiles were full of hope that God would soon usher in the age of blessing the prophets had spoken about in connection with the promise to David, but their enthusiasm for kingdom-building and revival waned as the years rolled by. The voice of prophecy fell silent in the fifth century and the emphasis gradually shifted to establishing a political and religious system that would ensure Jewish solidarity. Gradually the Judaism of the Book, with all its formal and legal ways, began to take shape. That actually had positive benefits, for it ensured that the Jews remained identifiably the LORD's people down the long centuries before Jesus'

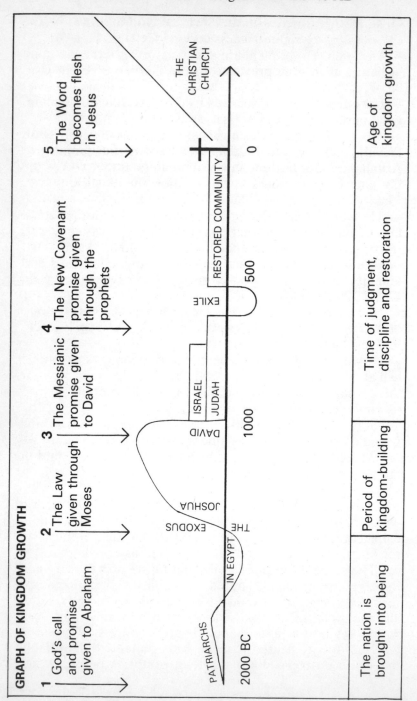

GRAPH OF KINGDOM GROWTH

1 God's call and promise given to Abraham

2 The Law given through Moses

3 The Messianic promise given to David

4 The New Covenant promise given through the prophets

5 The Word becomes flesh in Jesus

PATRIARCHS

IN EGYPT

THE EXODUS

JOSHUA

DAVID

ISRAEL

JUDAH

EXILE

RESTORED COMMUNITY

THE CHRISTIAN CHURCH

2000 BC   1000   500   0

The nation is brought into being

Period of kingdom-building

Time of judgment, discipline and restoration

Age of kingdom growth

birth, all the more learned in their sacred traditions, and so the better prepared for his coming. Judaism, religion for a waiting people, was crystallising.

Before continuing with the story into the New Testament, let us recall that it is all about the commission God gave Adam to increase in numbers, subdue the earth and rule over it. Adam lost his kingdom when he fell, but God's purposes were not to be thwarted. From Abraham he created a people; through Moses he taught them his kingdom principles; under Joshua he brought them into Canaan; and under David and his sons he established them there as a political kingdom. Thus he effectively re-planted a colony of heaven's kingdom on earth as a base from which he could proceed to recover the rest of the world-kingdom Adam had lost. There followed many years of training and discipline, interspersed with times of refreshing, but culminating in the judgment of exile. From among the scattered Jews a remnant returned to rebuild God's kingdom-colony and wait for Christ to come and restore David's throne as the prelude to an end-time thrust of Holy Spirit revival and kingdom-building leading to fulfilment of the commission of world rule given to Adam, and thus ultimately to restoration of Eden's Garden on Earth.

10

Jesus Christ and the Kingdom of Heaven

ST. MATTHEW'S GOSPEL

The various Jewish parties disagreed about how Messiah would come, but at least the expectation of his coming was virtually universal in Judaism by New Testament times. However, it was only a minority of Jews who recognised the fulfilment of that expectation in Jesus, and so Matthew's Gospel was written to present him as Messiah and show how the Old Testament promises about God's kingdom were fulfilled in his coming. It was probably written just before 70 AD.

We know next to nothing about the author. The traditional view is that he was Matthew, the apostle and former tax-collector named in 10.3, though many believe he was someone else who used a collection of Jesus' sayings compiled by Matthew. According to Papias, an early second century bishop, Matthew made some such compilation in Hebrew, which, he says, others interpreted as they were able (Eusebius, *Ecclesiastical History* III.39.16). Our Gospel-writer also seems to have made use of Mark's Gospel as the main source for his stories about Jesus, which is surprising if he was Matthew, for he had personally accompanied Jesus and would therefore have been well able to write his own account of his Master's ministry.

If the author was someone other than Matthew, but using Matthew's 'sayings' and Mark's Gospel as his two main sources, we can still see why his Gospel was described as 'according to Matthew'. That would also explain why it has so much in common with Luke's Gospel without either having borrowed from the other. Both probably drew on Mark and a common collection of Jesus' sayings, though they would have used them differently and would, of course, have added their own material as well. This discussion becomes quite complex and there are different opinions about its details, but such is by far the most widely accepted view about the relationship between the first three gospels (the Synoptic Gospels).

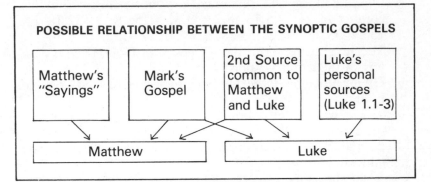

POSSIBLE RELATIONSHIP BETWEEN THE SYNOPTIC GOSPELS

| Matthew's "Sayings" | Mark's Gospel | 2nd Source common to Matthew and Luke | Luke's personal sources (Luke 1.1-3) |

| Matthew | Luke |

However, it is not so much the similarities between the gospels that concerns us here as their different portraits of Jesus.

— Mark's Gospel (slightly earlier than Matthew's, some time after 60 AD) was written as a dynamic account of what Jesus did, without too much emphasis on his teaching, presenting him as a man of faith, action, authority and power.

— Luke's Gospel (probably written about the same time as Matthew's, but as the first half of a fuller work telling the story of the beginnings of Christianity, Acts being the second half) gives a very detailed account of Jesus' life and ministry, with a strong emphasis on its charismatic and prophetic aspects.

— John's Gospel (written towards the end of the century) is as much concerned with the meaning of the events of Jesus' life as with the stories about them. For example, the miracles are seen as 'signs' of who Jesus is – the Way, the Truth and the Life.

— Matthew's Gospel, with its teaching on the kingdom and Jesus as the Messianic King, clearly offers us the most appropriate sequel to the story we have been studying here.

Matthew demonstrates that the promises of the Old Testament are fulfilled in Jesus by:

1. Highlighting his descent from David (1.1–16; 15.22; 21.9,15).
2. Telling of his kingship (2.1–11; 4.17; 21.1–11; 25.31; 27.11,37).
3. Showing that his mission was specifically to Israel (10.6; 15.24).
4. Quoting many Old Testament prophecies fulfilled by his coming (1.23; 2.5,15,18,23; 3,3; 4.15; 8.17; 12.18–21; 13.14f,35; 15.8f; 21.5,42; 26.54,56; 27.9).
5. Teaching more about the Kingdom of God/Heaven than any of the other gospels.
6. Giving hints that Israel has been recreated as God's people in him.
   — The way he tells about Jesus going down to Egypt and returning to Palestine in his infancy, reminds us of Israel doing the same in its earliest years, in the days of Joseph and Moses (ch. 2).
   — He shows us Jesus giving his disciples a new interpretation of the law on a mountain-side at the start of his ministry, as Moses first gave the law to Israel at Mount Sinai (chs. 5–7).
   — He tells us that Jesus commissioned the Twelve to spread the kingdom through Israel (specifically so during his life-time, not the whole world), which reminds us of Joshua sending the twelve tribes out through Canaan at the conquest (ch. 10).
   — He arranges Jesus' teaching in five main discourses, which is reminiscent of the arrangement of the five books of the law in Genesis to Deuteronomy (chs. 5–7; 10; 13; 18; 24–25).

The purpose of Matthew's Gospel is very clearly to show (a) that Jesus is the long-awaited Davidic king, and (b) that he has come to usher in his kingdom. Hence its portrait of Jesus is primarily as king, and the teaching given by Jesus in this gospel is primarily about the kingdom.

The Gospel of the Kingdom

As we read the Old Testament story we repeatedly saw how God's kingdom operated on principles very different from those of earth's empires. Its progress was not assessed by political successes, though they often followed in its wake, but by the measure of faith, obedience and repentance. The kings who were commended were not the political giants like Omri, but the men who walked with God. The same principles control the progress of the kingdom in the New Testament.

Jesus told Pilate that his kingdom was not of this world (John 18.36), and yet he openly proclaimed its presence and power in this world. Basically the expression 'kingdom of God', or 'kingdom of Heaven' (only Matthew uses the second, but both mean the same), means 'the rule/reign/ sovereignty of God'. That is not a place, but something that operates wherever God is acknowledged as king and rules in people's lives. Essentially it is where the life-quality of Eden is experienced, where man lives in harmony with God, with other men and with his environment – where he feels he has arrived home, where he knows the security of being with God again, or as the letter to the Hebrews puts it, where he has 'entered his rest' (Heb. 4.1–11).

God's intention was never to come and make this world his kingdom, as many Jews believed. This world is fallen; it can never be God's kingdom. The political state of Israel, as we saw, was brought into being only as a base where men could be prepared for the coming of the kingdom and from which it could be launched into the rest of the world. God's plan was to come and establish, not this world as his kingdom, but his kingdom in this world, and it is found today wherever his rule is effective in the hearts of men, where there are people who pray, 'Your kingdom come; your will be done on earth', and who live in obedience to that will.

Jesus came offering entry to this kingdom now, in this life, not in the hereafter. He proclaimed that the kingdom of heaven was near and spoke of entry to it being by present repentance, that is, by changing allegiance and acknowledging God's sovereignty. Of course, the kingdom continued to have a future aspect. Jesus only came to bring it near, to establish its rule, and said he would return again to bring it to fulfilment, but he never taught that it was entirely future. He even said it is within or among you. He brought it as God's gift to men for now.

We shall see further implications of what all this means as we read on, but it is important before proceeding to realise that what we are reading about is something dynamic and powerful to change lives and enable men to live for God today. The challenges Jesus laid before us are impossible to fulfil in our own strength, but with the power of the kingdom through the operation of the Spirit, they become a delight and joy to his kingdom-children. Read to lay hold of that joy and make it your own.

The Messianic titles of Jesus in Matthew's Gospel.
Christ – the Greek word for 'Messiah' (both mean 'the Anointed One'). Jesus never used the title of himself, but others did and he did not deny its truth.
Son of David – according to the promise of 2 Sam. 7.12–16 (cp. Matt. 1).
Immanuel – recalling the prophecy of Isa. 7.14 (Matt. 1.23).
King of the Jews – like David, during his earthly life; he entered into his kingship over the rest of the world after the resurrection.
Son of God – after 2 Sam. 7.14 and Ps. 2.7.
Servant – after Isa. 42.1; 49.3; 52.13 (Matt. 12.18).
Son of Man – the only title Jesus ever used of himself. Its significance, which is much debated, is probably best explained in the light of Dan. 7.13f, which prophesies the coming of 'one like a son of man' to receive from God 'authority, glory and sovereign power' and a 'kingdom . . . that will never be destroyed'.

1. THE BIRTH AND INFANCY OF MESSIAH (CHS. 1–2)

Ch. 1: Jesus' genealogy, human and divine
The Gospel opens with the royal genealogy of 'Jesus Christ the son of David', tracing his ancestry back in three equal stages of fourteen generations each, through Jeconiah (Jehoiachin), the last ruling Davidic king, then David, to whom the Messianic promise was made, and finally to Abraham, the first forefather of all God's promises to Israel. Jesus was not only David's son, but also born in a generation that ideally qualified him to be the heir to his throne. The angel's greeting to Joseph pointedly emphasises again that

PALESTINE IN JESUS' TIME
(with places named
in Matthew's Gospel)

Sidon

PHOENICIA

SYRIA

Tyre

Caesarea
Philippi

GALILEE

ITUREA AND
TRACONITIS

Capernaum
Gennesaret
Magadan
Nazareth

Bethsaida

Gadara

DECAPOLIS

SAMARIA

R. Jordan

PEREA

Arimathea

Jericho

Jerusalem
Bethphage
Bethlehem
(Ramah)

Bethany

DEAD SEA

JUDEA

Jesus' earthly father was 'son of David' also (1.16,20).

But Jesus was not just David's son. Though the Jews of his day did not make much of them, there are passages in the Old Testament that suggest Messiah would also be God's son, even that he would be called 'Immanuel' or 'God with us' (cp. 2 Sam. 7.14; Ps. 2.6f; Isa. 7.14). And so, Jesus, whilst legally of David's line because his mother was married to Joseph (1.16), was actually conceived from the Holy Spirit to be the one who would save his people from their sins.

Ch. 2: 'Out of Egypt I called my son.'

Jesus is born in Bethlehem, David's town (1 Sam. 16.1), as Micah foretold he would be (Mic. 5.2), and there the Magi pay homage to 'the one born king of the Jews'. Herod recognises only too well what is happening. The story of how he slaughtered the infants, of Jesus' descent to Egypt, of the succession of Archelaus and Jesus' departure from Egypt all have echoes of the exodus story (cp. Exod. 1–4), as the citation of Hosea 11.1 in v. 15 also points out. What these similarities highlight is that in Jesus God was recreating his Israel. Jesus' followers will presently become the new people of God, but as the first Israel was God's son, so must be the new. As the old came into being after a time in Egypt and oppression by a brutal monarch, so must the new. Jesus has not come simply to help Israel, but to see Israel made new, firstly in himself and ultimately in his disciples.

2. FIRST MINISTRY AND DISCOURSE ONE (CHS. 3–7)

Jesus comes proclaiming the kingdom, calls some disciples – then teaches them the ways of the kingdom.

The plan was quite straightforward. Jesus started revival-preaching in the synagogues, then later in the open as well. He gathered some disciples, taught them about the kingdom by verbal instruction and by demonstration of its power, sent them on practice missions, and thus prepared them to further the kingdom-work after him. But first the way was prepared for his coming by another revival-preacher.

Ch. 3: The herald of Christ's ministry.
No king comes unheralded. About 27 AD John the Baptist began preaching, and with considerable success, for people from all round about came out to hear him and were responding to his call to confess their sins and be baptised (vv. 5f). His message, 'Repent, for the kingdom of heaven is near', was exactly what Jesus would soon be preaching (3.2; cp. 4.17), but, linking repentance and the kingdom, it is also reminiscent of the prophetic calls to revival we heard so many times in the Old Testament.

John was a revivalist prophet like those of old, but far more than that (11.9). He was also the herald of the king, the messenger sent to 'prepare the way' (Isa. 40.3; Mal. 3.1). According to Mal. 4.5 that herald was to be Elijah, and so John dressed himself with Elijah's camel-hair coat and leather belt (see 2 Kings 1.8). Jesus said of him later, 'If you are willing to accept it, he is the Elijah who was to come.' (Matt. 11.14; cp. 17.12).

If John was a revivalist prophet, so also was Jesus to be. Despite his unique conception and birth by the operation of the Spirit, he had had no prophetic or revival ministry as yet. Things had to be done in the proper way, 'to fulfil all righteousness', that is, to comply with all God required (v. 15), and a revivalist-prophet had to be a man filled with the Spirit. Thus, it was only after Jesus was baptised and the Spirit descended on him that his prophetic ministry could begin.

But Jesus, like John, was also more than a prophet, and so 'to fulfil all righteousness' meant something more still. He was the King, the Messiah, 'the Anointed One'. At the Jordan he was anointed with the Spirit for that role, as Isaiah had said he would be (Isa. 11.2; 42.1; 61.1). When the Spirit rested on him the voice from heaven announced his Messianic sonship (cp. Ps. 2.7), but more than that, also the nature of his Messiahship. The words 'with whom I am well pleased' are a clear echo of what is said in Isa. 42.1 about the LORD's servant in whom he puts his Spirit, but that servant was to suffer and die for men's sins (Isa. 53). The Jews were mostly looking for a political leader; Jesus knew from the start his Messiahship would be different.

Ch. 4: Christ's kingdom-revival ministry begins.
Powerful spiritual experiences are often followed by times of
doubt or testing. So it was with Jesus. Was he really the Son of
God? Should he try to prove it by turning stones to bread, or
jumping from the pinnacle of the temple? (vv. 1–7) Did he
really have to win the kingdom battle by suffering? Was there
not an easier way? (vv. 8–10).

In Jesus' wilderness experience, as well as seeing a man
tempted to doubt, we see the headlong confrontation of two
kingdoms at war with each other. Satan invited Jesus to
change sides and join him in ruling the kingdoms of the world,
but his vocation was to serve the Lord God only and bring in
his kingdom. Satan apparently realised that and was trying to
stop him right at the beginning.

Satan or the devil, if Isa. 14.12–15 refers to him, was an
angel of light who fell from grace when he tried to usurp
God's throne. In the Old Testament we occasionally see him
trying to undermine God's work (Gen. 3; Job 1–2; Zech. 3),
but still allowed access to his presence (Job 1.6; 2.1). We do
not read much about the activity of his demons, because
Israel's battle at that time was mainly with people, the pagan
inhabitants of Canaan. But when Jesus was born history
moved into another gear, for God then came among men as
never since Adam's day – and Satan came too, to defend his
kingdom of sin. In the wilderness we see the two rulers
meeting face to face before battle is engaged, with Satan
trying every trick to undermine Christ's confidence and get
peace on his terms, but to no avail, and when he leaves, we
see Jesus attended by the angels, his heavenly army. Thereafter we watch him march through Satan's domain driving out
his demonic hordes in victory after victory, reclaiming men
and territory for God's kingdom.

For the continuation of the story we have to go to Rev. 12f
where we find Satan and his band being finally thrown out of
heaven by Michael and his angels after Jesus' ascension. We
are told that 'they overcame him by the blood of the Lamb',
that is, by the power of the crucifixion, and since then he
ranges the earth 'filled with fury because he knows that his
time is short'. His onslaughts against those who are in Christ
can do them no harm, and so he summons other help, mainly
of a political sort, to attack the saints by persecution. His final

end is to be caught and thrown into the lake of burning
sulphur (Rev. 20.10).

Today he is still at war, but already he is a defeated enemy
fighting a rear-guard action knowing he has not long to go before the end. In the gospels we see Jesus in the heat of the
battle with him that was to lead to his expulsion from heaven
and his dislodgement from mastery over the world of men
(cp. Matt. 12.22–28).

When John was put in prison, Jesus took over. He made
Capernaum the base from which he conducted his early
ministry in Galilee, thus fulfilling an amazingly accurate
prophecy of Isaiah's. Galilee virtually became a Gentile
region when the Assyrians deported its Israelite population in
722 BC, then, after six centuries of pagan darkness, it was
brought back into Jewish hands by one of the Maccabean
kings about 104 BC. There, Isaiah had seen, the light of God
was to shine one day.

Jesus now set about his work of proclaiming the kingdom,
calling for repentance, healing the sick, driving out demons,
and sparking off the most amazing kingdom-revival Israel had
ever yet witnessed. Crowds came to hear him from the length
and breadth of the land.

Chs. 5–7: Kingdom living – the Sermon on the Mount.
During his early ministry Jesus began to put together a team
of disciples. One day on a hillside, like Moses at Sinai, he
began teaching them the quality of life expected in God's
kingdom. These chapters are so well known that only a few
comments here will suffice.

The opening beatitudes portray the richness of kingdom-
life and indicate the sort of people to whom it will most readily
appeal (5.1–10; cp. Isa. 61.1–3). It is a richness that should
bring joy to all the Lord's people, even in the most adverse
circumstances, and bring a new, wholesome flavour or light to
the rest of society (5.11–16).

The old kingdom-teaching of the Law and the Prophets is in
no way abolished by Jesus' new kingdom-teaching, but rather
taken to a deeper and more advanced level. The Law was like
primary education; Christ's kingdom calls for maturity, a new
life-style rising out of hearts and minds come of age, even the
perfection of God himself (vv. 17–48). Many groan as they

read the impossible demands of Jesus' new ethic, but the gift of the kingdom includes the power to fulfil them, as the prophets of old had promised it would (Jer. 31.31–34; Ezek. 36.26f).

In almsgiving, prayer, fasting, indeed in every activity, seeking personal acclaim and honour must yield to the priority of the kingdom. Our first prayer must be, 'Your kingdom come, your will be done'. In God's kingdom there is no place for seeking security through hoarding earthly treasure or serving a second master. His call is to total commitment, to seek first his kingdom and his righteousness, but that should not generate anxiety, for God is Father as well as King (that is emphasised several times) and knows our every need. Faith, not fear, is the mark of his kingdom (ch. 6).

Looking sideways at other people only leads to disgruntlement and takes your eyes off the kingdom. Get yourself right with God, seek him with all your heart, and stay on that right way (7.1–14). Watch out for the counterfeit; it can be recognised by its fruit. And make sure you get the foundations of your own kingdom-life right by heeding this teaching (7.15–27).

3. MIRACLE MINISTRY AND DISCOURSE TWO (CHS. 8–10)

Jesus demonstrates the power of the kingdom in action – then commissions his disciples to do the same.

We have digressed several times to consider such matters as the kingdom-gospel, the kingdom-battle, the quality of kingdom-life and the Messianic calling. From this point we shall press on with the story and pause less often.

Chs. 8–9: Jesus' kingdom ministry.
1. Jesus heals the sick of leprosy, paralysis, fever, demonisation and all sickness (8.1–17).
— Reaction: two excited enthusiasts ask to join his ministry team and he warns them of the cost (8.18–22).
2. Jesus exercises spiritual authority over the elements,

demons and sin (8.23 – 9.8).
— Reaction: Matthew accepts the cost and follows Jesus;
others see nothing – apart from their own dogmas (9.9–17).
3. Jesus restores life and health to the dead, bleeding, blind
and dumb (9.18–33).
— Reaction: the Pharisees judge his ministry as demonic, but
that only causes Jesus to point out the lack of spiritual
leadership in Israel to his disciples, while he continues to take
the kingdom message and power to God's people throughout
Galilee (9.34–38).

In chs. 5–7 Jesus spoke with an *authority* that called for a
response of *obedience* (7.24–29). In chs 8–9 he ministered
with an *authority* that called for a response of *faith*. His
authority was recognised by a Roman centurion (8.9), by
demons (8.16), by his disciples (8.27) and by the crowd (9.8),
but not by religious folk like some of the Law-teachers (9.3),
John's disciples (9.14) and the Pharisees (9.11,34). The
conclusion the Pharisees came to was that his authority was
that of 'the prince of demons'!

Matthew tries to show Jesus' authority was truly of God by
pointing out firstly that his miracle ministry was in accordance
with scriptural expectation (8.17; cp. Isa. 53.4), secondly that
it had the power of God himself in it (8.29; 9.8; 8.27, cp. Ps.
89.9), thirdly that, as even the blind recognised, it was
Messianic (9.27), and finally that it was part of the total 'good
news' of the kingdom (9.35).

The responses demanded and prompted by Jesus' exercise
of authority, namely obedience and faith, are those called for
in every time of revival, as we have seen, and show again how
clearly Jesus stood in the tradition of men such as Elijah and
the prophets of Israel. Revival is given by God when men
acknowledge his authority, and he gives it to restore the work
of his kingdom, the very essence of which is faith and
obedience. Jesus' authority, whilst certainly Messianic, was
also very much in keeping with the whole continuum of the
kingdom-revival tradition of Scripture.

Ch. 10: The kingdom messengers.
Jesus gives his authority to the twelve (v. 1) to proclaim the
kingdom as he has done (vv. 7f), though for now only in Israel
to which his mission as Messiah is limited (vv. 5f). The details

of his commission make best sense if we think of the twelve being sent as King's envoys with a royal commission:
— You will be received like royal messengers wherever you go, so take no special provisions (vv. 9f);
— You will impart the King's blessing or judgment according to how you are received (vv. 11–15);
— You will encounter enemies and traitors (vv. 16–23), but
— You are to be fearless, knowing you have the King's protection and his ultimate reward (vv. 24–33);
— You must pledge the King total loyalty, even in the teeth of family opposition (vv. 34–39);
— You must go with the full assurance of knowing you stand in the King's place as his representatives (vv. 40–42).

Chs. 4–10 are best read as giving us an introductory survey of the pattern that was to embrace all of Jesus' ministry, showing us what it was all about and how it was received:
— He called some disciples (ch. 4),
— taught them the ways of the kingdom (chs. 5–7),
— demonstrated the kingdom in action (chs. 8–9),
— in the process encountered both recognition and opposition, but was finally rejected by the religious;
— then sent his disciples to proclaim the kingdom in Israel (ch. 10).
Chs. 11–28 are in many ways like a replay on a wider canvas. There is deeper teaching, more widespread ministry, further recognition and opposition, final rejection, and then Jesus sends his disciples out to spread the kingdom-gospel, this time through the whole world.

4. PROCLAMATION MINISTRY AND DISCOURSE THREE
(CHS. 11–13)

Jesus' claim to be Messiah is debated and asserted in the teeth of unbelief and opposition – then he teaches about the kingdom.

People have already been asking, 'Who is this Jesus?', but now we sense an urgency that some should begin to see the truth. However, Jesus never openly says he is Messiah, for that truth has to be recognised by revelation, as we shall see later.

Chs. 11–12: The King's claims and the opposition

When John's disciples asked, 'Are you the one?', Jesus replied: Look at what is happening and judge for yourselves. His summary of his ministry should have prompted the right conclusion, for it pointed them to the prophecies of Isa. 35.5f and 61.1–3. To Jesus, John was the promised Elijah, herald of the kingdom, and since his day the kingdom had advanced forcefully into Satan's territory (11.1–19).

Jesus was amazed that some of the cities he preached in failed to respond to his revival work and repent. But if the wise and learned cannot see the truth, little children can, and all who acknowledge him find peace (11.20–30).

Jesus' strongest opposition came from the Pharisees. They were offended by his claim to authority over the Sabbath, one of Israel's most sacred institutions, created by God himself (12.1–14).

His healing ministry fulfilled Isaiah's prophecies about the Lord's servant, though Jesus did not want that publicised, for the servant's call was to work quietly (12.15–21; Isa. 42.1–4). However, people were beginning to catch a glimmer of the truth and were now asking, 'Could this be the Son of David?', though the Pharisees again said his powers were demonic. Jesus left no doubt about his own view: 'If I drive out demons by the Spirit of God, then the kingdom of God has come upon you' (vv. 22–29) so beware of speaking against the Spirit lest you be found to be opposing God's kingdom. Indeed beware of all careless speech, lest your words condemn you (12.30–37).

Jesus had come as the Spirit-Anointed One, and in the power of the Spirit was dramatically ushering in God's kingdom with no shortage of accompanying signs. Hence, a demand from some Pharisees and teachers of the law for further signs only stirred him to anger. Such refusal to accept the signs already given would just lead where it had led Jonah, into the darkness of judgment, all the more so since one greater than Jonah, or even Solomon, is here (12.38–45).

However, in the end it is not discussion about who Jesus is

that will be rewarded, but active response and obedience (12.46–50).

Ch. 13: The secrets of the kingdom.

From this point Jesus uses parables, and only parables, to teach those who are not his disciples (v. 34). The disciples themselves are surprised at this new development (v. 10) and Jesus has to explain that his teaching operates at two levels (vv. 11f). The parables are essentially like the miracles: they present the message and challenge of the kingdom. And like the miracles, they are only meaningful where there is faith – to the eyes that see and the ears that hear (vv. 13–17). Then they impart 'the knowledge of the secrets of the kingdom of heaven' (v. 11) and make rich in wisdom (v. 52).

The message of the parables is fairly straightforward. Their opening words, 'The kingdom of heaven is like . . .', immediately explain their purpose, to teach about the kingdom. And the picture they paint is also clear:
– The kingdom is not something everyone will receive with the same enthusiasm, but those who take hold of and retain it will experience a most fruitful life (vv. 3–23).
– It must grow in the world alongside other things (weeds) until the end, when a separation will take place and 'the righteous will shine like the sun in the kingdom of their Father' (vv. 24–30, 36–43, 47–50).
– It is something a man or woman must take for him or herself and use. It may seem a small thing at first, but it will change your whole environment (vv. 31–33).
– It is the most worthwhile thing in the world that a man can have (vv. 44–46).

The fact that Jesus speaks of 'secrets' (or mysteries, Greek *musteria*) and says the knowledge of them is 'given' to his disciples, indicates that the kingdom is not something man builds by natural means, but a gift from God, one that is received by revelation, and so by faith. That principle is one we saw operating repeatedly in the Old Testament, and as some of the old prophets also realised, without such revelation the teaching can even have a converse effect of dulling the understanding (vv. 10–17; Isa. 6.9f). The challenge of kingdom-ministry is still the same today.

THE PARABLES OF THE KINGDOM

In Matthew's Gospel:

The Sower	Matt.13.1-23	(Mark 4.1-20; Luke 8.4-15)
The Weeds	Matt.13.24-30,36-43	
The Mustard Seed	Matt.13.31f	(Mark 4.30-32; Luke 13.18f)
The Yeast	Matt.13.33	(Luke 13.20f)
The Hidden Treasure	Matt.13.44	
The Pearl	Matt.13.45f	
The Net	Matt.13.47-50	
The Lost Sheep	Matt.18.12-14	(Luke 15.4-7)
The Unmerciful Servant	Matt.18.23-35	
The Workers in the Vineyard	Matt.20.1-16	
The Two Sons	Matt.21.28-32	
The Tenants	Matt.21.33-46	(Mark 12.1-12; Luke 20.9-19)
The Wedding Banquet	Matt.22.1-14	(Luke 14.16-24)
The Fig Tree	Matt.24.32-35	(Mark 13.28f; Luke 21.29-31)
The Ten Virgins	Matt.25.1-13	
The Talents	Matt.25.14-30	(Luke 19.11-27)
The Sheep and Goats	Matt.25.31-46	

In Mark and Luke only:

The Seed Growing Secretly	Mark 4.26-29
The Good Samaritan	Luke 10.30-37
The Friend at Midnight	Luke 11.5-13
The Rich Fool	Luke 12.16-21
The Unfruitful Fig-tree	Luke 13.6-9
The Lowest Seat	Luke 14.7-14
The Great Banquet	Luke 14.16-24
The Cost of Discipleship	Luke 14.28-33
The Lost Coin	Luke 15.8-10
The Lost/Prodigal Son	Luke 15.11-32
The Shrewd Manager	Luke 16.1-9
The Rich Man and Lazarus	Luke 16.19-31
The Master and his Servant	Luke 17.7-10
The Persistent Widow	Luke 18.1-8
The Pharisee and the Tax Collector	Luke 18.9-14

5. REVELATION MINISTRY AND DISCOURSE FOUR
(13.53 – 18.35)

Knowledge of Jesus' identity is progressively confirmed by revelation
– then he unfolds the challenge of kingdom-servanthood.

This section marks the turning-point in Jesus ministry. Not everyone sees the truth, but once his own disciples get the revelation that he is Messiah his ministry in Galilee comes to an end and he sets his face to go to Jerusalem. It is as though with that insight they are at last ready to take over the kingdom-work from him, and so he can now go to complete his own calling.

13.53 – 17.27: Jesus' is revealed as Messiah –
1. Among friends and strangers (13.53 – 14.36):

At Nazareth, his home town where he was well known, people refuse to accept his identity and he is unable to do many miracles, because of their lack of faith (13.53–58).

Herod recognises his powers, but thinks he is John the Baptist resurrected (14.1–12).

The crowds flock after him in thousands and are miraculously fed by him (14.13–21).

His disciples acclaim him 'the Son of God' when he walks on the water (14.22–33).

At Gennesaret, where he was a stranger and not well known, people 'recognise Jesus' and bring their sick to be healed (14.34–36).

2. Among the religious and others (15.1 – 16.12):

The Pharisees are offended by his teaching (15.1–20, cf. v. 12).

A Canaanite woman calls him 'Son of David' and is blessed because of her faith (15.21–28).

The crowds flock to him again, bringing their sick for healing and again he feeds them miraculously (15.29–39).

The Pharisees and Sadducees come asking for miraculous proofs again and Jesus has to warn his disciples about their teaching that would blind the eyes of faith (16.1–12).

3. Among his own disciples (16.13 – 17.27):

At Caesarea Philippi, Peter realises that Jesus is 'the Christ, the Son of the Living God', whereupon Jesus explains for the first time that his Messianic calling must entail suffering. He also tells Peter about the empowering he is to receive for his own kingdom-ministry (and what it is going to cost him), even though he is not yet able to understand all he is being shown, particularly about Christ having to suffer (16.13–28).

At the Transfiguration, Peter, James and John are granted yet fuller revelation of Jesus' sonship, even hearing the very words Jesus heard at his baptism. Jesus again speaks of his suffering (17.1–13).

With such revelation the disciples now share in the Messianic calling themselves and so Jesus expects them to operate with the same faith as himself: 'Nothing will be impossible for you.' But again he repeats his warning about suffering (17.14–23).

The disciples also share in Jesus' sonship, and so as sons of God they should not have to pay God taxes! (17.24–27)

Ch. 18: The calling of the servant.

As Servant/Messiah, Jesus knew he was called to fulfil the life and ministry of the servant described in Isa. 42.1–6; 49.1–6; 50.4–9; 52.13 – 53.12. But if he modelled his own life on that pattern, he expected his disciples to do the same. Hence the highest qualities in the kingdom are humility, gentleness, caring for the little ones and the lost, forgiveness, mercy and the like.

Sharing Jesus' Messianic ministry brings royal blessings, but at servant costs. However, the end is always said to be resurrection, never death (16.21; 17.9,23).

6. CONFRONTATION MINISTRY AND DISCOURSE FIVE (CHS. 19–25)

Jesus goes from Galilee to Jerusalem to claim his kingdom – then speaks to his disciples about its consummation.

Jesus continues to teach his disciples as he goes up to Jerusalem, but his miracles and his preaching to the crowds begin to tail off. In Galilee he had proclaimed the kingdom, done battle with the demons, led the Lord's people in revival, and prepared the disciples who were to take over from him. Now he was intent on one thing, going up to Jerusalem to claim his throne. He had therefore no time at this stage for confrontation with Samaritans, to whom he was not sent anyhow (10.5; 15.24), so he crossed into Transjordan to skirt their territory (19.1).

Chs. 19–23: To Jerusalem and into Battle.
On the way Jesus discusses the main hindrances to accepting the kingdom (chs. 19–20), namely
— sex: on divorce, marriage and celibacy (19.3–12);
— money: 'it is hard for a rich man to enter the kingdom.' (19.16–30);
— power: 'whoever wants to become great among you must be your servant.' (20.20–28).
The economy and preference structures of the kingdom do not operate according to this world's patterns (20.1–16).

Note the reactions of those who meet Jesus on the road: crowds flock after him for healing (19.2), Pharisees try to trick him (19.3), children openly receive him (19.13–15), a rich man finds his challenge too costly (19.22), the disciples have already given up everything for him (19.27), the religious authorities will put him to death (20.17–19). The message is clear: the kingdom is promised to his disciples and to 'such as the children', those whose faith-eyes are not blinded by dogmas and selfish concerns and who are prepared to meet the cost.

As Jesus begins the last leg of his journey from Jericho to Jerusalem, he is acclaimed 'Son of David' by two blind men (20.29–34). A similar story stood at the climax of the first half of the gospel in 9.27–30. Their cry is like a herald's fanfare as the King (the Son of David) approaches his capital (the City of David).

Jesus makes his Messianic entry, riding on a donkey, as the prophet Zechariah had foreseen he would (Zech. 9.9), but now publicly recognised for what he is (21.1–11), and then, like the best Davidic kings of old, those that had led the nation in revival, he purges the temple (21.12–17; cp. 1 Kings 15; 2 Kings 11–12; 18; 22–23).

When his authority is challenged by the priests and other religious leaders (21.18–27), he tells them: 'tax-collectors and prostitutes are entering the kingdom ahead of you . . . the kingdom of God will be taken away from you and given to a people who will produce fruit.' (21.28–44). The parable of the tenants is so pointed that they are inevitably stirred to anger. But then, Jesus knows his time has come (cp. 20.17–19), that now is no longer a time for gentle teaching, but for open confrontation – and the powers that be know it too!

Jesus provokes further reaction by announcing that the invitation to join the kingdom is about to be thrown wide open to many the Jews would have thought quite unfit for it (Gentiles and sinners; 22.1–14).
— Pharisees try to trip him up (22.15–22),
— Sadducees also try (22.23–33),
— and one of their expert teachers tries (22.34–40),
— then finally, Jesus throws down the gauntlet by challenging the Pharisees to accept that as Messiah he is more than David's son, but also David's Lord (22.41–46).

In the end he has to denounce the Pharisees openly (in seven woes) and publicly warn against their teaching that would put a burden on their followers, undermine faith and ultimately keep people out of the kingdom. However, despite his strong language, we see Jesus at the end of the chapter almost broken-hearted at their lack of response to his gospel (ch. 23).

Chs. 24–25: The signs of the end and the consummation of the kingdom.

During his time with them, Jesus taught his disciples much about life in the kingdom and about kingdom-ministry, but now, in his fifth and final discourse, on the eve of his last and greatest battle, at the time it is most needed, he feeds them with vision and hope for the future progress and consummation of the kingdom after he is gone, just as Moses in Deuteronomy preached faith and vision to the Israelites on the eve of his departure and their entry to take the land.

The disciples ask about the date of the consummation, and Jesus tells them: Don't be led astray by false Christs who tell you it is now, for many things must happen first. There will continue to be wars on earth, as well as famines and earthquakes, but they will not signal the end. There will be persecution, some will fall from faith, but the gospel of the kingdom will be preached in the whole world. You will see the temple desecrated and Judea ravaged, but if they say at that time Christ has come, do not believe it. When the Son of Man comes with power and glory, heralded by angels and gathering in his elect, you will not fail to recognise it. No-one knows when that will happen, however, not even the Son, but only the Father. In the meantime watch, wait and be ready (ch. 24).

Make sure you are not left out when he comes because you are not ready, or because you have not made good use of all you have been entrusted with, for on that day the Son of Man will take his throne as King and will reward the faithful and pass judgment (ch. 25).

7. THE FINAL CONFLICT AND THE GREAT COMMISSION
(CHS. 26–28)

Jesus goes to his cross and resurrection
– then sends the disciples out to spread the kingdom to all
nations.

The story of Jesus' last hours is so familiar that we can review it quite rapidly here, highlighting its Messianic emphasis only. The same emphasis is every bit as evident in the other gospels, but here it is our primary concern to trace it.

Chs. 26–27: The King's last battle.
Though the chief priests are the ones who plan Jesus' death, his own repeated prophecies about it, even its precise date, show that he is clearly in control of his own destiny (26.1–5). Similarly, when he is richly and royally anointed, he acknowledges that as his 'anointing for burial' (26.6–13). He even shows that he is in charge of his very betrayal (26.14–25).

At the Last Supper he initiates the New Covenant (cp. Jer. 31.31), the fulfilment of the promises made to Abraham, Moses and David to which the whole of Old Testament faith looks forward (26.17–30).

Then, on the way to Gethsemane, as he tells Peter precisely how he will betray him, and in the garden itself we see him still very much in control, giving the final order to go forward to meet his enemies (26.31–46). He is also in charge of his own arrest: he tells Judas what to do, gives orders to Peter and even preaches a short sermon to the mob (26.47–56). He has the clear bearing of a king throughout.

Similarly, at his trial before the Sanhedrin, Jesus keeps regal silence in the face of false accusations that no king would disdain to acknowledge, but to the Messianic question he gives a direct, royal answer: 'In the future you will see the Son of Man sitting at the right hand of the Mighty One.' (26.57–68).

While Peter betrays him and Judas goes and hangs himself (26.69 – 27.10), he is taken for trial before Pilate, but there he responds exactly as before the Sanhedrin. Pilate keeps calling him 'Christ' (27.11–26).

As they lead him away to be crucified, the soldiers mock: 'Hail, King of the Jews' (27.27–31). The inscription Pilate has posted on the cross reads: 'This is Jesus, the King of the Jews' (27.32–44). And at his death the centurion in charge of the crucifixion exclaims, 'Surely he was the Son of God!' (27.45–56). Then, finally, he is given a royal burial in a rich man's tomb, which even has an official military guard posted outside it (27.57–66).

His enemies had him executed because he claimed to be the King of the Jews, and it was as the King that he died.

Ch. 28: *Resurrection-victory and kingdom-vision.*

The conclusion is also suitably majestic, befitting the King. A heavenly messenger directs the disciples to meet their risen Lord back in Galilee where they had been prepared by him for kingdom-ministry. There, on a mountain, like Moses on the eve of Israel's entry to the Promised Land, Jesus looks out over the kingdoms of the world that Satan had once offered to give him on his terms, now knowing they are his on his own and his Father's terms, and so finally he commissions his disciples to go with *all* his authority to *all* nations, teaching *all* he has commanded, and promising he will be with them *always*.

There is a sense of both satisfaction and challenge as we read the words of Jesus' last commission to his disciples. His work is now fully completed and the time all history has waited for so long has come at last:

— for the renewing of God's commission to Adam to be fruitful, increase in number, fill the earth and rule over it ('go and make disciples of all nations');

— for the fulfilling of God's promise to Abraham that through his descendants blessing would go to all mankind ('. . . all nations');

— for the spreading abroad of God's teaching about his kingdom's ways first given through Moses to Israel ('make disciples . . . teaching them to obey');

— and for the fulfilling of God's New Covenant promise of his abiding presence with his people by his Spirit ('I will be with you always').

11

The Flowering of Kingdom Witness in Palestine

ACTS 1–12

Let us again remind ourselves briefly what the story we are reading is all about. God's purpose from earliest times was to establish his kingdom's rule over the world, and so his commission to Adam was to fill the earth, subdue it and reign over it. After the fall that purpose did not change. God therefore chose Abraham and from his descendants planted a colony of his people in Canaan, as a base from which his kingdom could spread to the rest of mankind.

Their story was one of ups and downs as they alternately caught the vision and then lost it again. We saw exciting moments of hope, particularly in Joshua's and David's days, and in smaller or different ways at other times as well, but then we watched hope evaporate when they failed to press on into the next stages of their kingdom vision. That vision was for revival followed by kingdom-building followed by growth and expansion, but, as we discovered, the pattern only worked successfully when it was initiated and sustained by faith in the vision itself, obedience to God's ways in it and readiness to face the sacrificial cost involved in seeing it through (cp. p. 134).

Then Jesus came as successor to Adam, Abraham, Moses, Joshua, David and the kings, led God's people in revival, established a nucleus of God's kingdom among his disciples, lived a life of faith and obedience as no-one before him had ever done, and then paid the ultimate cost in the sacrifice of his own life. Both Joshua and David had attained some measure of progress in these things, but after initial waves of enthusiasm, much of what they gained was lost through the failure of their successors to walk with God. What will Jesus' followers do? He has shown them the ways of revival and kingdom-growth more fully than any of their forebears ever knew them, but will they be any more capable of sustaining the revival growth he has initiated?

The answer to the last question was a resounding yes, but the reason for that lay not so much with the capabilities of the disciples themselves, as with the fact that God did something new and powerful in and through them. Their story tells of men who continued Jesus' own ministry in the most amazing ways, partly because he had taught it to them during his lifetime, but also because they were led and empowered in it by the same Holy Spirit as had led and empowered Jesus himself.

More than that, their individual life-portaits remind us again and again of Jesus' own life and ministry – as also do the various phases of church growth, and even the whole story covered by Acts itself. The patterns are those we are already familiar with from the gospel:
— initial empowering by the Holy Spirit;
— revival-style preaching of the kingdom and repentance;
— mixed recognition and opposition from the hearers;
— suffering, persecution and even martyrdom;
— and finally resurrection.
We shall see how closely these patterns apply as we trace the stories, but before doing so, it helps to realise from the outset that it was this Jesus-style of life and ministry in the power of the Holy Spirit that was the key to the successful expansion of the early Church.

That is the reason why Acts begins by referring back to the gospel story as being 'about all that Jesus *began* to do and teach' (1.1). Luke wrote Acts as the sequel to his Gospel, but not just as a record of the apostles' ministries. His primary aim was to testify to what Jesus *continued* to do and teach through them by the power of the Holy Spirit. In fact, Acts is often called 'The Acts of the Holy Spirit'. It is therefore best to read it in the same way as we would read some of the more outstanding charismatic biographies and church-growth stories found in Christian bookshops today. They tell how individuals or groups have experienced an anointing of the Spirit that has led them into powerful preaching and miracle-working ministries resulting in fruitful evangelism and church-growth. Such stories are written to glorify God by bearing witness to his power and to encourage the readers to receive or stand firm in that power themselves. It is all beautifully summed up in the last recorded words of Jesus in Acts 1.8:

> *You will receive power when the Holy Spirit comes on you;*
> *and you will be my witnesses in Jerusalem, and in all Judea*
> *and Samaria, and to the ends of the earth.*

These words also provide a neat summary-outline of the story as Luke tells it in Acts, with the gospel being planted first in Jerusalem, then being carried out into the Palestinian home-lands (Judea and Samaria), and finally throughout the Roman Empire (to the ends of the earth, as it was then known). The chapter-divisions that follow correspond with that outline.

It is an unfinished story. It ends abruptly with Paul in prison in Rome awaiting trial, and Luke gives no hint of the outcome. He may have intended that for dramatic effect, because his picture of Paul preaching the kingdom and teaching about Jesus 'boldly and without hindrance' in Rome, the capital city of the Roman Empire and the heart of the ancient world, does make a powerful climax to the story of early Christian missionary expansion. On the other hand, he may have ended where he did simply because he wrote Acts about 64 AD (the date of the events at the end of ch. 28), and so could not tell us any more.

1. YOU WILL RECEIVE POWER WHEN THE HOLY SPIRIT COMES ON YOU (1.1 – 2.41)

Acts' story of the gospel's progress from Jerusalem to Rome carries us swiftly over thirty years or more after Jesus' death, particularly in its middle section. The pace slows down a little at the end, where the last eight chapters are devoted to Paul's arrest, imprisonment and trials (we shall see the reason for that later), but the general feel of the beginning is also slightly less energetic. That is because the early chapters focus on a mere handful of episodes from the times of the infant Church in Jerusalem, so that, as well as telling something of its story, they might paint for us, as it were, a series of sketches or portraits to illustrate the style and quality of life enjoyed by the first Christians. It is that life-quality that must occupy most of our attention here. The story sequence can be readily grasped by reading Acts itself and therefore requires little comment.

1.1–11: 'Wait for the gift my Father promised.'
If the apostles are to continue the work Jesus began in his lifetime, they must do it as he did. Hence, if Jesus' ministry only began after the Spirit came upon him, so also must theirs. If his ministry was a proclamation of the kingdom with power, so also must theirs be. It is surely significant that Jesus' last conversation with his disciples was entirely occupied with these matters: the kingdom, their witness in it, the Holy Spirit and his power.

In the opening chapters of Acts several streams of Old Testament tradition flow together, some of which we have studied in this volume, others not. Here we find two in particular: the kingdom and the Spirit. When Jesus called the Spirit 'the gift my Father promised', he was referring to such prophetic promises as Isa. 32.15; 44.3; Ezek. 36.26f; Joel 2.28f, but the vision underlying these passages was much more primitive. It found expression, for example, in the longing of Moses 'that all the LORD's people were prophets and that the LORD would put his Spirit on them.' (Num. 11.29). The promise of the Spirit is in fact as basic as the kingdom vision that we have been tracing so extensively here (discussed fully in Volume Three).

Jesus therefore bids the apostles wait. Their witness must be to a completed work. So much had already been accomplished with his coming as Messiah, his revival ministry, his sacrificial death and his resurrection, but, in addition to all that, the kingdom he had come to bring required the Spirit to be poured out as the Father had promised. That, of course, would also result in the apostles being empowered for ministry in the same way as Jesus himself had been – and the principle remains the same today.

THE PROMISE OF THE FATHER TO SEND THE HOLY SPIRIT

"I wish that all the LORD's people were prophets and that the LORD would put his Spirit on them!"

(Moses in Num.11.29)

. . . . till the Spirit is poured upon us from on high . . . .

(Isa.32.15)

For I will pour water on the thirsty land,
and streams on the dry ground;
I will pour out my Spirit on your offspring,
and my blessing on your descendants.

(Isa.44.3)

"The Redeemer will come to Zion,
to those who repent of their sins,"
declares the LORD .
"As for me, this is my covenant with them," says the Lord.
"My Spirit, who is on you, and my words that I have put in
your mouth will not depart from your mouth, or from the
mouths of your children, or from the mouths of their descendants
from this time on and for ever," says the LORD .

(Isa.59.20f)

I will give them an undivided heart and put a new spirit in them;
I will remove from them their heart of stone and give them a heart
of flesh . . . .

(Ezek.11.19)

I will give you a new heart and put a new spirit in you; I will
remove from you your heart of stone and give you a heart of flesh.
And I will put my Spirit in you . . . .

(Ezek.36.26f)

I will put my Spirit in you and you will live.

(Ezek.37.14)

I will no longer hide my face from them, for I will pour out my
Spirit on the house of Israel, declares the Sovereign LORD.

(Ezek.39.29)

And afterwards,
I will pour out my Spirit on all people.
Your sons and daughters will prophesy,
your old men will dream dreams,
your young men will see visions.
Even on my servants, both men and women,
I will pour out my Spirit in those days.

(Joel 2.28f)

When the apostles asked Jesus whether now was the time for the restoring of the kingdom to Israel they were perceiving that something had still to be, though they still did not understand properly what that would entail.

1.12–26: The new kingdom people prepare to meet God.

At the end of his Gospel, where he also records the ascension, Luke tells us that the apostles 'returned to Jerusalem with great joy. And they stayed continually at the temple, praising God.' (24.52f). They were excited men – not because they had bid farewell to Jesus for the last time, but because they knew the moment all history had been moving towards was on the point of arriving. Along with other disciples, they were to be the nucleus of God's new kingdom people, of his new Israel that was about to be launched into history with power.

In many ways they were so like the old Israelites at the point when God was about to form them into a nation, when they gathered at Mount Sinai and consecrated themselves in preparation for his coming on the mountain in fire. That is probably why they considered it so important to replace Judas: as old Israel had numbered twelve (tribes), so new Israel must also number twelve (apostles) at the moment of its birth.

2.1–4: The day of Pentecost – the Spirit comes.

God comes to his New Covenant People amid wind and fire, just as he came of old on Sinai with storm and fire (Exod. 19.16–19; cp. 1 Kings 19.11). Pentecost was the festival at which the Jews particularly remembered these things, how God came on Sinai to give the land and enter into covenant with his people. They even came to use Ps. 29, with its description of God coming to his temple amid wind and fire, as their appointed psalm for the festival. There could hardly have been a more appropriate moment for God to visit the people of the New Covenant.

2.5–13: The Spirit's anointing removes the curse of Babel.

There was another reason why the timing was perfect. When Jesus told the disciples they would be his witnesses to the ends

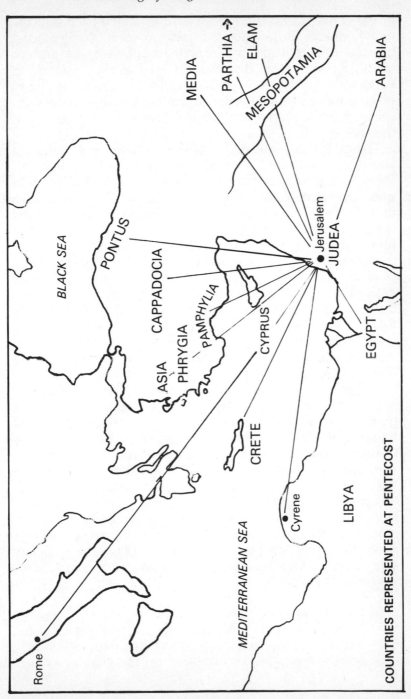

BLACK SEA

MEDITERRANEAN SEA

PONTUS

CAPPADOCIA

PAMPHYLIA

PHRYGIA

ASIA

CYPRUS

CRETE

MEDIA

PARTHIA →

ELAM

MESOPOTAMIA

ARABIA

Jerusalem • JUDEA

EGYPT

LIBYA

Cyrene •

Rome •

COUNTRIES REPRESENTED AT PENTECOST

of the earth, they could hardly have expected their international witness to be launched quite so soon. At Pentecost pilgrims gathered in Jerusalem from all over the ancient world. 3,000 of them discovered Christ as they listened to Peter and doubtless most of these would have taken the news of what was happening in Jerusalem back home. Many local churches in the Roman Empire probably traced their origin to this day.

The thing that particularly drew the pilgrims in amazement was that they heard the disciples 'declaring the wonders of God' in their own mother tongues. The miracle God wrought that day was more than a mere release of ecstatic utterance and charismatic enthusiasm, but a veritable reversal of the curse of Babel. That, of course, was a necessary part of the total kingdom-vision. Gen. 1–11 left us with man alienated from God, from other men and from his environment, in need of reconciliation. Today we can see how that problem is being radically dealt with through our experience in Christ, 'because God has poured out his love into our hearts by the Holy Spirit, whom he has given us' (Rom. 5.5). One of the most immediate blessings of that is in the gift of tongues which enables people of different cultural and national backgrounds to worship together in harmony, and sometimes even to cross language barriers in communication, as in Acts 2. Even more radical, however, is the Spirit's work in breaking down barriers of suspicion, envy, hostility, in the heart and replacing them with his love. In the power of these things it is possible to recapture something of the flavour of Eden today. God's ultimate purpose is still to restore Eden, and though he did not yet do so at Pentecost, he enabled one mighty step to be taken towards it.

Reactions in the crowd were mixed. Some entered into the enjoyment of Pentecost's benefits, others mocked. So it is every time the Spirit moves in power. There are similar stories in the Old Testament (cf. Num. 11.24–29; 1 Sam. 10.9–12), and equally so still today.

2.14–41: Repent. The promise is for you.

Peter's explanation of all that was happening is very simple:
— It is what the prophet Joel said would happen (vv. 14–21).
— It comes through Jesus of Nazareth, the wonder-worker

whom you killed, but God raised to life (vv. 22–32).
— 'Exalted to the right hand of God, he has received from the
Father the promised Holy Spirit and has poured out what you
now see and hear.' (v. 33).
— 'Therefore God has made this Jesus both Lord and Christ.'
(v. 36).

Peter's sermon, like the preaching of Jesus before him,
appeals to large numbers who are 'cut to the heart' by it and it
leads directly to a call for repentance. It is in true kingdom-
revival tradition. The continuing ministry of Jesus in the
power of the Holy Spirit is well and truly launched in the
witness of his followers.

2. AND YOU WILL BE MY WITNESSES IN JERUSALEM
(CHS. 2.42 – 8.1)

The Jesus-pattern that marked the birth of the Church
continues to characterise its life in Jerusalem and to be the
reason for its steady growth. As we trace its story we see its
Jesus-ministry unfold with powerful preaching and miracles,
with growing recognition and opposition, leading to persecution and eventually martyrdom, then to resurrection and new
vigour.

2.42–47: The new-born church in Jerusalem.
In these early chapters Luke paints a few little sketches of life
in the early church. What we see is a fairly small group (most
of the 3,000 of v. 41 were pilgrims), who 'devoted themselves
to the apostles' teaching and to the fellowship, to the breaking
of bread and to prayer', being blessed with signs and wonders,
a joyous and praise-filled life, respect from the community
around and steady growth. It is a kind of life many churches
long for and try to recapture today, but it has to be
remembered that it grew out of Pentecost and it has the
absolute stamp of Jesus himself. It can never be recreated
without these two basic ingredients.

Ch. 3: In the name of Jesus Christ.
Jesus' healing ministry is duplicated in the work of the first

leaders of his church. But they know that the anointing is Jesus', not their own, and that is what they continue to proclaim: 'It is Jesus' name and the faith that comes through him that has given this complete healing.' (v. 16). Peter again stresses that these things are continuous on the promises God made to the patriarchs and prophets and that their benefits are available only through repentance.

4.1–22: In the footsteps of Jesus.
As a result of their ministry Peter and John are dragged before the same court that sentenced Jesus and there they display the same conviction and authority that characterised Jesus' own encounters with the Jewish religious authorities.

4.23–31: The church prays for greater power to witness.
And as it does so, it is granted a renewed Pentecostal blessing. In 4.20 witness is defined as testimony to 'what we have seen and heard'. These early Christians had indeed plenty to tell, for they had seen and heard much. But the nature of witness has not changed today, for where God's Spirit is moving powerfully there is still plenty to tell. None the less, the Spirit's boldness is still needed to tell it.

4.32–37: All the believers were one in heart and mind.
Here we have Luke's second sketch of life in the early church. It offers a tremendous testimonial to the love God's Spirit had poured into the hearts of its members: 'they shared everything they had . . . There were no needy persons among them.'

5.1–11: Ananias and Sapphira.
Though the circumstances are not identical, we are reminded of what happened to Achan when he tried to keep some of the plunder of Jericho for himself (Josh. 7). In both instances the judgment may seem harsh, but it is a solemn reminder that we are not playing at games and that there is no room for deceit in God's holy presence. See also p. 36.

5.12–42: The apostles are flogged.
Signs and wonders multiply, as in Jesus' ministry before them

– and also persecutions. But they leave the court 'rejoicing because they have been counted worthy of suffering disgrace for the Name'. Clearly they recognise the Jesus-pattern in their ministry themselves.

6.1 – 8.1: Then finally martyrdom.

Persecution reaches its climax when Stephen, one of seven newly elected assistants, 'a man full of faith and of the Holy Spirit', is put on trial and executed. His trial before the Sanhedrin is so like Jesus' crucifixion, with him praying for the forgiveness of his executioners and committing his spirit into God's hands, that we cannot but see here the final touches to the Jesus-portrait of the early church in Jerusalem.

This church started its ministry when its members were baptised in the Spirit. That ministry was one of effectively preaching the kingdom message and calling for repentance, of performing the miraculous signs of the kingdom, of suffering opposition and persecution at the hands of the authorities, and finally of martyrdom. As persecution spreads to the whole Church (8.1), the Jesus-pattern is almost complete. The one thing that remains is resurrection, but that comes in a wondrous way when the Christians scattered by the persecution take the gospel through Judea and Samaria in the chapters that follow.

3. AND IN ALL JUDEA AND SAMARIA (CHS. 8–12)

The patterns that characterised the early Christian community in Jerusalem lived on in the Church as it spread out through the Palestinian coastlands. The same degree of success in kingdom/revival-preaching and church-growth ministry therefore continued to attend its witness.

8.1–4: Death, burial and resurrection.

The first missions were a direct consequence of persecution! Even after Jesus' commission to make disciples of all nations (Matt. 28.18–20) and the coming of the Spirit, it still took persecution to get the world-evangelisation programme going. In this section we shall see the early Church being repeatedly shaken out of Jewish traditionalism that almost

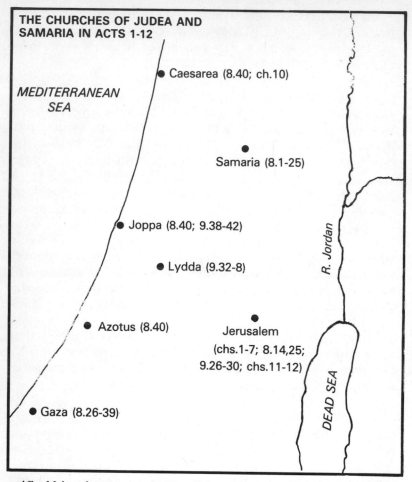

**THE CHURCHES OF JUDEA AND
SAMARIA IN ACTS 1-12**

MEDITERRANEAN
SEA

● Caesarea (8.40; ch.10)

● Samaria (8.1-25)

● Joppa (8.40; 9.38-42)

● Lydda (9.32-8)

● Azotus (8.40)

● Jerusalem
(chs.1-7; 8.14,25;
9.26-30; chs.11-12)

● Gaza (8.26-39)

R. Jordan

DEAD SEA

stifled kingdom-growth. Traditionalism is still the same today – a brake to the Spirit's work. The date is probably about 35 AD.

8.4–25: The gospel goes north.
Philip, one of Stephen's fellow-deacons, brings the gospel to Samaria, where his preaching is attended with the kingdom's signs and wonders. There the first new mission church is launched with a full and proper visitation of the Holy Spirit. If the church in Samaria and its members are to have the same Jesus-ministry as the Jerusalem church, they must start life in Christ in the same way.

8.26–40: The gospel goes south and west.

It is Philip who starts the evangelisation of the Judean coastlands as well, from Gaza right up to Caesarea (v. 40). The life of God that was extinguished in Stephen is truly risen again in this his fellow-deacon, and in even greater vigour. His convert is an Ethiopian courtier, with whom the gospel must have gone further south yet, into north-east Africa.

9.1–30: The gospel goes further north.

Saul, the leader of the persecution, is converted and in the same way as Jesus and the apostles, is also filled with the Holy Spirit. He then begins evangelising in Damascus. (We shall look more closely at Paul's life and ministry presently.)

9.31–42: On the northern coastal plain.

With the cessation of persecution, the churches in Judea, Galilee and Samaria enjoy a time of quiet growth. Meanwhile Peter's ministry continues to bear the full stamp of Jesus, accompanied by the same kind of signs and wonders, even raising the dead.

10.1 – 11.18: And so to the Gentiles!

If the conversion of Paul, the persecutor, took the Church by surprise, the conversion of the Roman centurion, Cornelius, causes a greater stir. Even telling him the gospel grates on all Peter's Jewish nerve-ends and it rouses a veritable hornets' nest of traditionalist anger in Jerusalem. However, the gospel has to go to all nations, and so God blesses this first Gentile convert and his household with the same Pentecostal endue-ment of the Spirit as the apostles experienced at the begin-ning. It is that fact alone that makes this new departure acceptable to the 'circumcised believers' in Jerusalem. As with every other phase of kingdom ministry before it, it too is seen to have the stamp of Jesus on its beginning.

11.19–30: Then on into the Gentile world.

The Palestinian mission reaches its further point when Barnabas, 'a good man, full of the Holy Spirit and faith', establishes the church in Antioch. This phase of missionary development is beautifully rounded off with the picture of Saul being invited to help Barnabas, and then himself, the man who had started it all off by his persecutions, taking gifts from his infant church to support the church he had once tried to destroy.

Ch. 12: Persecution again.

The Jesus-pattern of persecution and martyrdom concludes this phase just as it did the last. The apostle James is executed and Peter is imprisoned. However, Peter is miraculously released, Herod, the persecutor, dies, and 'the word of God continued to increase and spread'. (v. 24).

At this point Luke breaks off the story of Peter and the Jerusalem apostles. We meet them briefly again in chs. 15 and 21, but now he turns our attention to Barnabas and Saul, as they return to Antioch with Mark to prepare for the next phase of kingdom expansion (v. 25). Out of the ashes of Herod's persecution and James' martyrdom is to rise the final burst of resurrection glory that will take the gospel out to the rest of the Roman world.

The question with which we started this chapter, about how Jesus' followers would cope with the challenges of kingdom ministry, has been answered in a most encouraging way. Jesus clearly taught them the ways of the kingdom well and by the Holy Spirit working in and through them powerfully sustained the revival growth he had initiated. And thereby he established the patterns that all his predecessors sought after and that all his followers must adopt if they are to co-operate properly in the kingdom work to which God first called Abraham and has called every man of faith ever since.

PART FIVE

INTO ALL THE WORLD

46 — 67 AD

The second half of Acts tells of Paul's missionary work and paints the same portraits of Christ-like ministry as the first half. Paul is inspired and empowered by the Spirit, he proclaims the kingdom with effectiveness and demonstrates its power in signs and wonders, he is persistently persecuted and ends up, like Jesus, on trial for his life. However, the overall story is one of progression until the gospel finally reaches the capital city of the ancient world.

The story falls into several sections, corresponding mainly with Paul's various journeys, and that is how we shall study it here.

Paul wrote three sets of letters that have been preserved in the New Testament:

The Missionary Letters, written during his journeys, dealing with problems in his new mission churches and preparing the way for further missions: Galatians, 1 and 2 Thessalonians, 1 and 2 Corinthians, Romans.

The Captivity Letters, written during his imprisonment, encouraging Christians to stand firm in the faith he and others had taught them: Philippians, Colossians, Philemon, Ephesians.

The Pastoral Letters, probably written at the end of his life, instructing two of his closest disciples about pastoring the churches: 1 and 2 Timothy, Titus.

In the following pages we shall concern ourselves only with the missionary letters. They are like windows on the world of early church growth, through which we can look behind the historical narratives into the heart and life of the new converts and their young churches. Among the things we see are how much:

— the young churches were full of charismatic enthusiasm;
— the new converts urgently needed teaching and pastoring;
— Paul, the roving evangelist, cared for his converts;
— Paul suffered from opposition both outside and inside his churches.

Just as today, conversion brought release, healing, forgiveness, new revelation and understanding, love, joy, peace and new life, but the converts had to be taught how to live in this new dimension. They were like people who had changed citizenship to live in a new country having to learn a new language, new customs, new laws, a completely new way of life. In these letters we can trace some of their early adjustment problems as well as the freshness of their early charismatic enthusiasm. Acts tells the stories of how kingdom/revival-ministry got started in different places, the letters show us how its momentum had to be sustained in the face of opposition and every sort of danger.

Paul's letters therefore play a similar part in our presentation of the New Testament story to the part played in the Old Testament story by the historical reviews, in which Moses, Joshua, Samuel and others, at the end of each major phase of history, preached about the importance of maintaining the kingdom-vision (faith) and adhering to the kingdom-principles the LORD had shown them (obedience). Thus in Galatians, we hear Paul encouraging a forward momentum of faith and vision in the teeth of pressure to fall back into religion, in Thessalonians encouraging spiritual growth and warning against mere emotional exuberance, in 1 Corinthians pleading for personal and corporate growth according to the principles of kingdom living required in the New Covenant, and in 2 Corinthians pleading for proper recognition of authority and anointing in Christian leadership to enable kingdom-growth.

12

Into Phrygia and Galatia

ACTS 13–15 AND GALATIANS

The story of the expansion of Christianity from Antioch to Rome is very much Paul's story, just as the story of the Exodus was Moses' story and of the conquest Joshua's. That is how it tends to be in the Lord's work, for, as we have so often seen, his way is generally to choose a man to take the lead in revival or kingdom-growth. However, that only helps to make the story more personal and living for us.

Paul often looked back to his dramatic conversion when God called him not only to follow Christ, but also to take the gospel to the Gentiles. If it disturbed Peter to preach to one Gentile, how much more must it have disturbed Paul the Pharisee to be given such a call! Apparently it took him several years to come to terms with it, for his ministry as we read of it in Acts only began about ten years after his conversion. After an initial burst of evangelistic enthusiasm in Damascus (Acts 9.19–25), he disappeared for three years into Arabia (where exactly we do not know, Gal. 1.17). Then he must have gone home to Tarsus, for it was there about seven years later that Barnabas went to look for him to come and help him lead the church in Antioch (Acts 11.25). They had spent a year ministering together in Antioch when they visited Jerusalem with their famine-relief gift (vv. 26–30), and presumably it was in that same year that they left on their first mission trip. At the end of it they reported to the apostles in Jerusalem (Acts 15). All of that suggests the following dates for Paul's early ministry:

35 AD: Paul is converted,
35–38: goes to Arabia,
38–45: back home in Tarsus,
45–46: in Antioch with Barnabas,
46–48: first missionary journey,
48: reports to the Jerusalem apostles.

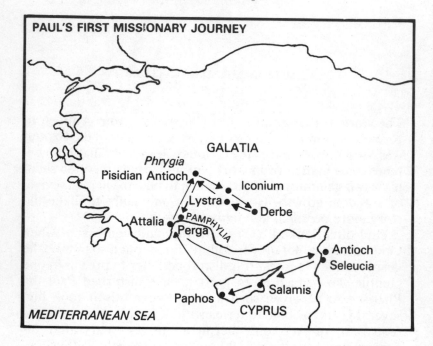

PAUL'S FIRST MISSIONARY JOURNEY

1. PAUL'S FIRST MISSIONARY JOURNEY (ACTS 13–15)

In Acts 1–12 the stories of the Jerusalem church, the Samaritan mission and the evangelisation of the Gentiles all began with accounts of baptism in the Holy Spirit according to the promise of Jesus. Only one of Paul's missions starts that way (Acts 19.1–7), but the others are equally clearly initiated by the prompting of the Spirit, as this first one certainly is.

13.1–12: Cyprus.
Barnabas, Paul and Mark go to Cyprus, which was Barnabas'

homeland (see 4.36). Their witness leads to the conversion of the governor, who was left 'amazed at the teaching about the Lord', just as in his day Jesus' hearers were by his own teaching (cp. Mark 1.22; 2.12; etc.).

13.13–51: In Pisidian Antioch.

When they cross to mainland Pamphylia, Mark returns to Jerusalem. We are not told why he did so, but Paul thought he was deserting them and later refused to take him on his second journey (15.38).

Paul and Barnabas press on to Pisidian Antioch where they have a successful mission, so much so that Jewish jealousy is roused and they are driven from the city. It is at this point that Paul takes his decision to 'turn to the Gentiles' (v. 46). The result is that the gospel, now freed from the shackles of Jewish tradition, spreads through the whole region. But at a cost, for Paul and Barnabas are now hounded and persecuted by the Jews throughout the rest of this mission.

Paul's evangelistic method was basically the same as Jesus' in his early ministry. He went first to the synagogues, to the people God had been preparing since Abraham's day for what was now happening. But there he would also have found Gentiles who were attracted to the Jewish faith – 'God-fearers' or 'proselytes'. Often he made more impact on them than on the Jews, which usually led to him preaching in the open or in other buildings, mainly to Gentiles. However, despite his decision at Antioch, he still continued to adopt the same initial approach right to the end of his ministry.

14.1–25: Iconium, Lystra and Derbe.

At Iconium they were able to escape from their Jewish persecutors, but at Lystra Paul was stoned and left for dead. However, in both places and at Derbe they won many for the Lord and established churches over which they appointed 'elders' in each place (14.23).

And so Paul's first mission, initiated as it was by the Holy Spirit, continued to bear the marks of Christ's ministry: powerful preaching accompanied by signs and wonders, responses in commitment and opposition, persecution and virtual martyrdom, then finally resurrection and the appointment of disciples to continue the work.

14.26 – 15.35: The Jerusalem Council.

Back in their home church in Syrian Antioch their reports about how the Gentiles had accepted the gospel were apparently well received. That is, until some Jewish Christians in Jerusalem, converts from among the Pharisees, heard the news and demanded that the new Gentile converts be circumcised and required to keep the laws of Moses. (We refer to these Pharisaic Christians as 'Judaisers' or 'the circumcision party'.) Paul and Barnabas went immediately to Jerusalem to defend their actions, but the outcome, once Peter had reminded them about how Cornelius received the Spirit, was that the Gentile mission was approved by the apostles and elders of the Jerusalem Church and by James, Jesus' brother, who was now its head.

Paul and Barnabas, accompanied by personal representatives of the Jerusalem apostles, returned to Antioch with a letter from James detailing some minimal observances for Gentile converts and the church was delighted.

The Judaising problem continued, however, for the circumcision party did not accept the ruling and continued to make trouble, both in Antioch and in the churches Paul and Barnabas had founded in and around Galatia. It was probably soon after this that Paul wrote Galatians giving his own account of the council and its consequences.

2. LIVE BY THE SPIRIT (GALATIANS)

Paul should never have had to write Galatians. The letter outlining the decisions of the Jerusalem Council should have resolved the dispute about Gentile converts and the law, but the Judaisers continued to insist that Paul's gospel was deficient and so he had to write to his new churches to re-establish them in the truth that faith in Christ sets us free from bondage to legalistic religion. Paul's tirade reminds us of Joshua's warning to Israel and David's to Solomon about the dangers of relaxing faith and vision and falling back into unregenerate religion (Josh. 23f; 1 Chron. 28). Though the historical circumstances are different, the principles of Church growth and kingdom-building are essentially the same.

It is uncertain when exactly Paul wrote Galatians. Perhaps it was soon after the council, perhaps after his second missionary journey, but Judaisers had already visited the Galatian churches and unsettled his converts, persuading some of them to submit to the Mosaic law. Though this letter contains many profound theological statements, it was not primarily written as a theological dissertation. Paul wrote in anger and distress.

Chs. 1–2: The gospel you heard from me is not deficient.

I am astonished at how easily you have been led astray (1.6–10). I assure you I did not invent the gospel I preached to you. Indeed I got it from no man, but straight from Christ by revelation (1.11–15). None of the apostles taught me it (1.16–24). In fact I hardly had any chance to consult them, but when after fourteen years I did finally meet with them at the council in Jerusalem, they approved all I teach (2.1–10). Peter himself approved it, though recently in Antioch he reneged when some Judaisers arrived, but I challenged him that in so doing he was denying the truth that we are now called to live by faith in Christ (2.11–21).

Here we have a virulent illustration of the power of tradition. Whilst it is understandable that new converts should have some difficulties in discerning the truths of their new-found faith, it is surprising that a man such as Peter who had walked and talked with Jesus, had himself been responsible for launching the Gentile mission, had defended it before similar Judaising pressure, had stood to support Paul at the council and had publicly approved of his gospel, that such a man should 'draw back and separate himself from the Gentiles because he was afraid of those who belonged to the circumcision group.' (2.12). But then, '*even* Barnabas' gave way before them (2.13), the very man who had accompanied Paul on the mission and was as much responsible as he was for the conversion of these Gentiles. Tradition does indeed die hard. The work of God's Spirit is hampered by the same pressure today, though in a different guise, as those involved in it well know.

Chs. 3–4: Faith means freedom.

Do not let anyone fool you. You saw for yourselves the power
of faith. Don't forsake the Spirit for the law (3.1–5). Look at
your Bibles – consider Abraham. God regarded him as
righteous because of his faith (3.6–9). What the law does in
fact is impose a curse on all who try to live by it, because they
cannot keep all its commandments, but the gospel is that
Christ has removed that curse by taking it upon himself in our
place (3.10–14). The tradition Jesus stands in is that of the
faith of Abraham; we were only given the law as a tutor to
take charge of us and teach us until he should come (3.15–25).

But now Christ has come, and by the gift of his Spirit in us
we are made like him, sons of God, not slaves (3.26 – 4.7).
Formerly you were slaves to many wrong things, including
'those weak and miserable principles' of ritualism and
legalism, such as 'observing special days and months and
seasons and years!' Don't let yourselves become slaves to
them again (4.8–11). Remember the joy with which you
received the gospel from me; don't let them steal it from you
(4.12–20).

Whose son would you rather have been, Sarah's or
Hagar's, the child of a free woman or a slave? It is the same
sort of choice you have now: the freedom of Christian faith
(of 'the Jerusalem that is above'), or the bondage of
Sinaitic/Jewish legalism (of 'the present city of Jerusalem')
(4.21–31).

Ch. 5: Stand firm in your faith and in the freedom of the Spirit.

You have been progressing so well, do not throw it all away
now for a Judaism (circumcision) that will be of no value to
you, or for men who are themselves in bondage (vv. 1–12).
Live in freedom, live by the Spirit. That will not mean
jettisoning all the good the law stands for, but living in love.
So be done with the old ways of sin, and let the fruit of God's
Spirit grow and mature in you (vv. 13–26).

Ch. 6: Rejoice in what Christ has done for you, not what you are doing by keeping laws.

Care for each other, encourage each other. Sow to the Spirit,
then you will reap the Spirit's harvest of eternal life.

Remember the only thing that counts is not law or circumcision, but that you are a new person in Christ.

Judaisers continued to frustrate Paul's progress throughout his missionary life. Some of them must have spread bad reports about him in Rome, which was one of the reasons why later on he had to write Romans – to allay anxieties about his gospel before he came to Rome himself. In it he incorporates and expands on a lot of his teaching in Galatians.

Paul's gospel is reviewed in Volume One of this series, that is, as he presents it in Romans, and so need not be discussed in more detail here. It is in itself his answer to the challenge of Jewish traditionalism. Basically it is quite straight-forward, though the language he uses does not always leave that impression (cp. 2 Pet. 3.16). In summary he preached that if Jewish religion (the law) could have saved us, God need not have sent us Christ. The law did prepare the way for him, but now he has come, what we need is faith in him, that by his death on the cross he achieved our release from the curse that sin brought into human life, and that subsequently he obtained for us the release of God's Holy Spirit. It is all a matter of faith in Christ and of living in the Spirit, which is a tremendously liberating thing. We know the good of it by our own experience, and it is foolish to fall back into the kind of things from which Jesus has set us free.

13

Over into Macedonia and Achaia

Unlike his first journey and unlike every other episode we have studied in Acts, Paul's second mission began in a most un-Christlike way, with a blazing row between Barnabas and himself. But even before that we do not read about the Holy Spirit guiding, but only about Paul making what seemed to him a good suggestion about going back to visit the young churches they had founded. To be sure he went on his way commended to the grace of God by the brothers in Antioch, and the churches he visited were strengthened and encouraged, but Paul experienced considerable frustration himself as he tried fruitlessly to find openings for evangelism in Asia, Mysia and Bithynia. In the end he tramped the whole way to Troas where he came to the sea and could go no further. Then at length God spoke to him and the doors began to open for what proved to be a very powerful mission indeed, though not at all in the regions he had expected (Acts 15.36 – 16.10).

If we see positive lessons about the effectiveness of Jesus-style ministry in other chapters, here we have the same lesson taught by showing us the frustration that comes from attempting ministry that the Spirit has not initiated. The date of this second mission must have been about 48–51 AD.

1. THE SECOND MISSIONARY JOURNEY (ACTS 15.36 – 18.22)

The churches Paul established on this mission were among the most vibrant of all he founded anywhere, at least, judging

184

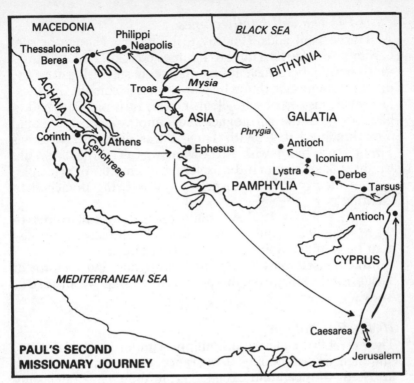

PAUL'S SECOND MISSIONARY JOURNEY

by the amount of correspondence they called forth from his pen. They were, however, very different from each other. The churches of Macedonia in the north seem to have been basically wholesome in their enthusiasm and though Paul had to write some corrective words to them, his letters to Thessalonica and Philippi, as well as his comments about them in 2 Cor. 8, betray a striking warmth of feeling. The churches in Achaia were also enthusiastic, but less well disciplined, and the Corinthians caused Paul a lot of heartache, as we shall see later.

15. 36–41: Off to a bad start.
Paul and Barnabas separate because of Mark (cp. 13.13). Paul takes Silas, one of the delegates sent by the Jerusalem council to carry their decisions to the young churches, himself also very much a man of the Spirit (15.32). Paul and Mark were later reconciled and Paul even came to find him a most helpful assistant (Col. 4.10; 2 Tim. 4.11).

16.1–10: The call finally comes.

At Derbe Paul adds Timothy to his team. Though he had earlier refused to let Titus be circumcised (Gal. 2.3), he insists that Timothy be, which at first may seem surprising after the decision about such things he had obtained from the apostles. However, his reasons are clear. On his missions Paul had to have access to the synagogues and Timothy's presence could have hindered that. With Titus it was different. Whereas Timothy was half Jewish anyhow, he was a Gentile, and what was at stake with him in Jerusalem was a matter of principle, of the integrity of the gospel that was being preached to Gentiles.

When, at Troas, Paul eventually receives his call to cross to the Macedonian mainland, we realise that the second journey is to be as much Spirit-led as the first after all!

Luke himself must have joined Paul, Silas and Timothy at Troas, for the story from this point is told using 'we' instead of 'they'.

16.11–40: Philippi.

They establish a church in Philippi without much difficulty, but then an astounding deliverance results in them being arrested, whipped and expelled from the city, though only after the jailer is converted! The picture of Paul and Silas in jail that night with their backs bleeding and yet praising God is a powerful testimony to the work of the Spirit in their experience.

17.1–9: Thessalonica.

Thessalonica was a key city in which to have a church planted. It was the capital of Macedonia and stood on the main highway from Rome to the East. The establishment of the church there, a thriving one at that judging by the letters Paul wrote to it shortly afterwards, was the result of a very brief, three-week mission in the synagogue, but Jewish jealousy brought that to an abrupt end.

17.10–15: Berea.

An equally successful mission in Berea is similarly halted by Jewish persecution and so Paul moves on to Athens, leaving Silas and Timothy to strengthen the new congregations.

17.16–34: Athens.

While waiting in Athens for Timothy and Silas, Paul preaches his memorable Areopagus sermon and a few come to faith, though his success is limited compared with what he achieved in Macedonia. It was there, after his companions rejoined him, that he wrote 1 and 2 Thessalonians.

18.1–17: Corinth.

The campaign in Corinth was different from any of the earlier ones, for Paul stayed there almost two years. Perhaps the work progressed more slowly, but it was certainly successful enough to stir up Jewish jealousy once more and engender further persecution. Paul's lack of tact in setting up his church next door to the synagogue was doubtless partly to blame for that, particularly since the synagogue ruler and his whole household moved next door with him. But then Paul actually saw it as part of his missionary purpose to arouse the Jews to envy in the hope that some of them might thus be saved (Rom. 11.13f).

While in Corinth Paul stayed with Aquila and his wife, Priscilla. Aquila was a converted Jew, a tent-maker like Paul. He had to leave Rome in 49 AD when the Emperor Claudius expelled the Jews, who, according to the Roman historian Suetonius (*Claudius* 25.4), were said to have rioted 'at the instigation of Chrestus' (= Christ?). Presumably the young Christian church in Rome was encountering the same Jewish persecution as Paul's churches suffered, and Claudius, who probably did not understand what was happening, just expelled the lot. The Jews were allowed to return to Rome when Nero became Emperor in 54 AD. Aquila and Priscilla must have gone home at that time too, since Paul sent them greetings there in Rom. 16.3.

Corinth itself was the capital of the Roman province of Achaia and a thriving centre of trade and commerce with two sea-ports. Here east and west met and intermingled freely. The result was a strange mixture of high culture, freedom of thought, variety in religion, and shameless immorality. The city was dominated by the temple of Aphrodite, goddess of love, with its extensive retinue of sacred prostitutes. It is therefore little wonder that a young church in such a setting should have had the problems of conduct and morality Paul had to deal with later in his letters.

18.18–22: *Home via Ephesus.*
On his way home to Antioch Paul dropped off Priscilla and
Aquila in Ephesus, where he did a little preaching in the
synagogue in passing. Judging by his farewell remark, he
seems to have sensed that what he was doing there was in fact
preparing the way for his next mission.

On Paul's vow in 18.18, see above, p. 54.

Despite the poor start, Paul must have returned home
satisfied, for again in this mission we see the usual marks of
Christ. The contrast between his initial frustration in Asia and
his subsequent whirlwind ministry in Macedonia is, however,
most telling. To be successful, Christian witness clearly has to
be led and empowered by the Spirit.

2. ADVICE TO YOUNG CHRISTIANS (1 and 2 THESSALONIANS)

It would appear that Paul only spent three weeks in Thessalonica before being driven out by persecution, but he left some
very enthusiastic young Christians behind him there. His first
letter to them must have been written only a few weeks later,
for after his brief mission in Berea, he went on to Athens to
wait for Timothy, whom he had sent back to see how the
Thessalonians were progressing, and it was when Timothy
returned with good reports that he wrote to them (1 Thes.
3.1–10), mainly to encourage them in their faith, though also
to restrain some youthful tendencies to over-exuberance.
There is no exact counterpart to this letter among the Old
Testament historical reviews, though it does perhaps remind
us of Samuel's attempts to curb some excessive enthusiasms
among the children of revival in his day, whilst still encouraging them to progressive maturity (1 Sam. 8 & 12).

1 THESSALONIANS

Ch. 1: *Thanks be to God for your exemplary faith.*
It delights me to recall how you first received the gospel, how
you responded as you did to the word and to the evidences of

the Spirit's power despite the persecution, and to hear how you are now living in it, indeed how you have already become an example to other Christians in Macedonia and down here in Achaia.

Chs. 2–3: I still care for you deeply.

After all we suffered at Philippi, our time in Thessalonica was certainly not easy and we had to work hard both to maintain ourselves and to bring you the gospel, but you responded to it beautifully. Then came the persecution that caused you suffering and tore us away from you. I have so longed to be back with you. I have been worrying about how your faith was standing up to the persecution, and that is why I agreed to stay here in Athens alone and send Timothy to you, but I am thrilled with the reports he has just brought back. May the Lord continue to make you strong.

Chs. 4–5: Now let me remind you about some of the things I taught you.

1. Your call is to be holy, so mind how you use your bodies (4.3–8).
2. Keep up the brotherly love God has given you (4.9f).
3. Let your life-style, your personal conduct and the way you work, be an example to others (4.11f).
4. Don't become anxious about those that die, because Jesus has broken the power of death by his resurrection and according to his own promise they will rise to meet him along with us when he comes again (4.13–18).
5. And don't worry about the time of his coming; it cannot be dated, but it will be sudden and unexpected (5.1–3).
6. So be watchful, keep living as children of light, and encourage one another (5.4–11).
7. Respect those over you in the Lord, live at peace with one another, admonish the idle, help the weak and rejoice, pray, give thanks always, keep the Spirit's fire aflame, test everything, hold on to the good (5.12–22).

2 THESSALONIANS

This second letter was written not long after to deal more fully with some subjects Paul had just touched on in the first, particularly in relation to Christ's second coming and to work. Some Thessalonian Christians must have become so excited by their new-found faith that they had given up working, perhaps with the thought that they should now be serving Christ 'full-time', and expecting his return to take place any minute. Paul had not had a long enough time with them to establish them in sound doctrine and discipleship, and so they were left with many unanswered questions to which he has now to address himself in writing.

Ch. 1: Thank God for your continuing faith.
We are delighted to hear of the growing faith and love you are experiencing among yourselves, even amid all the persecutions you are still suffering. Don't worry, your faith will be fully vindicated on the day Jesus returns.

Ch. 2: When will Jesus return?
That has not happened yet, nor will it be yet, for, as I taught you when I was with you, the rebellion has to take place first and the man of lawlessness has to be revealed. To be sure, his secret power is already at work, but he is being restrained at the moment. When he does appear he will be overthrown by the Lord Jesus at his coming. Before that, however, he will succeed in deceiving and deluding many, so in the meantime, while I thank God for choosing you, I bid you stand firm and hold to the teachings we gave you.

Paul never explains about 'the rebellion' or 'the man of lawlessness'. Apparently he spoke with the Thessalonians about these things during his stay (v. 5) and presumably what he told them would have been in agreement with what Jesus had taught his disciples in Matt. 24 and what John wrote in Rev. 11, about Christ's return being preceded by a time of persecution. That, however, is being held in check in the meantime, and so it is senseless to be alarmed by second-coming hysteria.

Ch. 3: Pray and work.
Pray for my ministry to reach more people. And don't any of you sit around in idleness; you will just become a burden to others. You did not see me do that. Get a job and earn your keep.

The Lord be with you all.

1 and 2 Thessalonians are particularly interesting, not just because they contain teaching about the second coming, but because they were written to people whose faith was just a few weeks old, and so show us some of the problems new converts faced in those early days of Christianity, as well as the joys they experienced. Perhaps what strikes us most is their enthusiasm – to love one another, to stand firm for Christ and to watch for his return. Maybe there was a bit of excess, but we could still do with some of their enthusiasm today. As we have repeatedly seen, revival flames are easily quenched. Paul knew that too (1 Thes. 5.19), but was certainly not without hope. Nor need we be!

14

In Asia

At the end of his second mission, when he left Aquila and Priscilla in Ephesus, Paul was actually preparing the ground for his third trip. He seems to have suspected that himself, and so publicly expressed his intention to return (18.19–21). However, further preparation occurred during his absence, probably unbeknown to him.

Another evangelist, called Apollos, had arrived in Ephesus. He was a well-educated man, with what today would be called an Arts degree from Alexandria University, one of the world's foremost centres of academic learning in those times. Furthermore, being a Jew, he knew the Bible thoroughly, and being a convert, he was every bit as enthusiastic as Paul. We are told that he knew and taught about Jesus accurately, but there was one deficiency, that 'he knew only the baptism of John'. On that matter Aquila and Priscilla soon put him right, however, and then they sent him over to Achaia with their commendation, presumably to the church in Corinth that they had just left (18.24–28).

When we meet some of Apollos' converts in ch. 19, we discover that the deficiency in his teaching was more than doctrinal or ritual. What was lacking in their Christianity was that they had no experience of the Holy Spirit. By John's own admission in the days of his ministry, his baptism was only with water for repentance and was no more than preparatory for the greater baptism with the Holy Spirit that Jesus would give (Matt. 3. 11). It is on that matter that Paul has to take action, and presumably also that Aquila and Priscilla had to as well.

PAUL'S THIRD
MISSIONARY JOURNEY

1. THE THIRD MISSIONARY JOURNEY (18.23–20.38)

This journey needs to be dated 53–59 AD (see further below, pp. 196–7).

53   Paul revisits the churches he founded on his first journey,

54–57   he spends three years in Ephesus (20.31),

58   he goes via Macedonia to stay in Corinth for three months (20.3),

59   he returns to Palestine where he is arrested.

Luke tells us very little about Paul's journeyings and concentrates on his time in Ephesus. What we have is therefore mainly the story of the Ephesian church, but it has all the characteristics of the revival stories we read in the Old Testament and still read today.

18.23 – 19.7: The Ephesian Pentecost.
After revisiting the Galatian churches, Paul came to Ephesus, where he found a small church already established with about a dozen members who, like Apollos, knew only John's baptism. As Paul ministered to them they experienced the same kind of Pentecostal outpouring of the Spirit that the church in both Jerusalem and Samaria had. From the signs we have already come to recognise, this mission looks as though it too will bear the marks of Jesus, in kingdom/revival-preaching, in accompanying signs and wonders, and in persecutions.

19.8–12: The first two years.
Surprisingly, after such a promising start, the impact of Paul's preaching at the synagogue during the first three months of his stay was apparently minimal, though sufficient to stir the Jews to anger. He therefore moved to a lecture hall, where he had two years of more fruitful ministry, reaching Jews and Greeks all over the province of Asia. Probably the church at Colosse and most of the churches mentioned in Rev. 2–3 traced their origins back to this campaign.

19.13–20: Breakthrough!
However, the real evangelism-explosion occurred, not when Paul was preaching, but after some Jews tried to perform deliverance ministry in the name of Jesus. The shock effect of what happened caused people everywhere to realise the truth of what Paul had been preaching, with the result that many people now became Christians openly and 'the work of the Lord spread widely and grew in power.'

Many Christians have been frightened about deliverance ministry through misapplication of this story. Jesus promised that he would give his disciples authority to overcome all the power of the enemy, that the spirits would submit to them and that nothing would harm them (Luke 10.19f). The sons of Sceva were not Christians and therefore had neither that authority nor that protection. It is wrong to assume that

Christian ministry operates on the same level as theirs.
Deliverance operates by faith, not fear.

19.21–22: Meanwhile in Corinth.
While the revival was gathering momentum in Ephesus, fairly
serious trouble was brewing in Corinth. It was about this time
that Paul wrote his letters to the brethren there. He also sent
Timothy to visit them and, as we shall see, took time off the
work in Ephesus to visit them himself.

However, in the midst of this busy work, establishing new
churches and attending to already established ones, Paul's
eye was already turning to the possibility of carrying the
gospel over new horizons. He thus began to plan a fourth
journey, this time to Rome.

19.23–41: Reaction to the gospel in Ephesus.
In every age revivals have disturbed social patterns, particularly the ungodly and superstitious ones, and have most upset
those who make their living by them. Today, depending on
the cultural setting, it is drinking-houses, betting-shops and
witch-doctors that are affected; in Paul's day it was idol-
makers. The riot they instigated reminds us of similar
episodes in the lives of John Wesley and others like him, and,
just as in later Christian times, neither the rioting crowd nor
the civil authorities had much understanding of the issues
involved.

20.1–16: Paul visits Corinth.
He visited his churches in Macedonia first and then went on to
Greece, that is to Corinth, where he stayed for three months.
It was there that Paul wrote Romans, outlining plans for his
fourth mission (Rom. 1.8–15; 15.19–33). Driven out by
Jewish pressure, he returned to Asia – first to Troas, where
Eutychus fell from the window.

When he left Corinth, he was accompanied by a delegation
of representatives from his churches in the area. One of Paul's
projects on this mission was to raise funds for the relief of
poverty among the saints in Jerusalem. He had already taken
them one gift from his home church in Antioch and at the
Jerusalem council had promised Peter and James he would
continue to help them (Gal. 2.10). He had therefore appealed

to his churches to make a collection and had asked for some
representatives from them to go with him to Jerusalem
bearing the gift (1 Cor. 16.1–4; cp. 2 Cor. 8–9).

20.17–38: Paul's farewell to the Ephesian elders.

Like Jesus at the end of his ministry, Paul now has his face set
to go to Jerusalem, already aware of the suffering he is to
endure. His last address to his disciples, the elders of the
young church, also reminds us of Jesus' teaching to his
disciples as his time approached: '(The Son of Man) must go
to Jerusalem and suffer many things . . . Watch out that
no-one deceives you . . . For false Christs and false prophets
will appear and perform great signs and miracles to deceive
even the elect – if that were possible.' (Matt. 16.21; 24.4, 24).

By the time Paul left them to sail for Palestine, the
Jesus-pattern in his mission had once more become unmistak-
able.

2. TROUBLE IN A DEVELOPING CHURCH (1 and 2 CORINTHIANS)

Paul's relationship with Corinth involved much more than
one evangelistic visit and a couple of letters. It required
several visits by himself and others, and he had to write at
least four letters, two of which are now lost. On the church in
Corinth, see pp. 186–7.

50–51 Paul visits Corinth during his second missionary
journey and stays there eighteen months (Acts 18.1–
18).

54 (?) He writes a first letter (now lost) urging a purge of
immorality from the church (1 Cor. 5.9).

54 Apollos preaches in Corinth (Acts 18.27 – 19.1).

54–57 On his third missionary journey Paul stays in Ephesus
for three years (Acts 19: cp. 20.31).

56 While there he sends Timothy to Corinth (1 Cor.
16.10).
He writes 1 Corinthians.
Then he visits Corinth himself, but finds the visit
'painful' (2 Cor. 2.1).

He sends Titus to Corinth with another letter (now lost), one written 'with many tears' (2 Cor. 2.4).

57 Paul moves on to Troas, then to Macedonia where he meets up with Titus (2 Cor. 2.12f; 7.5f).

He writes 2 Corinthians and sends Titus and two others back with it (2 Cor. 8.16–24).

58 Then he arrives in Corinth himself and stays for three months (Acts 20.3).

Clearly the developments during the first four years at Corinth had not all been happy ones and Paul had not exactly endeared himself to everyone there by the frankness of his first letter. His image was further tarnished when some began to compare his preaching with that of the eloquent and well-educated Apollos, but what finally goaded him to write 1 Corinthians was the appalling news brought by 'some from Chloe's household' (1 Cor. 1.11). Unable to visit Corinth himself at the time because of the expanding work in Ephesus, he sent Timothy to deal with the problems and wrote them this letter.

1 CORINTHIANS

In writing this letter Paul's purpose was not unlike Moses' when he reminded the Israelites in Deuteronomy about the need to uphold the ways of the law and return to God in repentance. The circumstances had vastly changed since his day, but that need to sustain kingdom-living in accordance with the forms given by God was still paramount, as Jesus himself also taught (Matt. 5–7). Because of the variety of material covered, what follows here can be little more than an introductory outline. But note how Paul, like Moses before him, keeps bringing us back to the basic principles of kingdom life, to holiness, righteousness, faith, obedience, repentance and, above all else, love. Some of his teaching, particularly about God's wisdom and the Spirit, is discussed more fully in Volume Three.

Chs. 1–4: Divisions in the church.

Chs. 1–2: Other preachers had visited Corinth, including Apollos and perhaps Peter (= Cephas; 1.12). Some of the

Corinthians were more attracted by their preaching than by
Paul's and the church was becoming divided. Paul's retort is
that the gospel is not about eloquence or cleverness, but
about the power of God and the unveiling of the mystery of
God (his secret and hidden wisdom) which is in Christ and is
revealed by his Spirit alone.

Chs. 3–4: Apostles and evangelists are only like gardeners
doing different jobs, such as planting and watering, but God
alone gives the growth (the life). Or they are like builders,
laying foundations and erecting superstructures, but it is all to
establish you as something solid and enduring, for you are the
temple of God's Spirit. Usually we have to work very hard to
do it and suffer a lot in the process. The important thing in the
end is Christ, not which apostle you like best.

Strangely, it seems to be where God's Spirit is most active
that divisions and jealousies focusing on individuals' ministries are most exaggerated. The problem is a very ancient
one. It divided Joseph from his brothers, it turned the
Israelites against Moses on more than one occasion, it roused
Saul to murdering anger against David, it caused prophet to
stand against prophet (e.g. 1 Kings 22), and it set Jerusalem's
religious leaders against Jesus. It seems that the man God
blesses with a strong call and anointing will inevitably have to
live with jealousy. And the result will be party strife, as some
follow one leader and others another, just as some once
followed Aaron and others Moses, or as some in more recent
times followed Whitefield and others Wesley. The church in
Corinth was far from unique. Strong ministries have always
resulted in strong personal followings. And the challenge has
always been the same, namely to reassert the centrality of
Christ and maintain unity in the body.

Chs. 5–10: Matters of Christian conduct.

5.1–8: The one unrepentantly living in sexual immorality
should be handed over to Satan. It is not clear what precisely
was involved in doing that, though it is commonly assumed
that it meant being expelled from the church, both for his own
good as well as everyone else's, as an act of discipline to bring
him to repentance (see also 1 Tim. 1.20).

5.9–13: Paul had written a previous letter about separation
from immoral people, but that had been misinterpreted. He

was appealing for purity within the fellowship, not for separation from the world.

6.1–11: You should not be taking your disputes to pagan law-courts; in so doing you are publicly denying the value of the Christian gospel.

6.12–20: Shun sexual immorality; it is more serious than other sins, for your body is the temple of the Holy Spirit.

Ch. 7: On marriage and divorce. It is better not to divorce, but if it becomes necessary, you must not remarry. The best thing is not to get married at all, then you can give yourself fully to the Lord's service, but if you have to, then marry rather than live in sin. Paul admits that some of this is his own advice, not the Lord's word (vv. 10,12).

Ch. 8: On food sacrificed to idols. The problem arose because most butcher-meat came from sacrifices at the pagan temples. To some that posed no problem at all, because for them idols were mere nothings and there was only one God anyhow. Others, the weaker brethren, still found it difficult to believe they were not polluting themselves by eating such meat. Paul pleads that they be loved, not criticised.

Ch. 9: On Christian freedom. Apostles and preachers have a right to be supported in their work. They need to be fed; that is the Lord's command. I do not avail myself of that right, but work with my hands to earn my own keep, because I want to preach the gospel free of charge. But I recognise the right for others. Our freedom is to serve all men in the gospel, whether Jews, the weak, or whoever. Go for the prize, for the crown that will last for ever!

Ch. 10: Do it all for the glory of God. Watch how you go; obey God; remember the lessons the ancient Israelites learned in the wilderness when they turned to idols (vv. 1–13). You cannot partake of both pagan sacrifices and the Lord's Supper – the one is a denial of the other (10.14–22). And so concerning questions of Christian freedom and food sacrificed to idols, the rule must be: 'everything is permissible, but not everything is beneficial'. Have a care, therefore, for your weaker brother (10.23–33).

Chs. 11–14: Matters of Christian Worship.

The various matters Paul discusses here suggest that church gatherings in Corinth had become quite undisciplined affairs.

His plea is neither that the women, nor the Lord's Supper, nor the spiritual gifts, should be banned from the church, but that there should be orderliness and love in all things.

11.1–16: Women should have their heads decently covered in church, men theirs uncovered, particularly when they pray or prophesy.

11.17–34: The Lord's Supper must be treated with reverence. It is a sacred meal and a man ought to examine himself before he takes it, lest he dishonour the Lord's table and bring judgment on himself.

Chs. 12–13: There are varieties of spiritual gifts, but they are distributed in the church like the parts in a body. They should therefore work together in harmony, since there is only one body, namely Christ's. And they need to be exercised in love, otherwise they become worthless. (Cp. Rom. 12 and Eph. 4.)

Ch. 14: Prophecy, tongues and interpretation are inter-related gifts. In tongues an individual speaks to God, not men, and so edifies himself; in prophecy he speaks to others and so edifies the church. If interpreted, the prayer or praise spoken in tongues may also edify the church, for the hearers can then join in and say 'Amen'; otherwise it sounds like just so much noise and no-one is edified, apart from the speaker.

The gifts should certainly be used during worship, so that the church may be edified, but not in such a way as to make worship something disorderly. God is not a God of disorder, but of peace.

Paul was himself very much a man of the Spirit. He tells us here how fully he knew the power of these gifts in his own experience and ministry. He would surely have found it well-nigh impossible to conceive the kind of services many churches have today, where God's gifts are never seen or heard, and would equally have been very much at home in today's renewal and revival settings where they are fairly well understood and enjoyed.

Ch. 15: The Resurrection.

Vv. 1–2: If there is no resurrection, your faith is a waste of time.

Vv. 3–11: Historically the evidence for Jesus' resurrection is overwhelming, and I too can testify to having met him.

Vv. 12–34: Theologically it makes perfect sense, because Jesus came to reverse the curse of Adam, which is ultimately death.

Vv. 35–38: Scientifically (?) its physical process is also easy to comprehend: it is like a seed dying, being buried and rising out of the ground into a glorious new plant, only it will happen in the twinkling of an eye, at the last trumpet.

Ch. 16: Paul's plans to visit Corinth.

The instructions about a weekly collection relate to Paul's promise at the Jerusalem council that he would continue caring for the poor in Jerusalem (Gal. 2.10; see above, p. 195 and on 2 Cor. 8–9).

Paul's plans to visit the Corinthians were clearly tentative, because his evangelism in Ephesus was beginning to take effect. On his and Timothy's movements, see above, p. 196.

2 CORINTHIANS

Between writing 1 and 2 Corinthians the break-through in evangelism happened at Ephesus and Paul was kept so busy he was unable to do more than pay a flying visit to Corinth and send Titus with an intermediate letter. That inevitably raised further criticism against him, that he was unreliable. It seems he came in for a great deal of personal criticism in the interim and so much of this letter is taken up with defending his actions and his ministry. Because of that, however, Paul opens his heart to us here in a way that he never does in his other letters.

In the New Testament 2 Corinthians plays a similar part to Joshua 1 in the Old. There we find something of a definition of the authority of leadership, here we find a defence of it. In both places, however, proper recognition of authority and anointing is called for to enable continued kingdom-growth, not just to elevate the leader.

Chs. 1–2: Paul's travel plans.

Sorry I was not able to visit you in the way I had originally planned. You will have heard about all we had to go through at Ephesus. I can assure you my intentions were good, but it is probably a blessing that I could not come earlier considering

how painful my last visit was! However, enough time has now
passed, so you can forgive the trouble-maker, for I have
forgiven him.

I am on my way to you now, but have been delayed again,
for I stopped at Troas to preach and the Lord opened a door
for the gospel. But I could not settle there, because Titus had
not returned with news about you, so I have moved on and am
now in Macedonia. Nevertheless, I praise God for the
opportunity to spread the aroma of Christ further.

Chs. 3–5: The Validity of Paul's ministry.

Ch. 3: Some of you are disturbed that I carry no letter of
recommendation, but you yourselves are that letter, written
by the Spirit on our hearts, not by ink on paper. Which would
you rather have? The one gives life, the other cannot. Ask
any Jew who has become a Christian and he will tell you how
the Spirit removed a veil from his heart, unlocked the
Scriptures for him and let him know God's glory.

Ch. 4: I assure you there is no deception in what we do, for
we do not preach ourselves, but Jesus Christ. He makes the
light shine in our darkness, he puts this treasure in vessels of
clay. That is how we can endure anything and not lose heart.

Ch. 5: Hence we live for heavenly, not material benefits;
we live by faith, not sight; we live to please God, knowing we
shall have to appear before him and give account of what we
have done.

This is about the only letter of recommendation you can
expect to get from us to show to those who seem to need it (v.
12). Our motivation is Christ's love, that you may know his
reconciling power and know what it is to be a new creation in
him. We are Christ's ambassadors appealing for reconciliation and peace between you and God.

Chs. 6–7: Paul opens his heart to the Corinthians.

Ch. 6: We have done everything and suffered all sorts of
things to help you receive God's grace. Don't contaminate
what you have received by becoming yoked with unbelievers.

Ch. 7: Open your hearts to me. I have wronged no-one and
have great concern for you. You were upset by my letter, but
that was good, because it led to repentance. Titus' reports
have heartened me. He seems to have had a great time with

you. I knew he would, for I have always had confidence in you.

Chs. 8–9: On the collection for the church in Jerusalem.

Ch. 8: The churches here in Macedonia have been generous beyond their means. I am sending Titus back to organise your contribution. You made a promising start last year – keep it up.

Ch. 9: Please don't let me down. I've been telling the Macedonians all about your eagerness to give, and some of them will be coming with me to Corinth. Remember that God will bless you as you bless others. And think of how many poor brethren will be thanking God for your generosity.

Chs. 10–12: On the authority of Paul's ministry again.

Paul picks up on chs. 3–5 and becomes angry as he thinks about the criticisms that have been levelled against him.

Ch. 10: Alright, I do speak strongly and boastfully in my letters. But I'll do the same when I come to you. Anyhow, my boasting is not about myself, like my critics' boasting, but about all the Lord has done through me. I boast for his glory.

Ch. 11: You know how I care for you, how I prepared you for Christ, how I never cost you anything. Don't be led astray by 'super-apostles' who teach you a different gospel. I have given up and suffered more for the gospel than any of them.

12. 1–13: I can also boast of visions and revelations, though I have been given a 'thorn in my flesh, a messenger of Satan to torment me' (a person rather than an illness?) and remind me that God's grace is sufficient for me. I have manifested all the marks of an apostle.

Personal outpourings of the heart in defence of charismatic or revival ministry, similar to what we find here and earlier in this letter, are not uncommon today. Sometimes they are publicly expressed in autobiographical publications, sometimes they are heard in sermons, sometimes they are just quietly spoken in private conversation. But they all express a deep conviction that a man's ministry has been like Christ's, bearing all the same marks as his, in preaching, miracle-working and suffering. The question is not just one of self-defence, but defence of the gospel that the preacher's life

and ministry have proclaimed, that is, defence of the gospel of
Jesus Christ himself.

12.14 – 13.14: Final appeal for reconciliation.
This will now be my third visit to you, but don't worry, I will
not be a burden to you. I write to defend myself, not for
financial gain, but for the sake of our relationship.

But when I come, as last time, I will not curry favour with
you by softness. Sin must be purged from your midst, so take
a good look at yourselves before I come. I want to see you
built up and made strong in the Lord.

My love to all of you in Christ Jesus.

These two letters to the Corinthians make an excellent
complement to 1 and 2 Thessalonians. There we saw something of the problems facing a new church only a few weeks
old; here we see something of the tensions that developed in a
city church as it grew beyond its first infancy, and just as in
Thessalonica, many of the problems confronting the Corinthian church look very much like those we still encounter in
churches today, particularly where renewal or revival is
happening.

Many Christians have concluded from what Paul wrote to
the Corinthians that charismatic activity has always been a
cause of turbulence and division and that it should therefore
be curbed and driven from the church. That is not at all what
Paul intended. The man who wrote 'Eagerly desire spiritual
gifts, especially the gift of prophecy . . . I would like every
one of you to speak in tongues . . . I thank God that I speak in
tongues more than all of you' (1 Cor. 14.1,5,18) and such like,
could never have contemplated quenching the Spirit's fire.
No! What he was pleading for was love, love between one and
another, love for weaker brethren, love between them and
him, and so forth – Christ's love. And that is still the plea
today.

It is not without reason that 1 Cor. 13 is one of the best
known passages in the New Testament. What it says about
love is virtually a summary-description of Jesus' own personality. It is therefore sad that so many today, whilst they see
that to be true, fail to see that equally what 1 Cor. 12 says
about the gifts of the Spirit is virtually a summary-description

of Jesus' ministry. Paul's appeal is that the two should operate in harmony among Christ's followers, not that one be jettisoned in favour of the other.

In the end Paul's plea is that in everything Christians believe and do, they should be able to say, 'Christ's love compels us', for we are called to be 'Christ's ambassadors', or 'the aroma of Christ' to a lost and dying world (2 Cor. 5.14,20; 2.15). That is Christian witness; that is Jesus-ministry. It is for that that God 'poured out his love into our hearts by the Holy Spirit' (Rom. 5.5), that we might reflect Christ to men. That was how Paul and the other apostles lived, and that was the secret, as we have repeatedly seen, of their success in kingdom/revival ministry. By faith, obedience and repentance, the men of the Old Covenant laid a foundation in Israel, then Christ came to teach us the fullness of God's kingdom-ways, which Paul has captured so perfectly here in his teaching about Christ's love and his Spirit.

15

On to Rome

These last chapters of Acts play roughly the same part in the story of Paul's life as the last chapters in the Gospels do in the story of Jesus', from the time of his entry to Jerusalem on Palm Sunday up to the eve of his crucifixion. The parallels are often very obvious, as we shall see. The main difference, of course, is that Paul's story is left unfinished. That is either because Luke could tell us no more since he had brought us right up to the time he was writing, or because he also had another purpose in mind.

As well as being his conclusion to Paul's story, these chapters are also the conclusion to his story of the expansion of the early Church. Repeatedly Luke has shown us that successful Christian ministry bears the mark of Jesus' life and ministry, that it is accomplished with his revival-style preaching, with the miraculous signs of the kingdom, and with suffering, often leading to death, but always to resurrection. As the end of the gospel-story is resurrection leading to a new outflowing of life, so also must the end of the Church's be. And that is exactly how it is, for though our last report of Paul shows him still a prisoner, he is actually also enjoying considerable freedom to preach the gospel in Rome itself. The ending is thus far from sombre. It leaves us with a fresh mission in full swing in the city at the very heart of all the ancient world.

1. PAUL'S GETHSEMANE AND TRIAL (CHS. 21–26)

After his arrest Paul spent a few weeks in Jerusalem and two years in prison in Caesarea (24.27) before he was taken to Rome. These chapters must therefore relate to the years 59–61 AD.

21.1–14: Paul's Gethsemane.
Paul's Gethsemane took place soon after he reached Palestine at the end of his third mission. The parallels with what happened to Jesus are not exact, but the overtones in the two men's stories are unmistakably similar. There, in the home of Philip the evangelist at Caesarea, as his friends pleaded with him not to go through with what they could see coming, just as Jesus' disciples had pleaded with him when he was on his way to Jerusalem in the same circumstances, Paul showed that, despite the inner anguish he was suffering (v. 13), his resolve was firm, and so they had to leave off their pleading, saying 'The Lord's will be done', using the very words Jesus himself had in Gethsemane when he accepted his call to go forward to the cross (v. 14; cp. Matt. 26.39,42).

21.15–36: The arrest.
Paul was warmly received in Jerusalem by the apostles and the rest of the Jewish Christians there, but just over a week after his arrival in Jerusalem, despite every precaution to avoid it happening, he was arrested, the mob shouting, as they had done with Jesus, 'Away with him!' (v. 36; Luke 23.18).

21.37 – 22.29; The flogging.
While the details are, of course, never exactly the same, Paul's story continues to have many echoes of Jesus'. At his arrest, Jesus also pleaded his innocence (Matt. 26.55f), and he too was eventually led away by the soldiers to be flogged (Matt. 27.26). However, Paul was saved from that at the last moment because he was a Roman citizen.

22.30 – 23.11: On trial before the Sanhedrin.
Just like Jesus, Paul was put on trial in the Sanhedrin, and was

similarly struck in the face before the Jewish court (cp. Matt. 26.67). However, by cleverly playing on the party tensions among the Jews present, Paul was able to turn his trial into a fiasco and so it did not lead to the same verdict being reached as at Jesus' trial. Despite the similarities, Paul's story was not yet finished. And so the Lord showed him he had a further purpose for him, to testify also in Rome.

23.12 – 24.27: On trial before the Roman governor.
The way in which Paul came to be sent to Felix, one of Pilate's successors in the office of Procurator of Judea, was not the same as the way in which Jesus was brought before Pilate. This time it was because a Jewish conspiracy to take Paul's life was uncovered and the centurion in Jerusalem thought it best to move him to more secure prison quarters in Caesarea, where Felix had his headquarters. The story is therefore different from Jesus' in its detail, but the sequence is similar and the same overtones are all there.

At his trial before the governor, his Jewish accusers trumped up the same, old, false charges about blasphemous attitudes to the temple. Felix and his wife, like Pilate and his wife, both recognised something of the truth, but Felix, again like Pilate, desired to 'grant a favour to the Jews' (v. 27; cp. Matt. 27.19–24; Mark 15.15). However, the way he did that was not by having Paul executed, as Jesus had been, but by taking no action and leaving Paul in prison for the next two years.

Chs. 25–26: On trial before King Agrippa.
When Festus replaced Felix as governor, he consulted King Agrippa, just as Pilate had consulted Herod Antipas, Agrippa's predecessor as ruler of Northern Palestine (Luke 23.6–12). Agrippa seemed as keen to meet Paul as Herod had been to meet Jesus, but the interview had equally little effect on him.

In the meantime Paul had appealed to Caesar. But the repeated verdict on his case was the same as Pilate's on Jesus': 'This man is not doing anything that deserves death or imprisonment' (23.29; 26.31; cp. Matt. 27.23; Luke 23.22).

Once more we have seen just how closely Paul's ministry, like that of Peter, Stephen and others before him, conformed to the patterns of Christ, right through to the end. In 26.20 we also find an interesting little insight into what Paul considered his aim in preaching to be, one that further testifies to the similarity of his ministry to that of Jesus: 'I preached that they should repent and turn to God and prove their repentance by their deeds.' In Acts we are only given summaries of two of Paul's sermons, one in 13.20–41 and the other in 17.22–31, the first a call to Jews to accept Jesus as the Christ and the second an explanation of his faith to Gentiles. Although he does say in 17.30 that God 'now commands all people everywhere to repent', the call to repentance is not as strongly emphasised in either sermon as it was in Jesus' or Peter's preaching. It is therefore good to hear him say here in 26.20 (cp. also Acts 20.21) that to give that call was indeed the whole purpose with which he preached, for as we saw earlier, it was of the very essence of revival and kingdom preaching as we encountered it among the prophets of the Old Testament and, of course, in the ministry of Jesus himself.

2. PAUL'S FOURTH MISSIONARY JOURNEY (CHS. 27–28)

It had been Paul's intention for some time, ever since his stay in Ephesus, that his fourth mission should take him to Rome (19.21). While in Corinth in the winter of 58–59 AD, he wrote to the Christians in Rome telling them of his plans to visit them (Rom. 1.8–15; 15.17–29). He said that he felt he had done as much evangelising in the east as he needed to do, right round from Jerusalem to Illyricum (Rom. 15.19), and since the next country on the map was Italy, Rome should be his next port of call, that is if he was going to break new ground as he felt called to do. It is unlikely that at the time he envisaged it all happening in the way it did, with himself as a prisoner. The date of the events covered in these last two chapters of Acts is 61–64 AD.

27.1 – 28.10: The Sea-voyage to Malta.

Though we read of no Pentecostal outpouring attending the

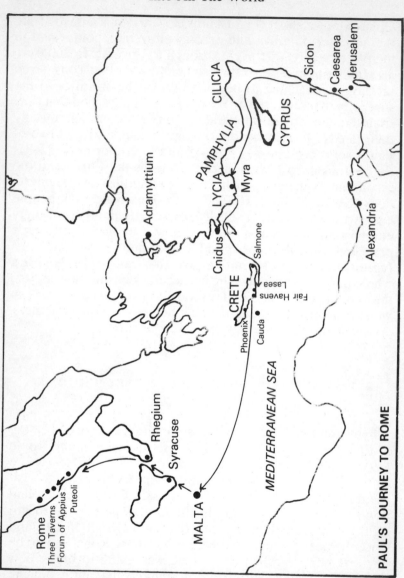

PAUL'S JOURNEY TO ROME

start of this journey, it was very much of the Lord's
appointing, not something that happened outside his
sovereign control. Two years before it began the Lord
revealed to Paul it would be taking place (23.11), and as it gets
under way and runs into trouble in the storms at sea, we
continue to see the evidences of God's controlling hand when

the crew are shipwrecked on Malta. And there, even before reaching Italy, the kingdom-ministry of healing and preaching begins, attended by miracles that leave the islanders astounded.

28.11–31: Rome.

On arrival in Rome, Paul was allowed to live in open house arrest with a considerable amount of freedom. He naturally used that freedom as an opportunity for the gospel, following his old missionary tactic of speaking first with the Jews. Though that bore some fruit, he soon found he had once more to turn to the Gentiles. For two whole years he used his rented accommodation as an evangelistic teaching centre, and there, in the city of Rome itself, 'boldly and without hindrance he preached the kingdom of God and taught about the Lord Jesus Christ', right at the heart of the ancient world, thus establishing the strongest possible bridgehead for the final thrust of gospel witness that would ultimately reach 'to the ends of the earth' (1.8).

3. PAUL'S FIFTH MISSIONARY JOURNEY.

The end of Paul's life is something of a mystery, but it seems likely that he did fulfil an earlier ambition to go on yet a further evangelistic mission.

It was probably during his two years in Rome that Paul wrote his letters from prison: to the Philippians, Philemon, the Colossians and the Ephesians. We shall be examining these in Volume Four, just as we studied Romans in Volume One. However, it is more difficult to date his letters to Timothy and Titus – which we shall also be looking at in Volume Four. The movements of Paul and his companions they refer to do not fit into any of the stories we have in Acts, suggesting that there was more to tell of his life-story than Luke has told us. Also, from information found in some post-biblical writings, it seems likely that Paul was released from prison in 64 and that he went on a fifth missionary journey. His correspondence with his two disciples would then belong to those later years, about which we know very little indeed.

About 95 AD, Clement, Bishop of Rome, wrote in a letter to the Corinthian church:

> *Through jealousy and strife Paul displayed the prize of endurance; seven times in bonds, driven into exile, stoned, appearing as a herald in both the East and the West he won noble fame for his faith; he taught righteousness to the whole world, and after reaching the limits of the West bore witness before rulers. Then he passed from the world and went to the holy place, having shown himself the greatest pattern of endurance.*

(Clement's *First Epistle to the Corinthians, 5.7*)

In Roman times 'the limits of the West' referred to Spain. Paul tells us himself in Rom. 15.24 that he intended to go there after Rome. Indeed, from what he writes he even gives the impression that, while he was looking forward to spending time with the church and ministering in the capital, he was viewing his visit primarily as a stop-over on his way West, partly to enlist the help of the Roman Christians to speed him on his way.

According to the third/fourth-century Church-historian, Eusebius, he was beheaded during Nero's persecution in 67 AD (*Ecclesiastical History*, II.25.5). So, presumably he was released in 64 and went to Spain, as he had originally planned. Judging by the movements alluded to in his letters to Timothy and Titus, he would subsequently have returned to the East and revisited Ephesus, Macedonia and Greece, possibly in 66. He must then have been arrested again, and it would have been during this second imprisonment that he wrote to Timothy and Titus, giving them instructions for making the churches under their supervision secure in their ministries and faith.

Then in 67 AD, Paul's life was offered up in the ultimate sacrifice of martyrdom, thus finally and fully completing the Jesus-pattern of his ministry to the glory of God.

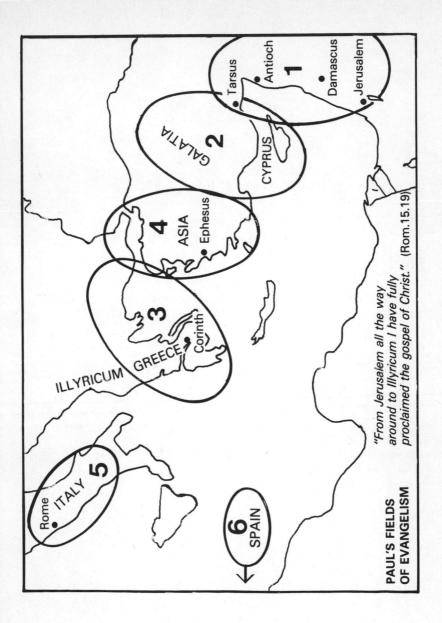

PAUL'S FIELDS
OF EVANGELISM

"From Jerusalem all the way around to Illyricum I have fully proclaimed the gospel of Christ." (Rom.15.19)

PART SIX

CONCLUSION

67 AD — TODAY

Eusebius tells us that Peter was also martyred in the Neronian persecution in Rome, by crucifixion. The Jewish historian, Josephus, tells us in his *Antiquities of the Jews*, 20.9, that James, Jesus' brother, head of the church in Jerusalem, was martyred by stoning at the instigation of the high priest Ananus after the death of Festus the procurator in 61 AD. But by the time the Jewish revolt erupted in Jerusalem in 66 AD, the main thrust of apostolic witness was complete. When the Romans destroyed the temple in 70 AD, the good news about Jesus Christ had already been proclaimed in every land in the Roman Empire where there were settlements of God's ancient people, the Jews, the descendants of Abraham, to whom the promise was originally given. Everything they had been waiting and watching for had been fulfilled and now God's kingdom was being built and was spreading over the earth in power, in ways that neither they nor their forefathers could have imagined possible. Furthermore, the old prophecies about the Lord's people being 'a light to the Gentiles' were also being dramatically fulfilled, so much so that many Jews found it hard to accept what was happening. Indeed, the gospel was now being carried rapidly, as Jesus himself had promised it would be, 'to the ends of the earth'.

And yet, the story was far from finished. What had happened so far, momentous though it was, was only the first launching of a new move of God on earth that was to continue to grow over the next 1900 years and more, down to our own day. As we followed the story of the first 2,000 years from Abraham to Christ, we saw how frequently faith fluctuated, how the kingdom-vision now flourished, now collapsed. Will the story of Christian Church-growth be any different? To be sure, its start was promising, but how will its end be? Will Christ's followers be able to maintain the patterns of kingdom-ministry he has taught them? Will they continue to operate in the power of the Holy Spirit he has given them? Or will they return to the same old ways that resulted in the Israelites needing to look to God for revival time and time again?

16

And to the End of Time

In the Old Testament we saw that the work of building the Lord's kingdom only progressed successfully when Israel relied in faith and obedience on his leading and not on its own strength. Similarly revivals came when the people returned to the Lord after times of disastrously trying to go it alone. At such moments the Lord would release his Spirit to work through specially appointed leaders who would restore faith and vision to the nation.

The greatest thrust of kingdom-building and revival of all time came to the Lord's people when Jesus appeared among them. The Gospels and Acts tell how it began with his own ministry and spread through the work of his kingdom-ministry teams that followed after him. In the same manner as the Old Testament revivals, it began with a call to repentance and an outpouring of the Spirit – for Jesus himself, and later for his followers – and at every new phase of its growth and expansion the same pattern was repeated. As we noted at the very beginning of this book, the whole key to revival and the growth of God's kingdom-work is contained in Peter's words in Acts 3.19:

Repent, then, and turn to God, so that your sins may be wiped out, that times of refreshing may come from the Lord.

And that is how it has been throughout Christian history. Sadly the work of kingdom-building and church-growth has declined from time to time, Christians have become disobedient in their way of life, their love and zeal have grown cold, but the Lord has continued to raise up men of the Spirit and has called them back to himself in repentance. And when they have responded he has indeed granted renewed and abundant times of refreshing.

We also saw how kingdom-growth and revival required vision. It was God-given vision that inspired and encouraged men such as Joshua, Samuel and David, and correspondingly the loss of it that undermined faith in the ages of the judges and the kings. Jesus gave his disciples plenty of vision for kingdom-ministry in his lifetime, but the Church needs it every bit as much today to sustain his ministry. To be sure, the Lord still speaks prophetically to the churches in our own time, but perhaps the most valuable vision he ever gave is recorded for us in the book of Revelation, written about 95 AD. It has encouraged many Christians down the centuries, it continues to inspire the Church today and it will do so for all time, because it speaks, not only of the future progress of history, but of The End.

JOHN'S VISION IN REVELATION

Chs. 1–3: A call to revival.
Though Christianity spread dramatically through the Roman Empire at first, it seems that by 95 AD a degree of laxity had crept into some of the churches which were by then already in need of revival themselves. So in John's vision Jesus dictates letters to seven Asian churches (which presumably are representative of the whole Church at large) in which he calls for repentance and perseverance. These letters contain a complete blue-print for revival in any age:

> *You have forsaken your first love. Remember the height from which you have fallen! Repent and do the things you did at first.*
>
> (2.4–5)
>
> *Do not be afraid . . . Be faithful, even to the point of death.*
>
> (2.10)
>
> *Repent, therefore! Otherwise, I will soon come to you.*
>
> (2.16)
>
> *. . . unless they repent . . . Hold on to what you have.*
>
> (2.22,25)
>
> *Wake up! Strengthen what remains and is about to die . . . Remember what you have received and heard; obey it, and*

repent.

(3.2f)

I have placed before you an open door that no-one can shut. I know that you have little strength, yet you have kept my word and not denied my name . . . Hold on to what you have.

(3.8,11)

You are neither cold nor hot. I wish you were either one or the other! Be earnest and repent. Here I am! I stand at the door and knock. If anyone hears my voice and opens the door, I will come in and eat with him, and he with me.

(3.15,19f)

Chs. 4–19: The course of history to come.

John is taken in vision before the throne of God in heaven to stand among the myriads of angels and men that worship in his presence (chs. 4–5). There he sees Jesus (the Lamb) open the seven seals of the scroll of history revealing turmoils to come, interrupted with visions of the redeemed in glory (chs. 6–7). Similar scenes are revealed as he watches seven angels sound their trumpets, this time interrupted with visions of the witnessing power of Christian martyrs (chs. 8–11).

He is then shown scenes of war in heaven and of the saints on earth engaged in battle with the devil and his beastly horde, culminating in the fall of 'Babylon' and the final harvest of mankind (chs. 12–14). By that point we are reaching the end of history as we know it. John watches seven angels empty bowls of God's wrath on the earth (chs. 15–16), and this time there is no interruption of the vision, which therefore passes directly to a final portrait of sin-ridden Babylon, an account of its fall and a vision of the victory procession of Christ (chs. 17–19).

Chs. 20–22: The End.

For a thousand years Christ and the saints rule on earth thus restoring Eden's kingdom-rule. Now at length we see the fulfilment of God's commission to Adam to rule the earth and his promise to Abraham that through his descendants blessing will be restored to all families on earth. Here indeed is Paradise restored, though not even yet in its full and final expression, for Satan, death and hell have still to be dealt with and the judgment of men has to take place, all of which John sees happen at the end of this millennium (ch. 20).

'Then I saw a new heaven and a new earth, for the first heaven and the first earth had passed away . . . He who was seated on the throne said, "I am making everything new." ' (21.1,5).

As John is shown the vision of this new heaven and earth, it has all the marks of the Garden of God in its original and absolute goodness, complete with the river of the water of life and the tree of life with its eternally available food and healing leaves (22.1–2; cp. Gen. 2.8–10; 3.22; Ezek. 47.1–12). There 'there is no more death or mourning or crying or pain' and God himself 'will wipe every tear from their eyes.' (21.4).

But at the end of all things we do not come just to a new place. We come to God himself, the One who was 'in the beginning' (Gen. 1.1), the One who now speaks from the throne and says, 'I am the Alpha and the Omega, the Beginning and the End.' (Rev. 21. 6). Our end is to be back home with God for ever, at rest in the restored harmony of his love in fellowship with his saints, where veritably he always intended us to be, from Eden's first beginnings – for there at the End, 'his servants will see his face.' (22.3f).

Throughout the centuries since John's day, churches have grown, declined and seen revival many times and in many places. The patterns we traced in the Old Testament have still applied, but history has also had a totally different dynamic since Christ's time. Despite continuing ups and downs, Christianity in one form or another today embraces about one third of mankind. And still God continues to do his kingdom-work powerfully among and through his people. Revival has become an increasingly common fact of Christian experience since the early eighteenth century, and since the beginning of this, the twentieth, churches world-wide have been witnessing outpourings of the Holy Spirit as at the beginning in measure unheard of before in human history. For many Christians today the things we read about in the Gospels and Acts have become familiar as seldom before in the history of the Church since the end of apostolic times: the baptisms in the Holy Spirit, the accompanying evidence of tongues, prophecy and interpretation, the powerfully effective preaching leading to numerous conversions, the healings and miracles, the increased joy, praise and love among believers, the growing churches and the persecutions. The marks of Christ are still plentifully with us. As Paul would have been delighted to hear us say, 'Not that we have already obtained all this, nor have already been made perfect, but we press on to take hold of that for which Christ Jesus took hold of us.' (Phil. 3.12). And as we do so, he blesses us continuously with times of refreshing from the Lord.

Surely the day of the fulfilling of that kingdom-vision first shown to Adam, then to Abraham, Moses and David, and in these last days to us who have believed in God's Son, our Lord Jesus Christ – surely that day hastens to its fulfilment in our generation as never before. The vision John saw of the End of it all has encouraged many saints down the ages and still it encourages us today. Though his words were spoken so many centuries ago, they were never more pertinent than now.

He who testifies to these things says, 'Yes, I am coming soon.'

Amen. Come, Lord Jesus.

(Rev. 22.20)

Chronology

The dates given to biblical events here are often approximations, some of them open to a great deal of debate. In the Old Testament, for example, some prefer to date the Exodus in the fifteenth century, or place Joel in pre-exilic times; Ezra's movements are notoriously difficult to pin down, as are dates for the kings of Israel and Judah. In the New Testament section there are also many problems. There are several views about dating Jesus' birth, the crucifixion can be placed any time between 29 and 33 AD, the dates for Paul's life are subject to a lot of discussion, and so forth, but the discrepancies seldom amount to more than two or three years. However, the dates used here are widely accepted ones and they do provide a constant framework for tracing the Bible-stories. Fortunately, precise dating of biblical events seldom affects our appreciation of spiritual truths very much.

The dates given to extra-biblical events are also generally open to discussion. Different scholars use different systems for the history of the second millennium BC, though the discrepancies are seldom much more than ten or twenty years either way. Dating becomes more precise the nearer we approach Christian times, though plenty of uncertainties remain.

THE SECOND MILLENNIUM B.C.

	PALESTINE	EGYPT	MESOPOTAMIA
3000		26–25th c.: The Pyramids	Sumerian City States
			2360–2180: Empire of Akkad
2000			
	The Patriarchs		Fall of Ur 1950 Rise of City States: Mari, Babylon, etc. Emergence of Assyria.
1720	Hebrews go down to Egypt	Hyksos ('Foreign Kings') come to power.	
1570		Hyksos expelled	Ascendancy of Assyria
1400		1400–1350: Amarna Period	
1290	The Exodus The Conquest	1290–24: Rameses II	
1224	The Judges	1224–11 Merniptah – battles with Sea Peoples	[Fall of the Hittite Empire]
	Philistines settle	1183–52 Rameses III – battles with Sea Peoples	Period
1100		End of Egyptian Empire	of
	Fall of Shiloh Samuel		weakness
1050			in
	Saul		Mesopotamia
1010	David		

THE DIVIDED KINGDOM

	JUDAH	ISRAEL	INTERNATIONAL
970	Solomon		
931	Rehoboam 931–14 Abijah 914–11 Asa 911–870	Jeroboam I 931–10	
900		Nadab 910–09 Baasha 909–886 Elah 886–85 Omri 885–74 Ahab 874–53	Expansion of Assyria begins
	Jehoshaphat 870–48	*Elijah* Ahaziah 853–52	Assyrian advance halted at Qarqar 853
850	Jehoram 848–41 Ahaziah 841 (Athaliah 841–35) Joash 835–796	Jehoram 852–41 *Elisha* Jehu 841–14	Jehu pays tribute to Shalmaneser III 841
800		Jehoahaz 814–798 Jehoash 798–82	
	Amaziah 796–67 Uzziah 767–42	Jeroboam II 782–53 *Amos* Zechariah 753–52 Shallum 752	
750	*Isaiah* Jotham 742–35 *Micah* Ahaz 735–15	Menahem 752–42 *Hosea* Pekahiah 742–40 Pekah 740–32 Hoshea 732–22 ------------------ 722	Tiglath-Pileser III takes Damascus 732 Sargon II deports the people of Samaria 722
700	Hezekiah 715–687 Manasseh 687–42		Sennacherib besieges Jerusalem 701
650	Amon 642–40 Josiah 640–09 *Jeremiah* *Zephaniah* *Nahum* *Habakkuk* Jehoahaz 609 Jehoiakim 609–597		Rise of Babylon Fall of Nineveh 612
600			

	JUDAH	ISRAEL	INTERNATIONAL
550	Jehoiachin 597 Zedekiah 597–87 *Ezekiel* ------------------- 587 *Obadiah* *Isaiah 40–55*		Nebuchadnezzar takes Jerusalem 597

THE POST-EXILIC PERIOD

	PALESTINE	INTERNATIONAL
	THE PERSIAN PERIOD	
539		Cyrus takes Babylon
538		Cyrus' Edict allows exiles to
537	Exiles start to return and Sheshbazzar is made Governor.	return.
535(?)	Zerubbabel is appointed Governor.	
520–15	The Temple is rebuilt. *Haggai & Zechariah*	
522–486		Darius I
486–465	*Joel*?	Xerxes I
465–424	*Malachi*	Artaxerxes I
458	Ezra arrives with more exiles.	
445	Nehemiah is made Governor.	
423		Xerxes II
423–404		Darius II
404–358		Artaxerxes II
	THE GREEK PERIOD	
336–323		Alexander the Great conquers and establishes his Greek Empire.
323		After his death, the Empire is divided between his generals.
	Palestine is taken under the rule of the Egyptian Ptolemies.	

	PALESTINE	INTERNATIONAL
200	The Seleucids take Palestine.	Antiochus IV Epiphanes (175–63)
168	The Temple is profaned and the Maccabean Revolt begins.	
164	The Temple is rededicated and Judas Maccabeus establishes the Hasmonean Dynasty.	

	THE ROMAN PERIOD		
63	Pompey takes Jerusalem		
39–4	Herod the Great rules Palestine.		
27		Augustus Emperor (– 14 AD)	
5	Birth of Jesus Christ.		
4	Palestine divided between Herod's sons: Archelaus (*Judea & Samaria*), Herod Antipas (*Galilee & Perea*) Philip (*Iturea & Traconitis*).		

THE EARLY CHURCH

	BIBLICAL		IMPERIAL
27	Jesus begins his ministry	14–37	Tiberius Emperor.
30/31	The Crucifixion	26–36	Pilate Procurator of Judea
35	Paul's Conversion		
38	Paul visits Jerusalem	37–41	Gaius (Caligula) Emperor
38–45	Paul in Syria and Cilicia	41–54	Claudius Emperor
43	Herod's Persecution (Ac. 12)	41–44	Herod Agrippa I, King of Judea
45	Paul & Barnabas in Antioch		

	BIBLICAL		IMPERIAL
45–46	Famine relief taken to Jerusalem		
46–47	First Missionary Journey		
48	Jerusalem Conference *Galatians* ?		
48–51	Second Missionary Journey *1 & 2 Thessalonians*	49	Claudius expels Jews from Rome
51–53	Paul back in Antioch	51–52	Gallio Proconsul of Achaia
	Galatians ?	52–60	Felix Procurator of Judea
53–59	Third Missionary Journey *1 & 2 Corinthians*	53–90	Agrippa II, King of Northern Palestine
	Romans	54–68	Nero Emperor
59	Paul arrested in Jerusalem		
59–61	Paul held at Caesarea		
61	Paul sails for Rome	60–62	Festus Procurator of Judea
62–64	Paul held in Rome *Philippians* *Colossians* *Philemon* *Ephesians*		
64	Paul freed & goes to Spain? *Mark's Gospel*	64	Neronian persecution
66	Paul returns to Asia? *1 & 2 Timothy* and *Titus*		
67	Paul & Peter martyred in Rome? Jerusalem Church moves to Pella *Matthew* and *Luke-Acts* ?		
70	Fall of Jerusalem	70–79	Vespasian Emperor
74	Fall of Masada		
		81–96	Domitian Emperor
95	*Revelation*	95	Domitian's persecution
	Clement of Rome's letters *To the Corinthians*		
95+	*John's Gospel* and *Epistles*		

Glossary and Index

(REFERENCES TO MAPS ARE IN ITALICS)

People

Aaron, Moses' brother and Israel's first High Priest 102, 198

Abdon, judge 49, 52

Abijah, 103, 104

Abimelech,Gideon's son, self-appointed king of Shechem (Judg. 8) 51f, 57, 62

Abner, Saul's cousin and commander of his army (1 Sam. 14.50) 77,87

Abraham, first patriarch (Gen. 12–25)5, 9f, 14f, 19–21, 25–28, 30, 32, 34, 37, 43, 57f, 90–92, 134, 140, 158, 172, 182, 219,

Absalom, David's son who usurped his father's throne (2 Sam. 13–18) 81–84, 88

Achan, Israelite who kept some of the spoil of Jericho (Josh. 7) 36, 168

Achish, Philistine king of Gath who gave David refuge (1 Sam. 27 & 29) 70

Adam, first man (the Hebrew word means mankind) 5, 7, 9, 18f, 25, 87, 90, 133, 135, 144, 158f, 201, 219–21

Adonijah, son of David, Solomon's rival to the throne (1 Kings 1–2) 83, 92

Agag, Amalekite king captured by Saul (1 Sam. 15) 67

Agrippa, king 208

Ahab, king of Israel in Elijah's time (1 Kings 16–22) 72, 105–112

Ahaz, apostate king of Judah in Isaiah's time (2 Kings 16) 113–118

Ahaziah, son of Ahaz 107

Ahijah, prophet in Jeroboam's time (1 Kings 11,14) 100, 102, 104

Ahithophel, David's counsellor who defected to Absalom (2 Sam. 16–17) 81, 84

Alexander the Great, founder of the Greek Empire. 128f

Amnon, David's son, murdered by Absalom (2 Sam. 13) 81, 82

Amon, apostate Judean king, 642–40 (2 Kings 21) 118f

Amos, eighth century prophet 112

Ananias and **Sapphira**, dishonest church members (Acts 5) 36, 168

Antiochus IV Epiphanes, Seleucid king who tried to eradicate Judaism 128f

Apollos, evangelist (Acts 18) 192, 194, 197f

Aquila and **Priscilla**, Paul's friends (Acts 18) 187f, 192

Araunah, whose threshing-floor David bought (2 Sam. 24) 86, 88

Archelaus, ruler of Judea during Jesus' childhood 129f, 142

Artaxerxes, Persian king in Ezra's time 127

Asa, reforming king of Judah 911–870 (1 Kings 15) 103f, 106, 108–110

Athaliah, daughter of Ahab, usurping queen of Judah (2 Kings 11) 108f, 111

Baasha, king of Israel 909–886 (1 Kings 15–16) 104f

Balak, king of Moab in Moses' time (Num. 22–24) 24

Barak, judge (Judg. 4–5) 45, 49f, 52

Barnabas, evangelist and companion of Paul (Acts 13) 171f, 177–181, 184f

Barzillai, faithful supporter of David (2 Sam. 17,19) 81

Bathsheba, Solomon's mother (2 Sam. 11–12) 82–84, 86, 88

Ben Tabeel, (Is. 7.6) 114

Caleb, spy who recommended entering Canaan (Num. 14) 31, 40, 45, 47

Chloe, her "people" told Paul of the problems at Corinth (1 Cor. 1) 197

Claudius, Roman emperor 41–54 (Acts 18.2) 187

Clement, Bishop of Rome at the end of first century 211

Cornelius, Roman centurion converted at Caesarea (Acts 10) 171, 180

Cyrus, Persian king who overthrew Babylon in 539 BC 125f

David, king of all Israel 1010–970 4f, 8–11, 15f, 30, 54, 60, 62, 67, 92, 95, 98–100, 124, 132–135, 138, 140, 142, 149, 152, 154–156, 180, 198, 218, 221

Deborah, prophetess who encouraged Barak (Judg. 4–5) 49f, 52, 87

Delilah, Philistine woman who betrayed Samson (Judg. 16) 55

Ehud, judge (Judg. 3) 30, 49f, 52

Elhanan, warrior who killed Goliath's brother (1 Chron. 20.5) 85

Eli, priest at Shiloh (1 Sam. 1–4) 59f

Places

Achaia, Roman province in southern
Greece 185, *185*, 187, 189, 192, *193*

Adam, where the Jordan blocked in
Joshua's day (Josh. 3.16) 34, *36*

Adullam, where David first hid from Saul (1
Sam. 22.1) *66*

Ai, village east of Bethel taken by Joshua
(Josh. 7–8) 35–8, *36, 39*

Aijalon, (Josh. 10.12; 1 Sam. 14.31) *36, 58*

Alexandria, Egypt's capital in Greek and
Roman times 192, *210*

Amalek(ite), desert tribe south of Canaan
31, *49*, 65, 67, 70

Ammon(ite), kingdom in Transjordan 15,
23, 24, *39, 41, 49*, 52, 64, 79, *80*, 82, 101

Amorites, people controlling southern
Transjordan in Moses' day 24

Antioch in Pisidia, early Pauline mission
centre (Acts 13) *178*, 179, *185*

Antioch in Syria, Barnabas' and Paul's
home church (Acts 11) 171f, 177f, *178*,
180f, 184, *185*, 188, *193*, 195, *213*

Aphek, where the Philistines captured the
ark (1 Sam. 4) 58, *58*, 60, *66*

Arabia, peninsula between the Red Sea and
the Persian Gulf *17*, 96, *165*, 177f

Aram(ean), region around Damascus,
modern Syria *17*, 48f, 79, *80*, *101*, 103,
109f, 113, 115, 117

Arimathea, home of Joseph who provided
Jesus' tomb *141*

Ashdod, Philistine city 53, *53, 58*

Ashkelon, Philistine city 53, *53, 58*

Asia, Roman province in what is now
western Turkey 7, 96, *165*, 184, *185*, *193*,
194f, *213*, 218

Assyria(n), kingdom in N. Mesopotamia,
empire ninth-seventh century BC 6, 14–
16, *17*, 105, 112–121,*117*, 132, 145

Athens, pre-Roman capital of Greece *185*,
186–188

Azekah, (Josh. 10; 1 Sam. 17) *36, 66*

Azotus, Palestinian church centre *170*

Babel, ancient city in S. Mesopotamia 5, 97,
164, 166

Babylonia(n), kingdom in S. Mesopotamia,

empire seventh-sixth century BC 6, 15f,
17, 117, 117–120, 128, 131, 219

Bashan, fertile area in N. Transjordan *23*,
24, *39*

Beersheba, southernmost town of Judah *53*,
80, 101

Benjamin, tribe in central Palestine *41, 49*,
50, *53*, 56, *58*

Berea, early Pauline mission centre *185*,
186, 188

Bethany, village near Jerusalem *141*

Beth Aven, (1 Sam. 13.5) *58*

Bethel, Israelite sanctuary town north of
Jerusalem *36, 39, 53, 58*, 65, *101*, 102,
104, 120

Beth Horon, (Josh. 10.10; 1 Sam. 13.18) *36*

Bethlehem, birth-place of David and Jesus
49, 53, 66, 141, 142

Bethphage, village beside Bethany *141*

Bethsaida, town by Sea of Galilee *141*

Bethshan (1 Sam. 31) *66*

Beth Shemesh (1 Sam. 6) *58*

Bezek (1 Sam. 11.8) *58*

Bithynia and Pontus, Roman province on
the shores of the Black Sea 184, *185*

Caesarea, home of Philip the evangelist 129,
170, 171, *185, 193*, 207f, *210*

Caesarea Philippi, where Peter recognised
Jesus' Messiahship *141*, 152

Canaan(ite), land taken by Israel 3, 5, 8–10,
15, *17*, 19–24, 28, 35–50, 56, 60, 76, 90f,
102, 135, 138, 144, 159

Capernaum, Jesus' ministry base by Sea of
Galilee *141*, 145

Cappadocia, Roman province in eastern
part of what is now Turkey *165*

Carmel, in Judah, home of Nabal and
Abigail (1 Sam. 25) *66*

Mount Carmel, NW of Megiddo, where
Elijah met the Baal prophets *101*

Cilicia, Roman province where Paul grew
up 96, *210*

Colosse, early church centre, not founded
by Paul himself (Col. 2.1) *193*, 194, 211

Corinth, trading city in Greece 185, *185*,
187, 192–205, *193*, 209, 212, *213*

Theological & Historical
Titles & Themes

Apostles, "the ones sent out", the Twelve 45, 138, 160, 162–172, 178, 180f, 186, 198f, 203, 205

Ark of the Covenant, symbol of God's throne in the temple 34, 41, 43, 59–61, 78, 87f, 93f

Day of Atonement, autumn festival for cancelling sin 132

Baal, Canaanite god 45, 47, 51, 106–111

Baptism, in water, in the Spirit xv, 7, 14, 143, 153, 169, 178, 192, 220f

Blessing, particularly God's 3–7, 19, 26, 37, 47, 64, 73, 78f, 91, 98, 133, 148, 153, 166, 221

Charismatic, endowed with gifts of the Holy Spirit xvif, 14, 18, 45–8, 61f, 65, 68f, 88, 106, 121, 137, 160, 166, 175, 203f

Church, whole body of Christian believers, or local expression of it xvii,3, 7f, 11, 18, 33, 45, 48, 130, 134, 160–221

Church-growth xvf,7–12,160f, 167–169,180, 216, 220

The Conquest, of Canaan led by Joshua 9, 11, 31–44, 55, 97, 138, 177

Covenant –
  Adamic (Gen. 1.26–30) 18f, 91f, 158
  Abrahamic (Gen. 12 & 15) 5, 19–21, 27, 91f, 133–135, 156, 158
  Mosaic (Exod. 20 & 24) 5, 22–5, 27, 37, 43, 48, 91, 156, 158, 164
  Davidic (2 Sam. 7) 5, 78f, 81, 91, 124, 132, 156, 158
  New Covenant (cp. Jer. 31.31 & Matt. 26.28) 6, 134, 156, 158, 164, 175

Creation 10, 12, 18f

Crucifixion/the Cross 6, 38, 144, 156, 169, 183, 206f, 216

Curse, particularly God's 5, 26, 37, 47, 73, 79, 164, 166, 182f, 201

Decline, in faith and morals 6, 8, 45, 48, 55–60, 72f, 95–98, 110, 112, 217, 220

Demons, spiritual beings hostile to God 7, 144–143, 153, 194

Disciples, followers of Jesus xviii, 7f, 138, 142, 145–164, 179, 190, 194, 196, 207, 211, 218

Elders, tribal leaders in OT, church leaders in NT 31, 67, 179, 196

End, of history 4, 7f, 145, 155f, 219–221

Essenes, semi-monastic sect of Judaism 132

Evangelical, approach to biblical interpretation 12f, 18

Exile, of the Jews after the fall of Jerusalem in 597 BC 6–9, 79, 93, 119, 124f, 128, 132–135

Exodus, from Egypt 9, 30, 97, 134, 142, 177

Faith (main passages only) 5f, 10, 20–52, 70, 75–7,95f, 99, 103, 110, 114f, 118, 121, 126f, 146f, 150, 152–155, 168, 175, 179–182, 189–191, 195, 217f

Fall, of man in Eden 5, 9, 19, 96, 159

Flood, in Noah's time 5, 97

Fundamentalism, approach to biblical interpretation 12–14

Gentiles, peoples other than Jewish 48, 145, 155, 171, 177–181, 186, 209, 211, 216

Glory, the manifestation of God's presence 34, 38, 93, 110, 156, 199, 202f

Gods (pagan) 25f, 43–58, 61, 96, 102, 105, 108, 111, 114, 118–120, 129, 187, 199

History, God's plan in it xv, xvii, 3, 8, 10–16, 18, 25–30, 44f, 59, 61–4, 72f, 81, 90, 98–100, 112f, 130f, 144, 157–159, 171, 217–221

Hyksos ("Foreign Kings"), Semitic rulers of Egypt c. 1720–1570 BC 15

Israel, God's chosen people 3, 8–10, 14–18, 24–98, 120, 125, 130–132, 138, 142, 144f, 147, 149, 157f, 164, 180, 197f, 217

Jews, name given to descendants of Israel after the Exile 6, 9–12, 124–136, 139, 142f, 145, 155, 157, 168f, 179f, 182f, 186f, 192, 194f, 199, 202, 207–209, 211, 216

Judaisers, circumcision party or party of Pharisees in the early Church 180f, 183

Judaism, the faith and culture of Jews after the Exile 127–136, 182

Judges, leaders in Israel in thirteenth-eleventh century BC 10, 30, 44–56, 61–6, 70, 72, 95, 97f, 119, 218

Kingdom of God/Heaven, God's rule in this

238

Summary Outline and Reading Guide

The following pages serve a double purpose:
1. They show at a glance the contents of the main biblical books covered in this volume.
2. They divide these books up in such a way that reading them can be spread evenly over a period of about six months.

As you read your Bible, keep your mind open to hear what the Holy Spirit has to tell you. Allow him to speak to you personally through its pages.

Watch carefully for what God does and says, and for how the men of Old and New Testament times respond to him, because that is what the Way of the Spirit is all about.

And don't forget to keep asking yourself what lessons you should be learning from their experience, so that you can apply them to your own life as a Christian.

(The reading scheme outlined here forms the basis of the home study course advertised on p. 248).

Week 1

Preparing the way for the Kingdom (Genesis – Deuteronomy)
Gen. 1–2: God's plan for his world – his covenant with Adam.
Gen. 3: Man's sin ruins God's primeval kingdom.
Gen. 12: God's plan for redeeming the world – his covenant with Abraham.
Exod 3: God sends Moses to rescue Abraham's descendants.
Exod 19–20: God's plan for his holy nation – his covenant with Moses.
Num. 13–14: The terrible cost of turning back.
Deut. 30: Moses' final challenge to Israel.

Week 2

Taking the Land (Joshua 1–12)
Chs. 1–2: Joshua takes up his leadership and sends spies into the land.
Chs. 3–4: The Israelites cross the Jordan into Canaan.
Chs. 5–6: They set up base camp at Gilgal and take Jericho
Chs. 7–8: The battle for Ai and the covenant renewal at Shechem.
Ch. 9: Tricked into a treaty with the Gibeonites.
Ch. 10: The conquest of southern Palestine.
Ch. 11: The conquest of the North and so of the entire land.

Week 3

The Distribution of the Land (Joshua 12–22)
Chs. 13–14: The Transjordanian tribes and Caleb.
Chs. 15–17: Judah and Joseph.
Chs. 18–19: The rest of the tribes.
Chs. 20–21: Cities of refuge and Levitical cities.
Ch. 22: Initial problems in Transjordan.
Ch. 23: Joshua's address to the leaders.
Ch. 24: Renewing the covenant at Shechem.

Week 4

Settling in the Land (Judges 1–12)
1.1–2.5: Failure to drive out the Canaanites.
2.6–3.6: Failure to remain faithful to God.
Ch. 3: Othniel and Ehud.
Chs. 4–5: Deborah and Barak.
Chs. 6–8: Gideon.
Ch. 9: Abimelech.
Chs. 10–12: Jephthah.

Week 5

Trouble in Central Palestine (Judges 13 – 21)
Chs. 13–14: Samson's childhood and marriage.
Chs. 15–16: Samson versus the Philistines.
Chs. 17–18: The migration of the Danites.
Ch. 19: Decadence in Benjamin.
Ch. 20: Civil War.
Ch. 21: The final state of the nation.

Week 6

Revival (1 Samuel 1–12)
Chs. 1–3: Samuel's birth, childhood and call.
Chs. 4–6: The fall of Shiloh and its consequences.
Ch. 7: Revival at last!
Ch. 8: The people ask for a king.
9.1–10.16: God chooses Saul and prepares him for his calling.
10.17–11.15: Saul is accepted by the people and crowned king.
Ch. 12: Samuel's review and challenge.

Week 7

The Reign of King Saul (1 Samuel 13–31)
Chs. 13–15: Samuel breaks with Saul.
Chs. 16–18: The LORD chooses David and Saul becomes jealous.
Chs. 19–21: David flees from Saul.
Chs. 22–24: He becomes a fugitive in Judah.
Chs. 25–27: He eventually goes over to the Philistines.
Chs. 28–31: Saul's last days.

Week 8

David's Early Reign (2 Samuel 1–12)
Ch. 1: David's lament over Saul and Jonathan.
Chs. 2–4: David moves to Hebron and becomes king over Judah.
Ch. 5: He becomes king of all Israel.
Ch. 6: He brings the ark into Jerusalem.
Ch. 7: God's Promise to David, or the Davidic Covenant.
Chs. 8–9: David's kingdom becomes an empire and he receives Mephibosheth.
Chs. 10–12: David's affair with Bathsheba.

Week 9

God's Hand of Judgment (2 Sam. 13–24)
Chs. 13–14: Amnon, Tamar and Absalom.
Chs. 15–17: Absalom's revolt.
Chs. 18–19: Absalom's death and David's home-coming.
20.1–21.14: Sheba's rebellion and the Gibeonites' vengeance.
21.15–23.39: David's songs and his mighty warriors.
Ch. 24: At the threshing-floor of Araunah.
1 Chron. 22–29: David's arrangements for the temple and his charge to Solomon.

Week 10

King Solomon (1 Kings 1–11)
Chs. 1–2: Solomon becomes king.
Chs. 3–4: A glimpse of Paradise.
Chs. 5–6: Solomon builds the temple.
Ch. 7: Other buildings and the temple's furnishings.
Ch. 8: The dedication of the temple.
9.1–9: God's second charge to Solomon.
9.10–10.29: The splendour of Solomon's kingdom.
Ch. 11: The cost of Solomon's splendour.

Week 11

Revolution and Revival (1 Kings 12–22)
1 Kings 12.1–24: The northern tribes separate from Rehoboam.
12.25–14.20: Apostasy in the North.
14.21–15.8: Meantime in Judah
15.9–24: Revival in Asa's time (details in 2 Chron. 14–16).
1 Kings 15.25–16.34: The slide into paganism.
1 Kings 17–19: Elijah leads the nation towards revival.
1 Kings 20–22: Ahab and the prophets during the wars with Syria.

Week 12

Revival in the Ninth Century (2 Kings 1–14)
Chs. 1–2: Elisha takes over from Elijah.
Chs. 3–5: Elisha's wonder-working ministry.
Chs. 6–8: More about Elisha's ministry.
Chs. 9–10: Jehu overthrows the house of Ahab.
2 Chron. 17–20: Meantime in Judah – Jehoshaphat's reforms and the vindication of his faith.
2 Kings 11–12: Decline and revival in Judah.
Chs. 13–14: Into the eighth century.

Week 13

The Age of Assyria and Babylon (2 Kings 15–25)
Chs. 15 & 17: Israel's last days.
Ch. 16: Apostasy in Judah.
18.1–12 and 2 Chron. 31: Hezekiah leads the nation back to God.
18.13–20.21 and 2 Chron. 32: The miraculous deliverance of Jerusalem.
Ch. 21: Manasseh's disastrous reign.
Chs. 22–23: Josiah's reforms (2 Chron. 34f).
Chs. 24–25: Jerusalem's last days (2 Chron. 36).

Week 14

Jesus brings the Kingdom (Matthew 1–10)
Ch. 1: Jesus' genealogy, human and divine.
Ch. 2: "Out of Egypt I called my son."
Ch. 3: The herald of Christ's ministry.
Ch. 4: Christ's kingdom-revival ministry begins.
Chs. 5–7: Kingdom living – the Sermon on the Mount.
Chs. 8–9: Jesus' kingdom ministry.
Ch. 10: The kingdom messengers.

Week 15

Preaching and Revelation (Matthew 11–18)
Chs. 11–12: The King's claims and the opposition.
Ch. 13: The secrets of the kingdom.
13.53–14.36: Jesus is revealed as Messiah among friends and strangers.
15.1–16.12: among the religious and others,
16.13–17.27: and among his own disciples.
Ch. 18: The calling of the servant.

Week 16

Confrontation and Victory (Matthew 19–28)
Chs. 19–20: To Jerusalem and to battle.
Chs. 21–22: Confrontations in Jerusalem.
Ch. 23: Jesus' final verdict on the religious.
Chs. 24–25: The signs of the end and the consummation of the kingdom.
Chs. 26–27: The King's last battle.
Ch. 28: Resurrection-victory and kingdom-vision.

Week 17

The Flowering of Kingdom Witness in Palestine (Acts 1–12)
Ch. 1: The new kingdom people prepare to meet God.
Ch. 2: The day of Pentecost – the Spirit comes.
Ch. 3: In the name of Jesus Christ.
Chs. 4–5: The cost of following in Jesus' footsteps.
Chs. 6–7: Even martyrdom.
Chs. 8–9: The gospel goes into Judea and Samaria and Saul is converted.
Chs. 10–11: The gospel goes out into the Gentile world.
Ch. 12: Martyrdom and persecution again.

Week 18

Into Phrygia and Galatia (Acts 13–15 & Galatians)
Acts 13–14: Paul's First Missionary Journey.
14.26–15.35: The Jerusalem Council.
Gal. 1–2: The gospel you heard from me is not deficient.
Chs. 3–4: Faith means freedom.
Ch. 5: Stand firm in your faith and in the freedom of the Spirit.
Ch. 6: Rejoice in what Christ has done for you, not what you are doing by
   keeping laws.

Week 19

Into Macedonia and Achaia (Acts 16–18 and Thessalonians)
15.36–16.40: After a bad start, Paul is called to Philippi.
Ch. 17: Then to Thessalonica, Berea and Athens.
Ch. 18: Finally to Corinth and then home via Ephesus.
1 Thess. 1–3: Thank God for your exemplary faith. I still care for you
   deeply.
Chs. 4–5: Let me remind you about some of the things I taught you.
2 Thess. 1–3: Thank God for your continuing faith. While you wait for Jesus
   to return, pray and work.

Week 20

In Asia (Acts 19–20 and 1 Corinthians 1–10)
Acts 18.23–19.41: Evangelism-explosion in Ephesus.
Ch. 20: Paul's visit to Corinth and his farewell to the Ephesian elders.
1 Cor. 1–2: On the power of God's wisdom compared to man's.
Chs. 3–4: The true calling of apostles and evangelists.
Chs. 5–6: Immorality in the church.
Chs. 7–8: Marriage and food sacrificed to idols.
Chs. 9–10: Christian freedom and responsibility.

Week 21

Teaching and Planning (1 Cor. 11 – 2 Cor. 2)
1 Cor. 11: Conduct at meetings and the Lord's Supper.
Ch. 12: The spiritual gifts and the body of Christ.
Ch. 13: The spiritual gifts and love.
Ch. 14: The spiritual gifts and worship.
Ch. 15: The Resurrection.
Ch. 16: Paul's plans to visit Corinth.
2 Cor. 1.1–2.11: Greetings and further travel plans.

Week 22

Paul Opens His Heart (2 Cor. 2–13)
2. Cor. 2.12–3.18: The glory of New Covenant ministry.
Chs. 4–5: The validity of Paul's ministry.
Chs. 6–7: The cost and the joy of Christian ministry.
Chs. 8–9: On the collection for the church in Jerusalem.
10.1–11.15: On the authority of Paul's ministry again.
11.16–12.13: More on the cost and the blessings.
12.14–13.14: Final appeal for reconciliation.

Week 23

On to Rome (Acts 21–28)
21.1–36: Paul's Gethsemane and arrest.
21.37–22.29: The flogging.
22.30–23.11: On trial before the Sanhedrin.
23.12–24.27: On trial before the Roman governor.
Chs. 25–26: On trial before King Agrippa.
27.1–28.10: The sea-voyage to Malta.
28.11–31: Rome.

A Bible Reading Course for Home Study

Tapes – Weekly Work Sheets – Tutorial Assistance

THE WAY OF THE SPIRIT
A Bible Reading Course

Part 2: TIMES OF REFRESHING

The present book can be used as the working manual for a complete six-month home study course which can be taken with or without tutorial assistance by correspondence.

The additional materials available are:
a folder of weekly work sheets and a set of six tapes, each with four 20-minute talks relating to the week's reading.

For details of this and other courses, and of the correspondence tutorial scheme, please write to:
The Way of the Spirit, Roffey Place Christian Training Centre, Faygate, Horsham, West Sussex RH12 4SA.